Modern Locomotives
of the UK

DEDICATION

To Harriet and Victoria

This book is dedicated to Harriet and Victoria, the two people in my life who keep me sane when deadlines are looming …

Modern Locomotives
of the UK

Pip Dunn

crecy.co.uk

First published 2019

© Pip Dunn 2019

ISBN 978 086093 6961

Printed in Turkey by Olas Solutions

Crécy Publishing Ltd
1a Ringway Trading Estate, Shadowmoss Rd,
Manchester M22 5LH
www.crecy.co.uk

Front cover: On 17 February 2017, DRS 68021 *Tireless* waits to leave Norwich with the 1205 to Lowestoft, a Abellio Greater Anglia train. *Pip Dunn*

Rear cover main:
GB Railfreight's 66738 Huddersfield Town crosses Rannoch Moor on 18 December 2017 with 6E45, the 0807 Fort William–North Blyth alumina tanks. No. 66738 was named by lifelong Huddersfield Town fan and Hollywood actor Patrick Stewart at the town's station on 16 July 2014 and commemorated the first English football club to win three consecutive top-flight titles. *Gary Lennon*

Inset from top:
No. 67029 and Driving Van Trailer 82146 work the DBS managers' on 29 May 2009 past at Ashwell. *Bill Atkinson*

Before the first locos moved to the UK, both the Class 68s and 88s were sent to the Velim test track in the Czech Republic for extended testing. In 2014, 68001 was stood next to a Vossloh Eurolight loco showing the obvious similarities in design. *Neil Bennett*

In 2016, GBRf won the contract to haul the summer Belmond luxury 'Royal Scotsman' trains and 66743/746 were repainted to match the coaches. On 7 July, 66743 passes Dalnacardoch, working north from Edinburgh to Boat of Garten. *Glen Batte*

Contents

Acknowledgments

Thanks to

I thank the following for their contributions of information, words, images or help: Bill Atkinson, Glen Batten, Cliff Beeton, Neil Bennett, Jack Boskett, Jaye Dry, Keith Fender, Steve Finn, Rob France, Ian Furness, Simon Grego, Anthony Hicks, Mel Holley, Ian Horner, Gary Lennon, Martin Loader, James Mayl, Jamie McEwan, Simon Metcalf, Brian Morrison, Ian Nightingale, John Patston, Mark Pike, Robin Ralston, Derek Riley, Jason Rogers, Paul Shannon, Karl Sharman, Paul Taylor, Steve Thorpe, Bob Tiller, Willy Ward, Karl Watts, Dale Williams and Alex Wood.

Opposite: In 1984 HSTs were introduced on the Highland Main Line and thirty-five years later they were still used on the 'Highland Chieftain' direct trains from King's Cross to Inverness. However, they were replaced by Class 800 Azuma bi-mode EDMUs from December 2019. On 8 July 2016, MTU-engined 43274 *Spirit of Sunderland* enters Blair Atholl with 1S16, the 1200 King's Cross-Inverness. *Glen Batten*

In the beautiful combination of snow and sunshine, GB Railfreight's 66738 *Huddersfield Town* crosses Rannoch Moor on 18 December 2017 with 6E45, the 0807 Fort William–North Blyth alumina tanks. No. 66738 was named by lifelong Huddersfield Town fan and Hollywood actor Patrick Stewart at the town's station on 16 July 2014 and commemorated the first English football club to win three consecutive top-flight titles. It is one of six GBRf Class 66s that had been named after football clubs by September 2019. *Gary Lennon*

Introduction

The introduction of new diesel and electric locomotives on the UK's railways has all too often appeared to be something of a feast and famine situation: mass orders followed by very little for a decade to two thereafter.

When the first main line diesels were tested in the late 1940s and early '50s, it led to British Railways almost panic buying them. Between 1957 and 1968, there were 3,434 main line diesel and electric locos delivered. From 1969 to 1994, when BR was privatised, just 433 locos were added to the fleet – not including the Class 59s or sixteen of the forty-six-strong Class 92 fleet, which were privately owned. You could add 197 Class 43 HST power cars to that number to make it 630.

The main reason for these massive differences was because the railway changed in three main respects. First was the Beeching report of 1963, which slashed the railway infrastructure by 30 per cent, and so reduced its need for rolling stock. Then the early 1980s saw loco-hauled passenger trains phased out in favour of multiple unit operation, and finally the decimation of the freight scene progressively in the 1970s and '80s.

In 1992, the then Conservative government announced it would privatise the railway, and in 1994 it had come up with a framework for doing that. The infrastructure would be publicly floated on the stock exchange, the freight operations sold off lock, stock and barrel and the passenger operation carved up into twenty-five franchises. The latter would be leased for set periods, typically of between seven and fifteen years.

The new operations would be able to source their own rolling stock. Most of the new trains were, understandably, multiple units, but for the freight operators, new locos were needed.

This book looks in detail at the new fleets of locos introduced by any main line operator in the UK. It also covers the major re-engineering projects. Included are the Class 66, 67, 68 and 70 on the diesel fleets – plus the Class 57, rebuilt from redundant Class 47s, and the Class 88s and 93s on the electric front, plus the two distinctly different Class 73 rebuilding programmes – two locos for Network Rail and eleven, and possibly more, Class 73/9s for GB Railfreight.

There is also a chapter on the HST re-engineering projects and another on other notable rebuildings, modifications and refurbishments such as the Class 91/1s and the forthcoming GBRf Class 56 project. The Class 59 and 92s have been excluded as they were introduced during the nationalised railway and not the privatised era.

It's not intended to be an overly technical book, and looks at the introductions, operations and subsequent changes to the different fleets. Such is the fast-moving nature of change on the UK's railways, it is inevitable that changes will occur as the text morphs from a word document on my computer to the finished book.

This subject of this book is constantly changing, and developing, so please remember that it went to print in October 2019 and events may overtake what was written in good faith at that time.

I hope you enjoy reading it.

Pip Dunn
Spalding, November 2019

1

The Railway
Before Privatisation

As mentioned in the introduction, this book looks at all the new locomotive types ordered for use on Britain's railways after privatisation, but before looking at these different machines, a bit of context and scene setting is required.

Britain's railways were nationalised in 1948 just after the end of the Second World War that had ravaged the country's transport infrastructure. British Railways started operating on 1 January 1948. There were a lot of benefits of a nationalised railway, most of all economies of scale and the ability to share resources where they were required. But it required huge subsidies from the British taxpayer, something that never sat easy with the Conservative governments over the years. As the competition from road vehicles, both cars and lorries, started to erode the railway's monopoly as a land transport provider, they started to lose even more money.

In 1961, the Conservative government then in power sought to reduce the costs of an admittedly over-staffed, outdated and over-resourced national railway system still reliant on steam and woefully lacking in customer focus. The 1960s were also the decade when car ownership rocketed and deregulation of the road transport industry further affected the railway's appeal and profitability.

Minister of Transport Ernest Marples appointed Dr Richard Beeching from chemicals giant ICI as the first chairman of British Railways and part of his remit was to cut costs. He did this by producing his famous report called *The Reshaping of British Railways*, which recommended massive closures across the network of stations, branch lines and what were deemed duplicate routes.

Over the next five years, swathes of the network were closed – although not all of his recommendations were implemented. He did also recommend modernisation and new freight yards. The introduction of air-braked wagons and the creation of the Merry-go-Round (MGR) coal train and the Freightliner intermodal system were all born out of his report.

In 1968 the last steam locos were retired, although the remaining modern traction fleet – most of which was still diesel-powered – was still reliant on vacuum train brakes and steam as the means of heating passenger trains. Electrification had been limited to the West Coast Main Line (WCML) from Euston to Liverpool and Manchester, several suburban lines in the home countries and other major conurbations such as Glasgow and Liverpool and the already obsolete 1,500V DC Woodhead line, which had more limitations than benefits.

The 1970s saw the introduction of more air-braked wagons and coaches and electrification through to Glasgow Central, plus the first air-conditioned coaches put into service. In 1976, the soon to be iconic HSTs were revolutionised inter-city travel. However, 1979 saw another Conservative government elected, combining with a recession in 1980–81. Costs had to be cut and that saw many locos laid up and scrapped. In 1981 the Advanced Passenger Train undertook a few passenger runs, but bad press and the need to cut the research budget saw this potentially excellent train shelved.

Sectorisation

In 1985 came the first signs that privatisation might be on the cards as the railway was split into 'business sectors' over the next two years. They were:

InterCity: already a brand name BR had been using for a decade and comprised all the fast main line routes mainly from London such as the East Coast, West Coast, Midland, Anglia, Great Western and CrossCountry Main lines.

Network SouthEast: The commuter lines from London termini to Salisbury/Exeter, Westbury, Oxford, King's Lynn, Ipswich, Peterborough, Kent, Sussex, Surrey, Portsmouth, Rugby, Banbury, and Essex.

An interesting meeting of Class 60s on coal trains at Foxhall Junction, Didcot, on 13 March 1997. Both locos are in temporary liveries applied by the shadow freight companies to the Trainload Freight grey. Loadhaul 60064 *Back Tor* has just run round its train near Didcot Parkway station and is approaching with the 6A64 loaded train from Avonmouth, while on the left Mainline 60086 *Schienhallion* waits with the 6C67 returning empties, which will shortly run round and head back to Avonmouth. *Martin Loader*

Railfreight: all freight services.

Provincial: all local and regional services across the country. This sector changed its named to Regional Railways in the early 1990s.

Parcels: all the mail and parcels trains

Departmental: all the infrastructure support trains.

The Conservative Prime Minister, Margaret Thatcher, was keen to privatise many of the utilities via public flotation, although she always thought the railways, because of their social importance, was a 'privatisation too far'. However, when she was ousted in late 1990 and replaced by John Major, he made privatising the railways part of his 1992 election manifesto. When Major won that election, the government set about implementing the plan.

The first signs of private operations was bus company Stagecoach leasing rolling stock to add to existing overnight trains, for which it would sell the tickets and take the revenue. This started in 1992 but did not last long.

The only other private operation had been Foster Yeoman and Amey Roadstone Company, which had acquired fleets of five and four Class 59s respectively from General Motors in 1986 and 1990. These were in direct response to BR's poor loco availability in moving stone from the Mendip quarries; the Class 56s BR provided were woefully unreliable and FY basically gave BR an ultimatum: 'Let us get 59s or the business goes to road.' Even the unions couldn't fight that one.

Major favoured a return to the days of the old 'big four' – regional companies that operated everything in their area, including maintaining their infrastructure. This was not favoured by others in government and instead they opted to sell off the infrastructure via a publicly floated company called Railtrack. Train operations would be split between twenty-five passenger franchises and six freight businesses.

Now owned by EWS but still in Loadhaul colours, 56118 approaches Potters Grange Junction, Goole, on 23 May 2001 with 6D51, the 0801 Doncaster–Hull Enterprise wagonload service. *Martin Loader*

The former would be let for defined periods, typically between seven and fifteen years. They would be the main InterCity routes, several regional franchises and several commuter lines from the old NSE area.

Shadow freight operators

In 1994 the Trainload Freight operations were totally recast into six operations. Three were business based; **Freightliner**, the container carrying intermodal operator, **Railfreight Distribution**, which covered wagonloads, some block trainloads of product and the forthcoming Channel Tunnel traffic; and **Rail Express Systems**, the mail and parcels arms.

Then the remaining Trainload operations were split into the regionally based operations; **Trainload Freight North and West**, **Trainload Freight South** and **Trainload East**. These were soon rebranded as **Transrail**, **Mainline Freight** and **Loadhaul** respectively, and each introduced its own liveries, as did RES, RfD and Freightliner.

Transrail inherited all thirty-one ETS Class 37/4s. No. 37404 *Loch Long* arrives at Garve on 10 August 1997 with 1H98, the 1325 Kyle of Lochalsh–Aviemore 'Royal Scotsman' luxury charter. The grubby Transrail loco is not exactly an ideal match for the well-maintained coaching stock and the following year EWS repainted 37428 to match the train. In 2005 the contract was lost and to West Coast Railways, which ran it from 2006–15 until GBRf took over. *Martin Loader*

The intention was that the three regional companies would have traffic allocated to them based on the origin of the flow. They would operate into each other's territory and the view was in the fullness of time, as contracts came up and new customers were enticed to rail, or back to rail, the three companies would be able to bid for the flows regardless of their main operating base. That would create the competition the government craved for the railways. The truth was, the railway already had competition from road!

The reality was two things. Firstly, there was not sufficient time between their creation and them being offered for sale to compete as intended. Secondly, there was limited appeal from the market to bid for the companies.

By 1996, it was clear the incumbent government, which would have to call a general election in 1997, was going to be given a beating at the ballot box with Labour taking power with a majority of 177 seats. Accordingly, in the run-up to going to the polls, the Major government was desperate to let the passenger franchises and sell off the freight businesses before the election, especially as Labour was indicating that it would halt and/or reverse the privatisation process (which, in fact, it never did).

The early part of 1996 saw the passenger franchises let almost every other day! On the freight scene, in November 1995, RES was sold to an American consortium led by Wisconsin Central Transportation Corporation. WCTC then went on to buy Loadhaul, Mainline Freight and Transrail in one go in February 1996. Eventually it would buy RfD, but that deal would not be ratified until December 1998.

Transrail 56119 passes Croome on 29 September 1995 with 6V69, the 1319 Brierley Hill–Cardiff Tidal steel empties. *Martin Loader*

The only part of the UK freight operations it did not buy was Freightliner, which was sold in a management buyout in in May 1996.

Many the new franchises let came with the promise of new rolling stock, all of which were multiple units, but the freight businesses were different, and WCTC's new operation – named initially North and South Railways until it changed its name in July 1996 to English, Welsh & Scottish Railway (EWS) – hit the headlines in typically American style with the announcement of 280 brand new locos. All would be built by General Motors, and they were the Class 66 and 67.

Interestingly, EWS's new maroon (or red, if you prefer) livery with a gold band first appeared in April 1996 – on 37057 *Viking* – some three months before the EWS name was official!

Later changes

Privatisation gave rise to new entrants into the market, both passenger and freight. Passenger businesses were called Open Access operators and they would run on routes and compete with the incumbent franchise holder, although they had many restrictions placed on them so they would not 'steal' too much business from the established operator.

Early examples of Open Access operators were Hull Trains, Grand Central and nationwide charter operators such as West Coast Railways and Merlin Rail. Other have put forward proposals, but not many get off the ground.

The freight market grew with new OA operators. First on the scene was Direct Rail Services, technically a nationalised company as it is a subsidiary of British Nuclear Fuels, in 1995. It was followed by GB Railfreight in 2001 and other companies have come – and some gone – such as Cotswold Advenza, FM Rail, Colas Rail

A clean 60044 *Ailsa Craig* approaches Wolvercote Junction on 30 June 1995 with 6M58, the 1725 Didcot Power Station–Toton MGR empties. The interim Mainline Freight livery was the blandest of the privatised freight company's colour schemes, made even more spartan here by the omission of the Mainline wording, which was normally below the logo. *Martin Loader*

Now in EWS livery, 56088 approaches the level crossing at Hambleton West Junction with 6G33, the 1057 Eggborough Power Station–Lindsey oil empties on 24 May 2001. It is just about to turn right on to the chord between Hambleton West and South Junctions, prior to joining the East Coast Main Line, which it will travel on as far as Joan Croft Junction, before turning left on to another freight-only link to Stainforth Junction. *Martin Loader*

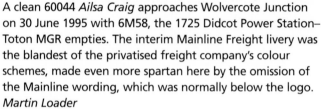

Freight, Jarvis Fastline, Rail Operations Group and also a number of small operators who only do certain bespoke operations such as moving track machines including Loram, Serco and Volker Rail.

Several of the freight companies have been sold – and in many cases, sold on again. EWS was sold to Canadian National Railway in January 2001, but the EWS name and logos were retained. In October 2005 it set up its Euro Cargo rail subsidiary for operating in France using redeployed EWS Class 66s, modified for use abroad. In June 2007 German state railways Deutsche Bahn (DB) bough the operation off CN and renamed it DB Schenker from January 2009, and in March 2016 it was renamed DB Cargo UK.

GBRf was sold to First Group in 2003, then Europorte in 2010 and more recently to Hector Rail in 2016. Freightliner was sold to Arcapita in 2008 and in 2015 it was sold on to Genesee & Wyoming.

Middle right: Freightliner still used Class 47s well beyond their sell by date and even had six painted in its new green and yellow livery, making them very hard to distinguish from a Class 57/0 at first glance. No. 47150 passes Culham on 21 June 2001 with 4M99, the 1647 Southampton–Trafford Park. *Martin Loader*

Right: In the initial post-privatisation Freightliner livery of simply putting a red triangle logo on the existing two tone grey, 47212 passes the derelict Aynho Junction signalbox on 18 June 1999 with 4M98, the 1704 Southampton–Crewe Basford Hall. *Martin Loader*

High summer at the site of Ashbury Crossing, near Shrivenham, on 23 June 1995 sees 47201 heading westwards with 6V22, the 1605 Longbridge Swindon Rover car panel empties. The loco sports the revised Railfreight Distribution 'European' livery. *Martin Loader*

Showing just how bad the two-tone sector livery was at wearing, and also highlighting to good effect the improvement in paint technology seen on newer locos such as the 66s, filthy 37019 passes the deserted and weed-choked Hinksey Yard on 25 June 1993 with the well-loaded 6M79 1508 Eastleigh to Crewe Basford Hall MoD stores trip. This Railfreight Distribution service was the successor to the Speedlink service, which finished two years earlier. *Martin Loader*

RES 47761 passes East Usk Junction on 18 August 1995 with 5M24, the 1420 Bristol Temple Meads–Cardiff TPO empty stock. At the time, this was still a British Rail train but three months later RES became the first part of the freight empire to be privatised. *Martin Loader*

National Power explored the privatisation process, set up as an Open Access Freight Operating Company and bought six Class 59s from EMD. No. 59204 passes Burton Salmon with 6D92, the 1130 Drax–Ferrybridge limestone empties on 25 October 1995. After witnessing the success of Class 59s in service with Foster Yeoman and ARC, National Power ordered a slightly modified locomotive in 1994, followed by a further five locos the following year. All were initially painted in this striking blue livery, although it is questionable whether white was the best colour choice for the underframes of a heavy freight loco. The 59 bodyshell was adopted for the Class 66 and in April 1998 EWS took over the NP operation and so acquired all six Class 59/2s. DBC offered the locos for sale in June 2019. *Martin Loader*

Railtrack and its demise

In October 2000 a serious derailment at Hatfield caused Railtrack to go into 'meltdown' as miles and miles of its track had to be given low-speed restrictions pending inspection over concerns on gauge corner cracking, cracks on the rails that had caused the rail to break and derail the GNER train at Hatfield. Railtrack did not know the condition of its track, so had to implement the precautionary speed restrictions until it could be assured it was in good condition. Emergency timetables came into force, swathes of trains were cancelled and the railway suffered immeasurably.

These speed restrictions were one of the major reasons why Railtrack was put into administration in October 2001. During its time in administration, in May 2002 a serious derailment at Potters Bar, which led to seven deaths, highlighted concerns over the award of maintenance jobs to private companies – in this case Jarvis.

In October 2002, Network Rail was created to take over from Railtrack. It was a 'not for profit' businesses – in other words it had no shareholders and while the government was desperate to say it was not nationalised, it was!

How privatisation affected new loco orders

All loco orders under the nationalised BR had to be funded out of BR's total budget and signed off by the Treasury. From the 1970s onwards, there are numerous examples of loco orders being cut back.

After a cull of locos in the late 1960s of the initial unsuccessful diesel types, more were slowly laid up in the 1970s and '80s, while at the same time very few new ones were ordered. Admittedly, the mass new builds of the 1960s combined with a contracting railway meant nothing much new was needed.

The Class 56s were ordered in response to the 1973 oil crisis when it was expected that more coal haulage would be needed, and this order for 135 locos was cut from an initial build plan of 142. This fleet was built – painfully slowly – from 1976 to 1984, overlapped by the fifty Class 58s being constructed in 1982–87. The next new diesel order was the 100 Class 60s built by Brush in 1989–92 and this was the last before privatisation.

The only bespoke passenger diesel locos built in the 1970s were the 197 Class 43 HST power cars. They were joined by the AC electric fleet growing in the 1970s/80s, with thirty-six Class 87s built in 1973–75 followed by fifty Class 90s in 1987–90 and – for the electrification to the ECML, the thirty-one Class 91s in 1988–91.

The last BR order for new locos was the forty-six-strong Class 92 fleet. This dual-voltage, 25kV AC and 750V DC, Brush locos were needed for the Channel Tunnel operation that was due to start from 1994.

The unique thyristor-controlled Class 87/1, 87101 *Stephenson*, passed into freight ownership while all its thirty-five Class 87/0 classmates were dedicated InterCity locos, so became something of an awkward one-off for many years. When operated by Railfreight Distribution, and sporting that sector's livery, 87101 passes Roade on 20 May 1991 with 6A28, the 0801 Bescot–Willesden Speedlink train. *Martin Loader*

A variation on the red theme at Woodborough on 28 July 1999 as RES red 47750 *Royal Mail Cheltenham*, EWS 47785 *Fiona Castle* and RES 47767 *Saint Columba* head west with a single Royal Mail van. When EWS took over RES, its new chairman only had scathing words about the reliability of Class 47s. *Martin Loader*

Of the fleet, only thirty were owned by BR, by its RfD business. The rest of the fleet comprised seven locos for Eurotunnel and nine for French operator SNCF. All forty-six locos were based in the UK at Crewe and initially were used indiscriminately, when they finally got the approval to run on the network. As you will read in this book, the

Loadhaul 56112 passes Cambois on 22 July 1996 with the 6G64 Blyth Power Station to Tyne Yard MGR empties. Blyth Power Station closed in 2001 after forty-three years of operation, so bringing to an end all coal movements along this line. *Martin Loader*

new Class 67s were woefully underutilised, but nothing compared with the 92s, some of which clocked up minor mileages and a couple are even good for nothing but scrap now after been withdrawn eighteen years ago having barely worked!

Of this fleet, the Eurotunnel locos were stopped in 2000 and offered for sale, but with no takers for these complex engines they were stored, followed by the SNCF locos. They were later bought by GBRf.

The thirty BR locos were taken on by RfD and then EWS, and many of these have now been withdrawn or redeployed in Eastern Europe for use by other DB subsidiaries.

Subjects in this book

This book looks at the new diesel and electric locos – and major rebuilds since privatisation. You could argue the Class 59s could have been included as they were never owned by BR, but they have been left out as they were operating on the network before privatisation.

The six Class 59/2s were ordered by National Power in 1994 with the view of running an Open Access coal haulage operation. This started in 1995 but did not last too long as in 1998 the locos were sold to EWS when it agreed to take over the NP operation. The locos were later redeployed in the Mendips but when this work was lost to Freightliner, they were effectively redundant and were offered for sale in June 2019.

Therefore, this book covers two main subject areas. Firstly, the brand new loco types ordered by the private operators, all of which are freight operators, so the Class 66s by EWS, Fastline Freight, DRS, Freightliner and GB Railfreight, the Class 67s by EWS, the Class 68s by DRS, the Class 70s by Freightliner and Colas and Class 88s by DRS.

It also covers the major rebuilds – Class 47s to 57s and Class 56s to 69s – plus the Class 73/9s projects as these are as complex and as thorough a rebuild as the 57s and 69s.

Also included are the Class 43 HST power car rebuilds where new MTU engines have been fitted. This rebuild is different to the 57s in the sense the locos look and perform the same, but it is a major modification all the same and within the remit of this book. There is also a look at the possibilities for the future – admittedly a tough thing to foresee, but worth an overview.

Although built in 2009, steam loco 'A1' 60163 *Tornado* – and any other new-build steam locos – are not included.

2

The Class 66s
The Loco That Changed Railfreight

The General Motors Class 66 has divided opinion amongst railwaymen, and enthusiasts, since they first arrived in the UK in 1998, but the fact is simple – they have proved the most successful freight loco in the UK bar none.

The last locos ordered by BR was a fleet of 100 bespoke freight locos, the Class 60s, built by Brush Traction in Loughborough from 1989 to 1992. They proved troublesome to start with – it took four years, until 1993, for all the fleet to reach the required reliability levels for them all to be accepted into traffic. They were also a heavy freight loco, good for moving heavy tonnages over shorter distances and not ideal for jobs such as hauling intermodal trains at faster speeds over longer journeys.

They had followed the Class 58s, which had only been a slight improvement, reliability-wise, over the pretty unreliable, although admittedly rushed, Class 56s as purpose-built freight locos. It had been the 56s' poor reliability that had led one of BR's biggest customers, Foster Yeoman, to order four General Motors Class 59s to operate its trains with to overcome the issue of delayed trains due to BR's poor traction. These were delivered in January 1986, with a fifth loco coming in 1989.

The 59s – which also received later orders of four by ARC in 1990 and six by National Power in 1994–95 – were the forerunners of the Class 66s, and the latter used the same bodyshell, bogies and a similar engine.

The dawn of the 66s

The Class 66s were a direct response to privatisation, and if the politicians wanted an example of new companies coming in to operate our railways that were privatised slowly from 1994 to 1998, then they were the real 'poster boys'.

No sooner had a consortium led by American Railroad company Wisconsin Central Transportation Corporation (WCTC), led by Ed Burkhardt, taken over all three of the regionally based shadow freight operations – Loadhaul, Transrail and Mainline Freight in February 1996, then

came the news of a massive order for 250 brand new freight locos.

WCTC had usually updated its traction fleet by buying second-hand locos and refurbishing them, but that was not a realistic option in the UK, where the restrictive loading gauge meant there was no real market for rebuilding locos – except for the kit BR had used. That was not an option in WCTC's eyes, so it turned to new build.

The UK's restrictive loading gauge was a major factor in that decision. Burkhardt added that General Motors was way ahead of other locomotive builders in terms of pricing, reliability and general design, and with the Class 59 bodyshell already designed, the costs could be kept manageable.

Having said that, Burkhardt ruled out buying a fleet of Class 59s as he said they were too old in terms of technological advancement, although there was no real new technology involved in the 66s – they were a simple piece of kit based on tried and tested components. The engine would be GM's 710 unit rather than the 645 unit in the 59s.

Initially there was dismay, especially from the rail unions, that this huge order had been placed with an American company and not with a UK loco builder, but the decision proved a wise one. Realistically, Brush could have been the only possible UK builder of new freight locos at the time, and the problems with getting the Class 60s into traffic were still fresh in the memory.

The Americans set about rebranding the three companies it had acquired, along with the Rail Express Systems mail and parcels services it had bought a couple months earlier, to English Welsh and Scottish Railway.

Later, WCTC also acquired Railfreight Distribution in 1998, so the company ended up buying five of the six railfreight businesses. That hadn't been the plan of the government in its quest to create a competitive freight market!

Burkhardt, now the head man at EWS, had told the press that one of the first actions of the new company would be to order new locos, and after a tendering process, it placed that order for 250 Class 66s with General Motors in May 1996, and delivery of the first loco was expected in 'late 1997'.

Acquiring new locos simply had to be a priority for EWS. It had inherited a truly mixed fleet of ex-BR locos that was ageing, unreliable and costly to run. It had gained a mixed bag of Class 31s, 33s, 37s, 47s, 56s, 58s, 60s, 73s, 86s, an 87, 90s and 92s.

Of these, only the 100 Class 60s, 90s and the restricted, and temperamental, 92s (of which EWS did not have even a fraction of a suitable workload for) could be classed as young, and while some locos, such as the Type 5s and AC electric Class 90s, and possibly the refurbished 37s, were not yet life expired, the rest was a collection of – not to mince words – elderly and essentially quite unreliable locos; there were only so many 'sticking plasters' that could be put on the fleet. Burkhardt was especially scathing about the reliability of the Class 47s.

EWS inherited just over 1,000 ex-BR main line locos, of which just over 800 were in traffic. The order for 250 Class 66s – and thirty Class 67s made shortly afterwards (see Chapter 3) – were aimed at eliminating 650 of these – the Class 31s, 33s, 37s, 47s, 56s, 58s, 73s and 86s. This would be achieved three ways – better reliability, eliminating double heading and better utilisation.

And this fleet restructuring also came at a time when EWS was being incredibly vocal about being out to win traffic and grow the business! There would always be scope to order more Class 66s if it needed to, which history tells us never happened, well, not for EWS. For other operators, it most definitely did.

With the ink dried on the contract, the design procedure was started, signed off in October and construction of 66001 then started at GM's London factory in Ontario, Canada, in May 1997. By February 1998 it had been painted and started and was ready for initial testing in Canada. On 23 March, it was officially handed over to EWS and a few days later, on 31 March, it moved to Albany ready for loading on board the MV *Fairload*, which set sail for Immingham the following day.

While 66001 would be shipped to the UK straight after construction, 66002 was sent to the Pueblo desert in May 1998 for extensive testing. The loco then moved to VMV at Paducah in Kentucky to be prepared for use before moving back to London, Ontario, in February 1999 for a few final tweaks before shipping to the UK along with 66094–105.

The 66s looks similar to a 59/1 or 59/2; there were subtle changes to the side grilles, but these are not that easy to spot. There were, of course, differences between a 59/0 and a 66 as the light clusters were totally revised, as they had been when the 59/1s appeared a few years after the 59/0s.

Maintenance on a Class 66 was made easier by the fact the centre part of the body can be easily removed at a maintenance depot to allow easy access to the engine. This led to them gaining the nickname 'shed' – after images of this section, removed and stood on the ground, looked just like a shed!

The examination schedule for the 66s was also extended compared with ex-BR locos. For example, a BR loco would have an 'A-exam' every sixty engine hours, so every six days or so. A Class 66 had exams every sixty days! And those exams could be done by a 'man in a van' going to the loco to undertake the routine examinations rather than the loco being taken out of traffic to be sent to a depot for the work.

Of course, 66s did have to visit depots for the heavier exams and also if any faults were found on those 'A-exams' that needed attention, but as a rule, these locos spent far less time stopped at depots than the locos they replaced.

The locos were also worked much harder, sometimes doing eighteen to twenty hours work a day and often on heavier trains.

BR locos would usually be overhauled every four years or so. That varied depending on classes, but even so the Class 66s have never been stopped for what we would regard as full, strip down and rebuild overhaul. They simply go on and on.

The first of many

It was 18 April 1998 when 66001 arrived at Immingham. After unloading it was taken to the nearby EWS Immingham depot by 56018 for a small media event the following day, which saw it run up and down the depot's tracks – these not being Railtrack infrastructure. Later that evening 60016 took the loco to Toton for initial checks.

On 24 April, 66001, still not passed to run under its own power, was taken to Chester for display with the Deputy Prime Minister of the time, John Prescott, one of those to see and 'inspect' the loco. It was taken back to Toton then on 27 March taken to the Railway Technical Centre at Derby for static tests, including weighing and measuring.

EWS had already had three drivers trained on the new type of loco out in Canada and they would train several driver trainers, who in turn would then 'pass out' the mass of drivers still employed by EWS at the time. EWS had a major training programme on its hands to ensure all of its 3,300 drivers would be able to handle the locos. If an EWS driver 'signed' Class 59s, then just a one-day conversion course would be needed, but for those trained on other locos, such as 56s, 58s and 60s, then a three-day course was implemented – including time in the classroom and handling the locos out on the network.

Opposite top: Brand new EWS 66001 was on display at Merehead on 28 June 1998 just two months after arriving in the UK. At the time it was the only 66 in the country and was still being used for testing and driver training. *Brian Morrison*

Below: EWS red 66040 has a relatively light load on 28 April 2008, as it passes Kings Sutton with 4O53. The 0433 Wakefield Europorte–Southampton intermodal. *Martin Loader*

Freightliner's maintenance on its 66s is mostly done at its Leeds Midland Road depot and at Crewe Basford Hall. Inside the Yorkshire shed on 22 August 2011 are standard loco 66526 and regeared Heavy Haul 66605, the latter having a slower top speed of 65mph. *Paul Shannon*

After a brief renaissance in the early 2000s, freight trains are now relatively few and far between on the Settle and Carlisle line. Freightliner's 66547 passes Kirby Stephen with a southbound loaded coal train from Hunterston to the West Yorkshire power stations on 29 September 2013. Such traffic is also now much reduced. *Rob France*

On 12 March 2014, Freightliner Heavy Haul's 66531 passes though Lazonby and Kirksowald with a coal train. *Rob France*

On 24 March 2014, DB Cargo's 66008 – still in EWS livery – heads away from Rylstone towards Skipton with an aggregates train. This traffic is now operated by GB Railfreight, as is the loco, which is now numbered 66780 and painted in Cemex livery. *Rob France*

On 21 May, 66001 worked on the national network for a first time, running light from the Derby RTC to undertake braking trials between Toton and Tapton Junction. On 27 May it hauled its first train, 6Z66, the 0930 Toton–Buxton with nineteen empty vans, a job it repeated twenty-four hours later. Then, on 2 June, it worked its first revenue-earning train when it piloted 58049 *Littleton Colliery,* which was shut down, on the 0400 Bentinck–Drakelow coal train. It was added to the train at Toton at 0430, which comprised thirty-six HAA hoppers. The new dawn had begun.

What was remarkable was the speed of introduction, in fewer than six weeks from arrival, the new type had gained approval to work. If this was rapid, then what followed was – by UK standards – even more remarkable.

Apart from 66001, which arrived at Immingham, all subsequent deliveries came through Newport Docks in South Wales. The 66s soon gained a reputation for docking, being unloaded on to the quayside and literally being filled up with consumables – fuel, sand, water and the like – and then being put into traffic.

Accordingly, the new locos would typically be in traffic the day after they docked. Although all allocated to Toton, most did not go to the depot and were sent in batches to start work. For example, a batch of locos went straight to Cornwall to displace Class 37s from china clay workings.

There was the odd occasion a loco was not passed for traffic straight away, for example 66022 arrived with some parts missing so spent nearly two weeks on the dockside awaiting rectification. Similarly, when 66064 arrived on 4 February 1999, it was found to be sitting too high on its bogies due to an issue with its suspension springs. Not only was it potentially out of gauge but there was an obvious issue with the loco that needed to be rectified before it could enter traffic, though it was only delayed by a couple of weeks or so.

As the new locos arrived, usually in batches of about ten, this allowed EWS to withdraw at least the same number of older locos, often more. The 66s also soon gained a reputation for reliability – 97 per cent availably was reached regularly, a figure that was a pipe dream for the older BR fleets, which typically struggled at 70 to 80 per cent availability.

The new locos could simply be worked harder. With clever diagramming, a single 66 could easily replace two 56s or 58s, and three or four older and smaller locos such as 31s, 33s, 37s and 47s.

No. 66073 leads 3J43, the 0529 Basingstoke–Didcot, via Westbury, Rail Head Treatment Train near Wootton Rivers on 20 October 2010. Surprisingly clean for an RHTT loco (at least on this side), 66073 shows the various modifications that it received for its redeployment in France working for Euro Cargo Rail, including a wasp stripe valance and additional stickers. Classmate 66026, on the rear of the train, is also an ECR loco. Both returned abroad and were only came back to the UK for the seasonal demand of RHTT workings. *Martin Loader*

DRS's 66422 passes Defford on 25 March 2019 with 4V44, the 1047 Daventry–Wentloog Tesco intermodal train.
Martin Loader

The next arrivals in the UK after 66001 were 66003–005, the first to dock at Newport. They arrived on 26 August and were unloaded by the following day. They were then collected by 66001 and, along with 37403 *Ben Cruachan*, taken straight to Toton for exhibition at the depot's open weekend on 29/30 August. After display, 66001/003/005 all moved to Bescot to start crew training, while 66004 was there on 2 September, working its first train to Bristol. This was piloting a pair of 37s but two days later 66004 worked the first train hauled by a solo Class 66 when it handled a Bescot to Longport trip. The 'red revolution', as it was called, really had started.

On 7 September, 66004 derailed at Bescot, but this was not a major incident and quickly rectified. Initial driver training was in the Midlands and South Wales.

Next to set sail were 66006–011 and they arrived in Newport on 2 October 1998, and deliveries continued until the last batch of the initial 250 for EWS, 66240–250, arrived in June 2000. But by then, there were other 66s, in different liveries, with other operators.

Less than two weeks into traffic, 15 October saw 66011 involved in a very minor collision to its cab front, which was repaired at Cardiff Canton. In later life, 66184/230 both had minor collisions that stopped the locos for extended periods.

Freightliner orders

In March 1999, Freightliner ordered its first five Class 66s, which would be numbered in the 665xx series from 66501. Unlike EWS, Freightliner – which was the only one of the six freight businesses not bought by WCTC – could not agree to a massive order like EWS could, even though it was clear its Class 47 fleet needed replacement.

The Class 57s – see Chapter 8 – had been a suitable loco to tackle the immediate issue of Class 47 reliability, but the lead times of getting them built had been longer than expected. By the time it placed the order, the landscape had change; the Freightliner business was doing well and it was able to secure new locos via a Rolling Stock Leasing Company, namely Porterbrook.

Labouring up the stiff and long climb to Beattock Summit, Freightliner's 66550 passes Harthorpe Bank in the Scottish Borders with 4S41 empty coal train on 18 April 2014. *Rob France*

The remaining nineteen Class 66s in the DRS fleet all sport a plain blue with a basic white DRS logo. On 13 March 2016, 66434 – now in its fourth livery – passes Arkholme, between Carnforth and Wennington with 6A01, the 0925 Hellifield–Crewe Basford Hall ballast infrastructure train returning from engineering work at Gargrave. Classmate 66302 is on the rear of the train. *Rob France*

On 24 April 2017 66738 *Huddersfield Town* and its train are seen snaking away from Rylstone as it heads to Skipton with 6D73. This loco was previously Freightliner's 66578. *Rob France*

The first Class 66 delivered to Freightliner back in 1999, 66501 *Japan 2001* passes Uffington on 16 April 2014 with 4L31, the 0903 Bristol–Felixstowe North container train. *Martin Loader*

Freightliner, which had been acquired by a management buyout, took delivery of 66501/502, painted in the company's new green and yellow livery, in July 1999 and they arrived on the same boat as 66128–136. The locos had been built alongside the EWS locos. The other three locos to make up the balance, 66503–505, arrived the following month, again, alongside some EWS locos.

Freightliner continued to order new Class 66s as and when the business allowed it. Orders varied, with twenty-seven the biggest at any one time. In 2000, it ordered twenty more locos – this time through Eversholt Leasing. Fifteen, 66506–520 were identified for a new contract with Railtrack, the then national infrastructure owner, which collapsed in 2001 and was replaced by the now-nationalised Network Rail.

Nos 66521–525 were for its new Heavy Haul operation, the business's decision to branch into the trainload freight market and go head to head for traffic that had been exclusively in the EWS portfolio immediately following privatisation. Also for the Heavy Haul operation were six locos with different gearing; numbered in the 666xx number series, 66601–606.

Eventually, following subsequent orders, twenty-five

Class 66/6s were to enter traffic with Freightliner, with 66601–606 arriving in November 2000, followed by 66607–612 in March 2002, 66613–618 in December 2003, 66619–622 in March 2005 and finally 66623–625 in February 2007.

The Freightliner locos were split between Intermodal and Heavy Haul operations. The former spent their time working container trains the length and breadth of the country, mainly from Felixstowe, Southampton and Garston to terminals inland.

The Heavy Haul locos worked oil, coal and aggregates trains, also nationwide, including as far north as Lairg in the Scottish Highlands.

GB Railfreight

The third Railfreight operator or take Class 66s was an interesting one as GB Railfreight, part of the GB Railways Group was a new business set up to serve the railfreight market. It ordered seven locos, numbered in the 667xx number series, on the back of a contract with Railtrack to provide logistical support to rail infrastructure projects. Nos 66701–707 arrived in March 2001 in a striking orange and blue livery.

GBRf bought ten Class 66s from DB Cargo in 2017 and caused something of a stir when 66250 – the last of the original EWS batch of locos – was outshopped in BR 'Large logo' livery when renumbered 66789. The loco – also named *British Rail 1948 –1997* – passes Baulking on 27 April 2019 with 6V32, the 1007 Tilbury–Trostre Works steel empties. This train was diverted via Gloucester, as the Severn Tunnel route was closed for engineering works. *Martin Loader*

The company soon won other traffic and – like Freightliner – ordered further locos in small batches. Nos 66708–712 arrived in June 2002, 66713–717 in May 2005, 66718–722 in April 2006, 66723–727 in December 2006 and 66728–732 in April 2008.

Of these, 66718–722 were delivered in Metronet livery, to tie in with a contract to offer infrastructure trains to Metronet, and 66723–732 were delivered in First Group colours following the takeover of GBRf by image-conscious First Group.

Direct Rail Services

It seems no one wanted to be left out of the Class 66 party and in 2003 Direct Rail Services, a subsidiary of state-owned British Nuclear Fuels Ltd, ordered ten locos through Porterbrook. This was after a trial with the class, having hired 66710 from GBRf, to which it temporarily added DRS logos.

These were initially going to be numbered in the 668xx series, but this was changed when it was realised those were already taken by some EMU coaches!

Instead, 66401–410 were allocated by the Rolling Stock Library for the Carlisle-based operator's new toys. They docked in two batches, 66401–405 in October and 66406–410 the following November. They sported a new livery with a compass logo.

In 2006, DRS ordered ten more locos, of which 66411–413 arrived in May 2006 and then there was a lengthy gap until 66414–420 docked on October 2006. Nos 66421–430 arrived in September 2007 – not all on the same ship – giving the company a fleet of thirty locos.

DRS acquired the last twenty locos through the new ROSCO, Macquarie. The ten Porterbrook locos were only leased for an initial five years, and surprisingly, DRS did not renew the contract, instead opting to acquire four new locos, 66431–434, also financed through Macquarie, which arrived in November 2008. These four were originally earmarked for Victa Westlink Rail.

In late 2008, DRS relinquished the lease on its first ten locos and they were returned to Porterbrook and redeployed with other operators. Nos 66401–405 were moved to Freightliner's Leeds Midland Road depot for warm store in October 2008 before being moved to the PRDC site at Willesden in May 2009. They were then taken on by GB Railfreight and taken to St Leonard's for preparation for their new operator in July 2009. They were renumbered 66733–737 in February–July 2011.

The DRS fleet had a fairly unspectacular life, although 66428 was involved in a bad accident at Cumnock in Ayrshire on 1 August 2015 when on hire to Freightliner. It was soon repaired.

Advenza

The other five of the initial batch of ten DRS locos were 66406–410 and they were initially moved to Glasgow Works in November 2008 for store before a deal was agreed for them to be taken on by fledgling spot hire and bit-part railfreight operator Advenza Freight.

They were repainted and renumbered 66841–845 in early 2009, and the first of the quintet moved to Gloucester Horton Road, the base for the company, in February.

However, while these five locos were being prepared

for use, their new user went bust. No. 66410 therefore never made it to work for its new operator – it would have been 66845 – while 66844 didn't exactly do a lot for it, barely working before being repossessed. Accordingly, 66410 moved to the PRDC at Willesden in August 2009, although it did have some spot hire with GBRf. The loco then moved back to Willesden on October, then to Tonbridge in January 2010 and then was moved again toe Midland Road in March. Eventually it, and 66841–844, would move to Colas.

With Advenza in administration, the locos passed initially on short term 'pay as you use them' basis with GBRf before being taken on by Colas Rail Freight.

Fastline

While Freightliner and DRS were enjoying their new locos, another operator came on to the scene: Fastline Freight, part of the Jarvis empire. It started its freight business in 2005 with three refurbished Class 56s, two it owned, 56301/302, and a third it had on hire from FM Rail, 56303.

One of the twenty EWS Class 66s fitted with RETB for working on the West Highland and Far North lines, 66114 passes Achallader, near Bridge of Orchy, heading south with 6E16, the 1800 Fort William–North Blyth, on 8 June 2006. *Bill Atkinson*

During its brief spell working for Fastline Freight, 66304 passes Wichnor Junction with 4G81, the 1330 Ratcliffe–Daw Mill, empty coal hoppers on 30 June 2008. *Bill Atkinson*

These were a stopgap, but in 2007 it ordered five Class 66s, and 66301–305 arrived in June 2008. It also did a deal with DRS to have 66434 re-liveried into Fastline grey livery. However, it too failed to make a go of the railfreight business and when its parent company collapsed in October 2010, still suffering from the fall out of the Potters Bar derailment, combined with the downturn in coal traffic, the operation ceased.

During their short life with Fastline, the 66/3s were predominately used on coal trains in Yorkshire but they did occasionally travel further afield.

After Fastline went bust, the five 66/3s transferred to DRS, allowing it to relinquish the lease on ten more Class 66/4s, and 66411–420 were all taken on by Freightliner. This allowed Freightliner to relinquish the lease on 66573–581. Of these, 66577–581 were snapped up by GBRf and renumbered 66738–741, and they entered traffic with their new numbers still on their green livery.

Nos 66573–577 moved to Colas and were renumbered 66846–850, which allowed 66841–845 to transfer to GBRf. They were duly renumbered again, this time to 66742–746.

Colas Rail Freight

Colas started operations in 2006, initially with three Class 47s, and in 2009 took the five ex-Advenza locos 66841–845 into its fleet, having them repainted at Eastleigh into its colours. They had the Colas hard hat logos on their bodysides and Colas Rail branding.

They were used on timber traffic serving Chirk, Teigngrace, Ribblehead and Carlisle before also starting coal operations from Wolsingham to Scunthorpe and from Thoresby to Ratcliffe.

These five locos were only on a short-term lease and soon moved to GBRf in July 2011, being renumbered 66742–746, but they were replaced at the same time by 66573–577, which were ex-Freightliner locos. They were duly renumbered to 66846–850 and given the same livery with subtle differences, namely the hard hat logo on their cabsides and Colas Rail Freight branding.

More recent work has seen them handling steel trains to Boston, infrastructure, RHTT and cement haulage. The Colas fleet has grown, but not with 66s, and now it has Class 37s, 56s and 70s at its disposal.

66137 crosses the iconic Forth Bridge with 7G70, the 1440 Hunterston–Longannet Power Station coal train on 18 April 2003. *Martin Loader*

Fastline 66303 passes Hinksey on 9 January 2010 with 6Z37, the 0923 Daw Mill–Didcot Power Station coal. *Martin Loader*

No. 66402 passes Wootton Rivers on 22 June 2010 with 4E31, the 0625 Taunton Fairwater–Whitemoor scrap sleepers. The loco had recently been taken on by GBRf, but still sports DRS livery, although with all branding removed. It was soon repainted and renumbered 66734 but was to be written off almost two years to the day, on 28 June 2012, when it derailed at Loch Treig. *Martin Loader*

One of – to date – eight Class 66s acquired by GBRf from operators in Europe, 66750 *Bristol Panel Signal Box* runs alongside the Kennet & Avon Canal near Crofton on 23 August 2016 with the late-running 6V42 0813 Wellingborough–Whatley Quarry stone empties. Nos 66747–751/790–792 have all been acquired when their European users no longer needed them. *Martin Loader*

Lower emissions

To meet more stringent legislative requirements to reduce harmful exhaust emissions, EMD had to develop a more environmentally friendly engine. This was the 12N-710G3B-U2, which required various modifications to the existing Class 66 layout.

The cooler group needed more space and the only way to do this was to infringe on the internal walkway between the two cabs, so an additional bodyside door was added to improve access to the engine room.

The new locos were also going to be heavier, so to reduce weight elsewhere, to keep the loco's overall weight the same, it was necessary to reduce the amount of fuel carried – so smaller fuel tanks were fitted. This lowered the fuel capacity from 1,440 to 1,133 gallons, which meant the locos had a reduced range.

The first two locos to be built for the UK to this new specification were 66951/952 for Freightliner, although 66951 initially went to Pueblo for testing, allowing 66952 to ship to the UK first. It arrived in April 2004, with its classmate arriving in October. There was a suggestion the lower-emission 66s may have been classified as Class 68, but this never happened.

This new specification was to be adopted for later Class 66 deliveries for the UK market, namely 66301–305, 66411–434, 66585–599, 66623–625, 66723–732/752–779, 66953-957, while 66747–749 were also to this specification and 66750/751 were not.

Advenza Freight had four Class 66s for a matter of months, so pictures of them at work are comparatively rare. On 2 June 2009, 66841, formerly DRS 66406, heads 4E71, the 0925 Tilbury–West Burton empty Cemex tanktainers, at Australia Farm crossing, between March and Whittlesea. *Bill Atkinson*

GBRf takes on more locos

GBRf continued to source more locos. It took three from the Netherlands and two from Germany, which became 66747–749 and 66750/751, but only after a few modifications to make them compatible with the UK railway. Nos 66747–747 arrived on December 2012, painted in all-over grey, and were taken to Swanwick at the Midland Railway Butterley for modifications to allow them to run in the UK. They entered traffic in the summer of 2013.

Meanwhile, 66750/751 arrived in June and August 2013 respectively, both painted in the blue livery of their previous user, Rush Rail. They also needed modifications to make their driving desks compatible for the UK and this work was undertaken by EMD at Longport near Stoke. All five locos initially ran with GBRf branding and large numbers on their existing paint before they were later all re-liveried in GBRf colours at Arlington Fleet services.

In 2013, GBRf announced it would be ordering another twenty-one Class 66s, 66752–772, with the option for five more, and these would be the last of the type built for the UK before changes in emission regulations rendered the design unsuitable for the European market.

Unlike previous Class 66s, they would be built by EMD's subsidiary Progress Rail in Muncie, Indiana, as opposed to Canada after the London plant in Ontario had been closed in 2012.

They were delivered in 2014 with the last, 66772, arriving in December 2014. However, around the same time 66766–772 were docking GBRf had decided to exercise an option it had for five more locos plus another two new locos using the engines recovered from 66734 – which was written off after it derailed in Scotland in June 2012 – and another 66 withdrawn in mainland Europe, which was written off in a crash and also had its engine returned to America. These locos, 66773–779 would be the last ever Class 66s built after a production run totalling 683 – 480 for the UK, 162 for Europe and forty-one for Egypt.

By 13 April 2010, the Advenza Class 66s had become part of the Colas fleet and had been repainted in the company's livery. One duty they were sometimes used on was the Washwood Heath to Boston steel job and 66841 passes Ancaster with 6Z56. This loco is now with GBRf as 66742. *Bill Atkinson*

After DRS returned 66411–420 to their leasing company, they were snapped up by Freightliner, which was in no rush to repaint the locos. The second loco to carry a Stobart Rail wrap was 66414 and when it moved between operators it was debranded and ran in plain blue for a few months. On 3 May 2014 it worked 4M41 Ipswich–Crewe past East Goscote between Melton Mowbray and Syston Junction. This loco is now in Freightliner Powerhaul colours. *Bill Atkinson*

One of the five Class 66/3s ordered by Fastline, but now working for DRS after the former went bust, 66305 approaches Craigenhill summit on a Newton to Carlisle engineering train on 31 March 2019. *Robin Ralston*

The Spalding Flower parade held every May bank holiday used to attract several loco-hauled trains each year until the mid-1980s. On 1 May 2010, there was just one, a UK Railtours' charter from King's Cross top and tailed by 66186 and 66193. After depositing its punters at the town, 66193 heads the ECS back to Peterborough for stabling and approaches South Drove level crossing. *Pip Dunn*

No. 66148 emerges from the trees as it comes to the end of its journey with 6B30, the 0955 Margam–Bridgend, on 22 August 2017. Although DB Cargo is slowly repainting its 66 fleet into its corporate red livery, many are still in their original EWS livery applied at new, a testament to the quality of the paint jobs they were given when built. *Paul Shannon*

The first of three Class 66s to carry a Stobart Rail wrap was DRS's 66411 and on 8 March 2011, it worked 4M71, the 10.53 Tilbury–Daventry past Chelmscote on the WCML south of Rugby. *Bill Atkinson*

In recognition of 66779 being the last Class 66 off the production line, GBRf decided to commemorate the fact and it was delivered in lined BR Brunswick green livery. It arrived with 66773–778 at Newport in February 2016 but the loco was under a tarpaulin wrap to hide its look.

It was kept under cover until taken to the National Railway Museum on 10 May 2016 and named *Evening Star*. The nameplates were in the same style as those applied to the last steam locomotive built for British Railways in 1960, '9F' 92220, also named *Evening Star*. GBRf announced the loco would be offered to the national collection when its working life was over.

In 2017, GBRf agree a deal with DB Cargo to buy ten Class 66s from it, and the locos identified for sale were 66008/016/046/058/081, 66132/141/184 and 66238/250. Initially some of the locos went into traffic with their new owner in the existing EWS liveries, but soon they were moved to Arlington at Eastleigh for repainting into GBRf colours, although only six appeared in GBRf livery!

In 2019, GBRf was in discussion with owners of at least another four Class 66 in mainland Europe and in June it announced it had agreed deals to acquire three of the locos through Beacon Rail. They were former Norwegian locos T66403–405, which used to be operated by Cargonet and had later moved to Sweden. They were renumbered 66790–792.

After some modifications in Gothenburg in Sweden, the locos were moved to the UK, the first being 66790 (ex-T66403), which was collected from Immingham by 66741 *Swanage Railway* on 3 June 2019 and taken to the EMD site at Longport for conversion to UK specifications. This including fitting UK safety systems, air conditioning, and reliability improvements. The loco looked a little strange as its bufferbeam was modified to accommodate a heavy-duty snowplough – a vital requirement for use in Scandinavia. No. 66791 arrived on 18 July and was taken to Longport on 23 July, while 66792 arrived in October 2019.

GBRf has made no secret that it will try to acquire any Class 66s that come on the market anywhere in the world if they can be made suitable to work in the UK and, of course, if the price is right!

GBRf has been acquiring locos from European operators and having them modified to be compatible with Network Rail signalling. The first three were 66747–749 and once ready for use they were put to work in their plain grey liveries before repainting into GBRf livery. No. 66747 passes Turves, between March and Peterborough working 6E88, the 1224 Middleton Towers–Goole Glassworks. After a spell in GBRf livery, this loco was repainted into Newell & Wright company livery in July 2019. *Bill Atkinson*

Three casualties

Three Class 66s have been written off in the UK. The first was Freightliner's 66521, which was only three months old when it was hit by a train that had derailed at speed when a car and trailer came off the M62, ran down an embankment and landed on the ECML at Heck on 28 February 2001.

The 0445 Newcastle–King's Cross hit the obstruction and was pushed into the path of a northbound coal train worked by the new locomotive. Sadly ten people died, including the drivers of both the Freightliner and GNER trains. The damage to 66521 was so severe it was eventually written off. It was moved to Doncaster Works on 13 March. After the enquiry into the collision had been concluded, 66521 was moved to Freightliner's Leeds Midland Road depot in June 2004, then sold to CF Booths at Rotherham and it moved there on 24 June 2006. It was scrapped straight after it was delivered.

The next Class 66 to be written off was an EWS loco, and to date is the only one of the EWS order of locos to be withdrawn. In late 2009, DBS won the contract from DRS to operate the Stobart Intermodal trains, and this included one train a day from Inverness. No. 66048 was re-liveried into Stobart colours, as DRS's 66411 and later 66414 had been, and it was sent to work the inaugural DBS train from the Highland Capital on 4 January 2010.

Sadly, due to excessive snow and bad weather, on the descent to Carrbridge, ice had built up in the brake system and the loco failed to slow down. It derailed on the approach to the station, crashing into trees. No one was badly injured, but the loco was badly damaged. It was retrieved and taken by road to Inverness depot, where it was dumped for several months until being received and taken by road to Toton for stripping.

The bodyshell of the loco was later sold to EMD and taken to its Longport maintenance facility near Stoke, where it was sprayed in all-over black and left on accommodation stands. It was still there in early 2019, though rebuilding seems highly unlikely.

The third Class 66 to be written off was GB Railfreight's 66734 *The Eco Express*. This loco had started its life as DRS's 66402 but moved to GBRf in June 2011 and was renumbered and repainted. It was named on 18 January 2012 at the National Railway Museum at York.

At just past 1900 on 28 June 2012, the loco was hauling the twenty-four-wagon 6S45 North Blyth–Fort William Alcan train, weighing just over 900 tonnes. Bad weather including heavy rain in the West Highlands had caused a landslide and resulted in mud, rock and other debris sliding on to the track on the section where the line skirts Loch Treig, between Corrour and Tulloch.

The train hit this blockage at 30mph, derailed and the 66 was pushed partway down the embankment. The driver was badly injured but there was no loss of life. However, where the loco had landed made it impossible to recover it in one piece. No. 66734 only had minimal damage and under normal circumstances it would have been easily repaired. It was made safe so it would not slip further down the embankment and risk ending up in the loch.

Eventually, in September 2013 QTS Group staff set up a system to scrap the loco on site and the recovered sections were then removed. The cabs were taken to Longport and one section was later used for a GBRf driver simulator at Peterborough, which came into use in 2019. The engine was reused in 66779.

Interestingly, this was not the first simulator to use a Class 66 cab as EWS had a fully fitted out Class 66 cab done up, and even registered on TOPS as 66499, built and stationed in Doncaster to teach its new recruits to drive trains.

To date these have been the only Class 66s scrapped, although one other loco, 653-06, was written off in the Netherlands in 2009.

Class 66 Operations

The Class 66s were a success from day one. They were simple, but rugged and reliable. They were dated and the technology was not state of the art, but they were bulletproof in many respects.

With more locos – by the end of 1998, 66001/003–044 were in the UK and hard at work – they were used in the Home Counties and in London as well as in Yorkshire, Westbury and the North-east.

GBRf has painted several Class 66s in customer liveries and 66780 – formerly 66008 and one of ten 66s bought from DB Cargo – sports Cemex livery. It is working 6M60, the 1112 Whitemoor Yard–Mountsorrel, ballast empties past Copleys Brook, near Melton Mowbray, on 5 March 2019. It has since been named The Cemex Express. *Bill Atkinson*

EWS 66004 and DB Schenker red 66152 pause in Newtondale on the North Yorkshire Moors Railway with a ballast train to complete winter track renewals at Kingthorpe, near Pickering, on 24 February 2016. The train ran from Tees Yard, having been stabled from Doncaster Local Distribution Centre, where the wagons were loaded with stone originating from Mountsorrel quarry in Leicestershire. Because of axle weight restrictions on the line from Middlesbrough to Whitby the wagons could not be fully loaded. *Ian Horner*

They also broke new ground, reaching places where Type 5s had hitherto been a pipe dream. For example, in May 2000, the first 66s started operating on the West Highland Line to Fort William. For decades, this route had been a complete no-go area for anything heavier than a Class 37, but with their steering bogies, the 66s did not risk damaging the track.

They were then cleared in 2001 for the Far North Line from Inverness to Georgemas Junction and then the branch to Thurso – but not Wick – and in more recent times the class has even been cleared for Kyle of Lochalsh and Mallaig. Oban remains some way off. They have been to Aberystwyth and it's only the introduction of ERTMS to Pwllheli that makes them unsuitable for that line.

The class has gained pretty much UK-wide clearance, with just a few bits and pieces here and there that remain barred to the type, but few places they actually need to go. Part of the change has been brought about by the freight operators demanding more of NR to make the network open to bigger locos, and the infrastructure provider has undertaken its fair share of track improvements as well.

The locos have traditionally been used mainly on heavy trainload work, although for the heaviest trains Class 60s were still preferred by EWS and the need to have a better tractive effort led Freightliner to order its Class 66/6s, which had a reduced top speed of 65mph.

The EWS/DB locos were used on all sorts of traffic including intermodal, infrastructure, petroleum, coal, metals, aggregates and charter trains. They also work Railhead Treatment Trains (RHTTs).

The Freightliner locos were split in allocation to the two businesses, Intermodal or Heavy Haul. The former mostly worked container trains while the latter were also used on petroleum, coal and aggregates trains.

The DRS locos mostly worked intermodal and infrastructure trains. The Fastline locos were used mostly for coal trains in their short time operated by that FOC.

Colas 66848 passing Gants Mill, near Bruton, working 6C22, the 0100 Exeter St Thomas–Westbury engineers' train on 28 February 2016. *Mark Pike*

The Advenza locos, which also had a very short operation, were used on cement and scrap metal trains, including a flow from West Burton to Thurrock. The small stud of five Colas 66s were used on petroleum, cement, timber and infrastructure trains. This has taken the locos across the country from Inverness in the north to Cornwall in the South-west.

The GBRf locos also work all manner of trains, with intermodal and trainload work both key parts of their day-to-day work. They also travel the length and breadth of the country, including the West Highland line on freight trips.

Several locos have had Radio Electronic Token Block (RETB) signalling equipment in their cabs. The first were EWS 66095/114 for trial runs on the West Highland and Far North lines. When 66s were passed for these routes, EWS fitted 66096–113 with the in-cab equipment to give it twenty locos in one block. Nos 66095–098/109 have since had their RETB removed as there is little demand for EWS locos with the equipment.

However, 66301–305 from DRS have it fitted as they often work nuclear fuel trains to Georgemas Junction, while GBRf's 66733–740 had it fitted for West Highland line work, although 66734 was written off. More recently, 66743/746 have been modified as they work on RETB lines with the Royal Scotsman while 66735/739 have also had the equipment removed. When Freightliner locos

work on RETB routes, which they sometimes do on infrastructure trains, they use portable RETB receivers in their cabs.

Passenger work

Despite being a bespoke freight loco, the 66s have done their fair share of hauling passenger trains. The first passenger working came on 28 November 1998 when 66011 worked from Paddington to Cardiff for Hertfordshire Railtours. It was then joined by 66009 to top-and-tail to Cwmgrach and Onllwyn, with 66009 hauling the train back to Paddington.

The first service train passenger work came on 19 January 1999 when two locos were pressed into action. The first was 66016 when it rescued Virgin's 1A21, 0649 Shrewsbury–Euston, at Admaston, 2 miles west of Wellington, and worked it through to Wolverhampton after 47709 *Dionysos* failed.

Later that day, 66035 was sent to assist another Virgin train. This time 47847 failed at Stoke Works Junction, north of Cheltenham while working 1M31, the 1555 Plymouth–Manchester Piccadilly. The train was assisted by 56126 to Bromsgrove – having been removed from a freight train – and it was then switched for 66035, which worked the train forward to Birmingham NS.

No. 66413 was the first loco repainted into Freightliner's parent company's livery, Genesee & Wyoming, and later repaints have used a much darker orange, making this loco unique. No. 66413 was nearly redeployed to Poland, but remains in the UK. It leads 66558 as they pass Basingstoke with 6O26, the 1019 Hinksey Sidings–Eastleigh Yard on 3 October 2018. *Mark Pike*

Two days later, 66053 was a third Class 66 to rescue a Virgin train, coming to the aid of 47711 *County of Hertfordshire*, which failed before setting off with 1M01, the 0640 Poole–Manchester Piccadilly. The train was cancelled and the 66 worked the ECS to Reading.

Equally unusual was 1 February, when 66033 worked a RES train, taking charge of the 1030 Doncaster–Heaton with just four vans.

In recent times, the GBRf locos have seen some use on passenger work. As well as standing in, occasionally for other locos, such as 57s on the Cardiff–Taunton shuttles for First Great Western in the early 2010s.

In 2017 it was commonplace for a GBRf 66 to work in multiple with a Class 73/9 on 'sleeper' trains. This was because the newly built Class 73/9s needed a modification that mean they could not take power in their final 'notch'. This left them underpowered for the sleeper trains, so the solution was to run them in multiple with a 66/7 with the 73 inside providing train supply. This is the only time you can realistically say a Class 66 was booked for passenger work on service trains.

Charter work has taken 66s to a variety of places, sometimes at the request of the promoter, sometimes for the operational convenience of the operator.

Over the last twenty years most Class 66s have worked passenger trains, but not all. For a start, early condemned

66521 only had a few weeks in traffic so never got close to working passenger trains. Most of the EWS locos have, except several that were redeployed abroad before they had a chance to work a charter, including 66010/029/033/049/073/146/179/191/196, 66202/203/205/209/212/215–217/223/225/228/233–235/240/243. Some Freightliner, DRS and GBRf also still have yet to work a passenger train.

The 75mph limit of a 66 does sometimes preclude them from undertaking charter work, especially on the main lines out of London, but at weekends, when most charters run, then it is less of a problem.

EWS locos move to France...

In January 2001, Canadian National Railway announced it was to acquire Wisconsin Central, and so EWS as well, and this deal was concluded in October that year. It did not affect the operations, or indeed the name, of the company and all 250 Class 66s remained in traffic, in EWS colours.

An exciting development for the Class 66s came on 10 October 2005 when 66083 was sent via the Channel Tunnel to Calais Ville in France. This was for re-railing tests and other gauge clearance tests in preparation for a plan to redeploy spare Class 66s to work in France. It returned three days later and went back to work in the UK.

The Royal Scotsman

In 2016 GBRf won the contract to operate the summer luxury Royal Scotsman train. These operations saw the class break new ground, firstly working to Mallaig and then to Kyle of Lochalsh – lines that had never before welcomed a Class 66. The train has its own on-board generator, so supply from the locomotive is not needed. For the contract, GBRf usually supplies one of either 66743 or 66746, which were re-livered to match the train.

The typical working of the Royal Scotsman is Edinburgh to Keith, where it stables overnight. It then continues to Kyle of Lochalsh, running round at Invergordon and again at Dingwall. It often stables overnight at Kyle, with the passengers sleeping in their berths in the station. It also takes in the Highland Main Line and works to Mallaig, the leg from Fort William being top-and-tailed due to the length of the train precluding a run round at Mallaig.

Each year the train does a tour of the UK and that has seen it work to Plymouth, Chester and Peterborough amongst other places, with its dedicated Class 66s in charge. Sometimes a 66 in GBRf livery is used if either 66743/746 are unavailable, and 66735, 66738 *Huddersfield Town* and 66740 *Sarah* have all been used.

In 2016, GBRf won the contract to haul the summer Belmond luxury 'Royal Scotsman' trains and 66743/746 were repainted to match the coaches. On 7 July, 66743 passes Dalnacardoch, working north from Edinburgh to Boat of Garten.
Glen Batten

The last Class 66 off the production line, after 683 units, was 66779 and it was specially painted in British Railways' Brunswick green and named *Evening Star*. On 4 September 2017 it was on display at Old Oak Common HST depot open day. *Jack Boskett*

By this time, EWS was no longer the 'default' first-choice railfreight haulier in the UK and it was losing traffic to other operations, such as GBRf and Freightliner. As a result, it not only had surplus traction in the UK, but CN also identified that the only area growth was going to come was in mainland Europe. With this in mind, getting an operator's licence in France was seen as key.

The next stage as part of the approval process for running 66s in France had already started when, in July 2005, EWS stopped 66215 at Toton for the start on the conversion work to allow the loco – and indeed the type – to be cleared to run in France.

By 22 December the loco had reached Dollands Moor and on 3 January 2006 it moved through the Channel Tunnel and started testing the following day in France on the Plouaret to Plourerlin section of the Rennes to Brest line. More tests were conducted in January 2006.

The next loco to move was 66049 in May 2006 for static driver training at Champigneulles, followed by 66022 in June, 66029 in September, 66010 in October and 66032/036/038 in November.

In 2007–08, more locos moved, namely 66026/ 028/033/042/045/052/062/064/071–073, 66123/179/190/191/193/195, 66201–205/208–214/ 216–219/222–226/228/229/231–236/239–247/249. In total sixty-four locos were redeployed in France alone.

Several locos were identified for movement to France but not actually modified. They include 66031/037/ 039/051/206, while 66110 – one of the locos fitted with RETB – was also moved into the ECR pool, but not actually modified. It was sent to France on 6 March 2007 for static test and returned to the UK on 21 April.

Most of the conversion work was undertaken at Toton, but to spread the workload to meet the commitment for shipping locos abroad, some were modified at Crewe Electric depot, namely 66179/195, 66202/203/216/217/223–225/228/231/233/242/247.

Many locos returned to the UK for routine maintenance at Toton, but this practice soon stopped as it was cheaper to keep the locos in France for any repairs or routine exams. The locos are based at a depot at Alizay, where several ex-EWS Class 58s have been dumped for several years following their withdrawal after a hire contract in France.

Some locos also returned to the UK and were put back to work back with EWS/DB Schenker, and this was especially true during the autumn when EWS ran many Railhead Treatment Trains (RHTTs) and required extra traction. Locos returned to the UK for this purpose were 66010/022/028/029/033/042/062/072, 66123/191, 66209/ 211/218/225/242 and some of these made several returns to the UK.

The final Class 66s made in America for GBRf docked at Newport, South Wales, on 13 February 2016. They were 66773–779, with 66779 covered with a tarpaulin to hide its green livery. No. 66775 is craned off the ship ready to land on UK soil. *Jack Boskett*

As well as the sixty-four ex-EWS locos transferring to Euro Cargo rail operation, ECR also then acquired its own sixty brand new Class 66s – numbered as 77xxx – from Canada in 2007–09.

In June 2007 it was announced that the German operator Deutsche Bahn had agreed to buy EWS and this deal was ratified in November of the same year. On 1 January 2009 the company was rebranded as DB Schenker, and in March 2016 the company again changed its name, to DB Cargo, the one it operates under at the present time.

... and to Poland

As well as sending locos to France, now under the DB empire, and with surplus traction in the UK caused by restructuring and losing traffic, in April 2010, DBS sent the first of its EWS Class 66s to Poland, with 66220, which had been sent to the ECR fleet, making the switch from France.

It was followed by fourteen more locos during 2011, with 66146/153/157/159/163/166/173/178/180/189/196/227/237/248 all moving, and these remain at work in the country to date. Nos 66221/232 were both earmarked for use in Poland, but were never sent and remained in the UK.

Many of the locos were initially laid up in Poland as issues were resolved before they could be put into traffic, but they are all now working there. Six – 66163/178/189/220/227/248 – have been repainted into DB red, without any yellow panels, and while all have been renumbered with UIC numbers, each loco retains its TOPS number as part of that. All are numbered in the 92 70 0 066xxx-x series. They occasionally work into Lithuania and Germany but tend to remain in Poland. Those not repainted into DB red retain EWS colours, as do those in France.

The Polish locos lost their swinghead couplers, a modification that was also implemented on some of the ECR French Class 66s.

Freightliner sends locos to Poland

Freightliner also found itself with surplus motive power in the UK and started to send Class 66s to Poland. It had already acquired seven brand new Class 66s via Angel Trains for use in Poland, and 66001–004 were delivered in February 2007, joined by 66005–007 in April.

The first of its UK locos to move was 66586, which was shipped from Immingham on November 2008 and taken to Kostrzyn before moving to the Unikol works for modifications. It was renumbered 66008.

The next transferred were 66582/583, which moved to Immingham in late May 2009, then taken to Cuxhaven and then on to Olesnica works for conversion in June. No. 66584 joined the fleet in August 2009, then 66624/625 in June 2010.

There was a steady stream of transfers in 2011, with 66608 moving in February, then 66609/611 in March, 66612 in July and ex-DRS 66411 in November. In 2012 two more ex-DRS locos moved to Poland; 66417 in March and 66412 in October.

There was a lull in locos heading to Poland until 2016, when 66527/530/535 all moved in March, and more recently 66954 and 66595 have made the move in January and April and 2018 respectively. Another ex-DRS loco, 66413, was also considered for transfer but experienced some issues when at Immingham waiting to ship, so its move was cancelled and it later went on to be the first of the company's locos repainted into the Genesee & Wyoming orange and black livery in 2017.

All the 66s moved from the UK for Freightliner PL have been renumbered in the 660xx series for the 66/5s, while the six 66/6s transferred have been renumbered but still in the 666xx series. These nineteen departures mean there are nineteen Class 66/6s and 92 Class 66/5s left in the UK.

The original seven Freightliner PL Class 66s, those that were not former UK machines, are now owned by Alpha Trains, which is the European arm of Angel leasing but is a leasing company in its own right. Nowadays they tend to work mostly in Germany with occasional trips into Poland.

Class 66 liveries

The 250 locos for EWS were delivered in the company's corporate livery of all-over red (or, as some called it, maroon) with a gold or off yellow band. However, unlike other locos that had been painted in this livery prior to the Class 66s' arrival, the yellow band was in a zigzag style. This livery was seen on 66001–250.

Even the 66s look tiny when compared with the size of the ship and the cranes used to move them. No. 66777 is in the air as it becomes the last Class 66 to be unloaded of this final order of seven locos. *Jack Boskett*

No. 66778 touches down on the dockside at Newport. The last twenty-eight Class 66 were built in Muncie, Indiana, in two batches, 66752–772 and 66773–779. *Jack Boskett*

Freightliner's locos were delivered in all-over green with wrap round yellow cabs, and seen on 66501–599, 66601–625 and 66951–957.

DRS's locos were in blue, with small yellow warning panels, and a Compass logo and DRS branding added using vinyls on the side. Locos in this livery were 66401–434.

GB Railfreight opted for a blue and orange livery, the bodysides were blue and the cabs orange, with orange GBRf branding and large bodyside orange numbers, and this was applied initially to 66701–717.

Fastline Freight chose a predominately grey livery with a black roof and upper band with yellow and white angled stripes and full yellow ends. This was applied to 66301–305 at construction and DRS's 66434 was also repainted in this livery as part of a short-lived hire agreement.

Repainting locos – or re-liverying as more often than not vinyl wraps were used as opposed to actual paint – has been big business in the privatised world. Often locos were re-liveried as part of a tie-in with a customer where a loco or two were re-liveried in a customer's colour scheme or with branding.

Following its sale to DB, some of the first 250 locos started to appear in DB Schenker all-over red, and this was seen on 66001/058/097, 66101/114/118/152/185,

66200. This was changed, slightly, to the DB Cargo red, which had a full-height DB logo and no Schenker branding. This is progressively being applied to the remaining locos in EWS livery and by August 2019 had been seen on 66001/009/016–021/027/034/035/041/044/ 055/065/066/070/074/077/078/082/085/094, 66100/104/105/107/113/115/117/124/128/130/131/134/135–137/149/150/165/167/175/182/185/192/206/230. Of these, 66016 was later sold to GBRf and has lost its red livery. Additionally, 66136 sports DB Cargo red with China–London branding. Some of the other locos still in their original livery had their EWS lettering removed and their three beasties logos replaced by DB stickers, with at least 66002/012/014/023/031/039/040/043/053/078/080/ 084/088/090/095/096/098/099, 66103/108/109/111/112/114/121/127/139/143/145/155/156/168/172/174/176/188/197/200 running like this.

DB also repainted some locos in customer colours. The ill-fated 66048 emerged in Stobart livery, similar but not the same as the livery applied to some DRS locos. As mentioned, it only worked one train in this colour scheme before crashing.

In spring/summer 2019, six DB Cargo loco were painted in Maritime blue with cabside DB logos, these being 66005/047/051/090 and 66142/162, while shortly afterwards in April, 66109 was unveiled in a similar blue livery but one to support another customer, PD Ports.

Of the locos moved by DB to Poland, some have been painted in DB red – without yellow panels – and at least 66163/178/189 and 66220/227/248 have been reported as such.

Freightliner locos branded for customers have been 66522 in Shanks Waste livery, which was actually only half the loco, the other half being in standard Freightliner green. It has since lost this livery for standard Freightliner colours.

No. 66623 was initially branded in Bardon Aggregates blue, but it later lost the branding for a large bodyside Freightliner logo. Both the locos were re-liveried from base Freightliner green.

Nos 66601/612 and 66738–741 ran for periods in unbranded Freightliner livery – the latter four doing so while in operation with GBRf after their transfer and renumbering.

When the Class 70s arrived, they were in a new livery – called Freightliner Powerhaul – and this has since been applied to a handful of 66s, namely 66414/416/418/420, 66504/528 plus 66411/412/417 for Freightliner Poland.

The green and yellow went out the window in 2018 when the company was taken over by Genesee & Wyoming Railroad company and it has started to apply its orange and black livery to Freightliner locos. No. 66413 was the first in August 2018, followed by ex-Bardon blue 66623 in March 2019 and 66415/419 in April. No. 66413 was a much lighter shade of orange but the later repaints were a much darker hue.

In June 2019, Freightliner unveiled 66587 in a striking pink and white livery at an event in Southampton to tie in with a partnership deal with Ocean Network Express (ONE). The loco was also 'named' AS ONE, WE CAN.

On 8 September 2014, the second batch of newly constructed locos to arrive from Muncie were moved from Newport to Doncaster Roberts Road for commissioning. Using 66753 as the train loco, it having been delivered in the first batch of Muncie locos two months earlier, in order are 66757, 66758, 66765, 66759, 66760, 66762, 66761, 66764 and 66763, as the convoy passes Cheltenham. *Jack Boskett*

Maintenance on Class 66s is made much easier by the ability to lift off the main body section, which when left next to the loco, as shown in this view of 66427 in the Electromotive depot at Longport on 9 February 2012, earned them the nickname 'sheds'. *Jack Boskett*

GBRf 66737 *Lesia* approaches Bridge of Orchy on the West Highland line with the Alcan aluminium train on 3 May 2017. This loco is named after the wife of GBRf's Managing Director John Smith, and the wording was added when Lesia celebrated 'a significant' birthday. No. 66737 was chosen as she often joked she was only 37 when ever asked her age, and hence the 37 part of the number are much bigger! *Jack Boskett*

Of the ten locos Freightliner took from DRS, 66411–420, three were exported to Poland and repainted into Powerhaul, but the others ran in traffic in unbranded DRS livery and in the case of 66413/416, they actually spent lengthy periods in their previous owner's livery! However, some had a full de-brand (66418/419), and others had a partial de-brand (66413/416/420). Most still in some form of DRS livery had the old-style Freightliner logos added to the cabsides and fronts, and 66419 ran for a period with the new-style Freightliner branding on its cab fronts only.

No. 66414 was taken on by Freightliner in base light blue after its Stobart wrap was removed and had no Freightliner branding. It was an early recipient of the Powerhaul livery.

GBRf's livery changed on locos during delivery of the batches, plus the company has been the most prolific in branding locos for customers and adopting special liveries for other reasons.

For a contract to provide infrastructure support for Metronet, part of the London Underground, 66718–722 were delivered in April 2006 in a lighter blue, still with orange cabs, but with Metronet branding. The next two batches of locos, 66723–727 and 66728–732, were delivered in First Group livery as by the time of their arrival in December 2006 and April 2008 respectively GBRf had been acquired by First Group, in August 2003.

When GBRf was taken over by Europorte in June 2010 it reverted back to its initial livery style with subtle changes to the original scheme seen on 66701–717. This was applied to 66702–708/710/712/713/715/719/722/728–746/747–778, with 66701 keeping its original livery albeit with the GBRf in the newer, correct, narrower font.

After it derailed in June 2012, the body of 66734 *The Eco Express* remained perched on the hillside by Loch Treig for more than a year until a safe method of working could be finalised to dispose of it on site. On 22 June 2013 the loco, covered by a tarpaulin, was photographed from a passing train. It was broken up in situ in September 2013. *Pip Dunn*

Even then, there have been some subtle changes to certain locos. No. 66775 *HMS Argyll* sports large F231 numbers instead of 66775, its correct TOPS identity in small black numbers on the cab. No. 66723 *Chinook* is similar, with ZA723 instead of 66723.

Following the sale of GBRf to Hector Rail in October 2016, another newer version of the GBRf livery is now being applied and is seen on 66724–726/781/786/788, while 66782 is similar but has Charity Railtours branding.

DB Schenker's 66048 – only just outshopped in Stobart rail livery – derailed on 4 January 2010 at Carrbridge. The damaged loco was recovered on 2 March and taken back to Inverness depot, where it was dumped for a few weeks until it was made safe to move by rail back to Toton. On 4 April, three days before it was collected, it was still on shed. *Pip Dunn*

Still in First Group livery, as applied to 66723–732 when new, 66724 *Drax Power Station* crosses the viaduct at Colbrookdale with 4F68, the 0900 Ironbridge–Liverpool Bulk Terminal, on 8 April 2014. This freight-only line in Shropshire has recently been mothballed. *Paul Shannon*

Resplendent in DB Cargo red and named *Resourceful* – a name previously carried by 47594/739 – 66035 arrives at Dagenham Dock with 6L35, the 1739 from Mossend, on the morning of 17 February 2018. *Paul Shannon*

Class 66s arrived in Cornwall at the end of the last millennium and immediately replaced Class 37s. Such has been the decimation of the china clay traffic in the county, by 2019 just one loco was needed to cover all trips in the area, usually staying in the county for several weeks at a time. On 12 April 2011, 66147 backs its rake of CDA hoppers into the railhead at Kernick with the 6P07 Fowey–Treviscoe trip. *Paul Shannon*

One of the EWS 64 Class 66s shipped over to France to work for Euro Cargo Rail, 66228 works an aggregates train through Noyelles in the north of the country on 17 April 2016. The loco still sports it original EWS livery with just a few minor tweaks. *Keith Fender*

Freightliner has progressively been moving Class 66s to its Poland operation. One was ex-DRS 66417, which has been repainted in the Powerhaul livery and renumbered 66014. It was at Sokolka on 29 May 2013 hauling a coal train. *Keith Fender*

Variations have affected the GBRf fleet – 66705 had small black cabside numbers when full-height union flag logos were applied in the space where the running number would have been as part of the Queen's Golden Jubilee in 2002.

No. 66709 has carried two special liveries. Initially in July 2002 it was painted in Medite black, and having orange cabs meant it was not too dissimilar to the Loadhaul livery of the late 1990s. It had large cabside numbers in this livery and MSC logos either side of Medite branding in capitals. Its nameplates were in yellow. It was re-liveried in April 2012 with graphics of an MSC ship on the side.

No. 66720 was re-liveried in 2011 featuring colourful artwork designed by then 6-year-old Emily Goodman, with a markedly different design each side.

In 2013, 66718/721 were re-liveried to celebrate 150 years of the London Underground, which saw 66718 in a predominately black livery with LUL graphics while 66721 was painted all-over white with a reproduction of the famous Harry Beck tube map.

In spring 2015, 66711 was painted in Aggregates Industry's light blue and turquoise livery – similar to that applied to some of the Class 59/0s. The winning of the Royal Scotsman contract in 2016 saw GBRf repaint 66743/746 in the deep plum maroon livery to match the train.

No. 66727 was painted in Maritime blue in October 2016, sometime before six DB Cargo locos were repainted, and it differed by having large bodyside numbers and blue over the headlight and the top of the bufferbeam. Its different light clusters also made it stand out compared with the DBC locos.

No. 66779 emerged in Brunswick green in 2016, but when GBRf acquired ten locos from DBC some were not repainted in to GBRf livery. The biggest shock was 66789 appearing in British Rail 'Large logo' livery, while 66783 was painted red with orange cabsides for Biffa waste. No. 66780 was the last of the ten locos to be repainted and it appeared in a red, white and blue Cemex livery. It ran like this for several months before being named *The Cemex Express* in June 2019.

One minor tweak was 66737, which had the 37 part of its number in a much larger font after its naming. After their acquisition from Europe, 66747–749 ran in all-over grey with orange numbers and GBRf logos, while 66750/751 did likewise in all-over light before being painted into GBRf livery. In July 2019, 66747 *Made in Sheffield* was outshopped in a white and turquoise livery as part of a GBRf customer tie-in with Sheffield-based container haulier Newell & Wright Transport. In August 2019, 66773 was given

DB Schenker moved fifteen EWS Class 66s to its DBS Polska operation. One of the locos, 66173, was stabled at Sokolka on 29 May 2013. *Keith Fender*

additional rainbow embellishments and named *Pride in GB Railfreight.*

DRS also had several locos rebranded. These all arrived in base DRS blue and the company's compass logos were added. However, 66411/414 were both soon outshopped in Stobart colours.

The livery on the three Stobart Rail locos all differed. The first was DRS 66411 and this had Stobart Rail branding on its bodyside with Rail in upper case and only the height of half of the bodyside. The second loco, also from DRS, was 66414, which had Stobart Rail with Rail in lower case but the full height of the bodyside. Both had red upper bufferbeams. Nos 66411/414 were delivered in DRS Compass livery and both had these decals removed and operated in base DRS blue before the Stobart wraps were applied.

No. 66048, a DB Schenker loco, had the same bodyside lettering as 66414 but with yellow upper bufferbeams. No. 66048 also had the original Bmac light clusters, whereas 66411/414 had the later headlight design.

DRS also had some locos re-liveried into Malcolm Group livery as another customer tie-in. They were 66405/412/434. The three locos with Malcolm branding also differed. All DRS locos, the first of which was 66405, had 'Malcolm Logistics Services' on the bodyside with

Malcolm in upper case and the company logo in between Malcolm and Logistics. Underneath Logistics Services they had 'Networking with European Industry' and under Malcolm they carried the company's website address. The DRS logos were on the cabsides under the driver's side and behind the cab on secondman's side.

The second loco re-liveried was 66412, which had Malcolm in uppercase large letters on the top of the body towards No. 1 end and underneath was the word Rail, also in uppercase and with triangular flashes. The company logo was behind the cab windows at No. 2 end and small DRS Compass logos on the doors. This loco also had red and yellow stripes on the extreme bottom edge of the front valance.

No. 66434's Malcolm livery was more striking, with Malcolm Rail in the middle of the bodyside and the company lion logo next to the grilles at No. 1 end. On the bodyside was the branding 'Committed to the environment'. The bodyside was a light blue with a seeping dark blue that extended up behind the Malcolm branding. It too had a yellow/red-striped lower valance, while the cabsides had black numbers and Malcolm Rail branding. This loco had previously been in DRS and then Fastline Freight liveries. When DRS lost the Malcolms contract, the loco had its vinyls removed and it was left in plain DRS blue with white compass logos.

As mentioned, several DRS locos passed to other operators and ran in de-branded DRS blue before being repainted into the livery of their new owners. When the company took 66301–605 from the failed Fastline business, they were repainted into Compass livery.

Nos 66401–405 went to GBRf, as 66733–737, while 66406–409 initially went to Advenza, as 66841–844, and appeared in that company's livery, which was similar to BR blue with yellow fronts and side window frames with Advenza branding. This livery, like the company, was short-lived before the locos headed to Colas Rail Freight, along with 66410, which became 66845. These were duly repainted into orange, yellow and brown livery. They then moved to GBRf as 66742–746, while 66846–850 joined the Colas fleet, being ex-Freightliner 66573–577.

DRS meanwhile rebranded its Class 66s into a plain blue with white compass logos and this has now been applied to all its remaining fleet: ex-Fastline 66301–305 and 66421–434.

One minor livery embellishment worth of note was EWS's 66111 running with (unofficial) Highland Rail stags on its bodyside.

Names

The first 66 named was Freightliner's 66506, christened *Crewe Regeneration* in July 2000. The event, which cemented the haulier starting a contract to supply infrastructure trains to Railtrack, saw it bestowed with blue Railtrack branding on the cabsides. The nameplates were standard BR corporate style font.

Freightliner's 66601 *The Hope Valley* was the next to be named, in November 2000, and then GBRf named 66701 *Railtrack National Logistics* in March 2001.

Freightliner and GBRf continued to name 66s occasionally, but it was March 2003 when the first EWS Class 66s were named. Unlike previous namings, which used BR-style nameplates fitted to the loco's bodysides, when 66002 was

With a dramatic backdrop, on 19 November 2015 Freightliner's 66597 *Viridor* passes Brotton on the freight-only Boulby branch. *Rob France*

named *Lafarge Buddon Wood* in September 2002 a different font on thinner nameplates was used, and the plates were fitted to the cabsides as opposed to the bodyside.

No. 66002 was then renamed *Lafarge Quorn*, while 66022 was named *Lafarge Charnwood* respectively in March 2003. These were followed by 66042, which gained the *Lafarge Buddon Wood* nameplates in July 2003. Again, all three had cabside thinner plates as also used on the earlier EWS Class 67 namings.

Since then many other Class 66s have been named (see Appendices, page 248). The vast majority had their names in the standard BR corporate-style font. No. 66618 was likewise but had small additional nameplates for the three different winners of a competition, which were changed.

The nameplates on 66723 are in the standard font but also had a cutout graphic of a Chinook and three squadron crests, while 66741 *Swanage Railway* is similar with a cutout of Corfe Castle. Some GBRf locos also had crests within their plates, such as 66739/763.

Another GBRf loco, 66715 *Valour*, has a shaped nameplate with the inscription 'In memory of all railway employees who gave their lives for their country' in upper case. It also had separate square plaques with coats of arms to the left of the nameplates. No. 66716 *Locomotive & Carriage Institution Centenary 1911–2011* had its second name in a circular wheel crest with 1911/2011 in the centre.

GBRf has also named several locos after football clubs, with 66725 *Sunderland*, 66726 *Sheffield Wednesday*, 66729 *Derby County*, 66735 *Peterborough United*, 66736 *Wolverhampton Wanderers* and 66738 *Huddersfield Town* all having the old LNER-style football curved nameplates, in upper case and with a football underneath them, albeit a flat ball rather than the half spheres the steam locos had back in their days.

EWS's 66172 *Paul Mellany* and 66200 *Railway Heritage Committee* both had their names in uppercase in a non-standard font, while Freightliner's 66503 *The Railway Magazine* had its nameplate in the same style at the

In the beautiful north Yorkshire countryside, 66086 approaches Sherrifs Brow, near Settle, with 6S00, the 1705 Clitheroe–Mossend loaded cement train, on 3 July 2017. *Rob France*

Railway photography does not get much better than this. No. 66083 crosses Ribblehead Viaduct with 6S00, the 1705 Clitheroe–Mossend loaded cement train on 20 April 2018. *Rob France*

DB Cargo red 66085 passes Steventon on 24 February 2019, with 6C03, the 1314 Southall–Severnside Sita binliner. *Martin Loader*

One of the most striking liveries applied to a Class 66 is the pink and white on 66587 – also named *AS ONE, WE CAN*. The 'pink wafer' passes Eastleigh with 4O05, the 0719 Birch Coppice–Southampton Maritime on 26 June 2019. *Mark Pike*

magazine masthead. The nameplates on 66593 *3MG Mersey Multimodal Gateway*, 66731 *interhubGB* and 66744 *Crossrail* are all in company logo or font style.

Nos 66048/411/414 had their 'names' in transfers above the cab windows and on the cabsides under the windows. Several locos have lost their names, including 66002/022/042/077/200, 66411/414, 66576/581, 66612, 66701 (twice), 66720, while 66709/716/718/727 have been renamed.

Detail differences

The majority of the differences that have affected the Class 66s have been cosmetic and centred around the headlight clusters. Standard Bmac light clusters were fitted to the first locos for EWS, Freightliner and GBRf, namely 66001–250 had standard Bmac light clusters and these were fitted to 66501–537, 66601–606, 66701–707 but later locos – namely DRS's 66401–420, Freightliner's 66538-581, 66607–622, 66951/952 and GBRf's 66708–727 – all had bigger headlights, which were very powerful.

The original style of light clusters, but with LED lights, were fitted to later locos built, namely Fastline's 66301–305, DRS's 66421–434, Freightliner's 66582–599, 66623–625, 66953–957 and GBRf's 66728–732/752–779.

Renumbering means 66738–746/841–850 have the larger headlight style. More recently, new black-framed light clusters with LED lights have been fitted to Freightliner locos and this programme is ongoing.

The DBS locos have cab wing mirrors fitted but these have been removed from those locos sold to GBRf and renumbered. Nos 66003–250 have swing-head 'knuckle' couplers fitted. These were fitted from new on 66201–250 and retrofitted to 66003–200. EWS's 66055–059 have an additional spotlight and drawbars on their cab fronts for working as Lickey bankers – 66058 is now GBRf's 66783 and retains this modification.

No. 66001 also differs by having an additional pipe running horizontally across its bufferbeams. The EWS locos also had a number of modifications to improve the cab comfort and this led to the horn grilles being changed to a protruding type. This was fitted from new to 66200 and retrofitted to the remainder of the EWS fleet.

Early on in their careers some of the rail unions complained about the cab comfort in the Class 66s and a few modifications were undertaken to the windows and the heating to make them more comfortable to work in.

Another modification the DB Schenker undertook on its 66s was fitting them with a start-stop mode. This shuts

One of the original EWS batch of 250 Class 66s, 66111, crosses Lunds Viaduct and approaches passes Grisedale Crossing on the Settle and Carlisle line with 6S00, the 1705 Clitheroe–Mossend loaded cement, on 16 June 2014. *Bill Atkinson*

The colourful 66720 has artwork designed by Emily Goodman when she was just 6, with a different drawing on each side. On 1 September 2016 the loco passes Rugby with a Felixstowe to Hams Hall intermodal train. *Ian Nightingale*

Ownership

All Class 66s were initially leased, with Angel Trains and Porterbrook the main companies leasing the locos in the early days, but later HSBC, Beacon Rail and Macquarie bought some for customers. The Angel locos acquired for EWS have since passed into the company's outright ownership and ten were recently sold to GBRf.

Because locos were leased, some locos have changed operators. Of the Class 66s left in the UK, GBRf owns 66747–749/752–789, Beacon owns 66301–305/596–599/738–746/750/751/790–792/846-850/953/955–957, Macquarie owns 66413–416/418–434/585/587–594/623, DB Cargo owns 66001–007/009/011–015/017–021/ 023–025/027/030/031/034/035/037/039–041/043/047/050/051/053–057/059–061/063/065–070/074–080/082–099, 66100–122/124–131/133–140/142–145/147–152/154–156/158/160–162/164/165/167–172/174–177/181–183/185– 188/192/194/197–200, 66206/207/221/230, Eversholt 66506–520/522–525/538–543/554–572/613–622/701–727/ 951/952, Porterbrook 66501–505/526/528/529/531–534/536/537/544–553/601–607/610/728–737.

the engine down automatically when the loco is stood for several minutes so as to save fuel. This is useful when the locos are sat in loops waiting for other trains to pass. This is being steadily rolled out across its fleet.

In 2004, Freightliner's 66951/952 were the first to be built with modified lower-emission engines and this became the norm for most deliveries thereafter – namely 66301–305, 66411–434, 66582–599, 66623–625, 66718–732/752–779, 66953–957.

Those locos sent abroad have had a few cosmetic changes. The French ones have small red-and-white-striped panels on both ends, while the lower portion of the bufferbeams have black and yellow stripes. The EWS branding has been changed to the Euro Cargo Rail logo, although the three beasties EWS logo is retained. Large number panels are on the cabside with the locos' new UIC number.

The global story

The Class 66s proved a success in the UK for their simplicity and their reliability, and accordingly they soon attracted the attention of overseas operators. Whereas most other railways could have much bigger locos due to their more generous load gauges, the Class 66 was a proven piece of kit and available 'off the shelf'.

The first operator to take note was German operator HGK, which took delivery of two locos, DE61/62 in September 1999, and these were two locos actually diverted away from the EWS build – it is understood they were destined to be 66154/155.

Swedish operator TGOJ took two in August 2000, numbered T66 713 and T66K 714.

Between 1999 and 2011, 162 more Class 66s were taken by non-UK operators and found work in many European countries.

Norwegian company Cargonet took six locos in January 2003, numbered, coincidentally (or otherwise!), 66401–406, and Class 66s have also been operated by Rush Rail, Heavy Haul Power, Trainsport AG, ACTS, Railion, DB Cargo, Rail4Chem, ERS Railways, DLC, Shortlines and others. The locos were usually owned by leasing companies including Porterbrook, Angel and

HSBC Rail – the three main ROSCOs in the UK. Other leasing companies to own them were Mitsui Rail Capital, Beacon Rail, and even EMD itself.

Freightliner set up its Polish operation with seven new locos, numbered 66001–007, and then bolstered that fleet with eighteen further locos moved from its UK operation due to dwindling traffic and improved operating practices.

EWS also sent sixty-four surplus Class 66s to France to create its Euro Cargo Rail operation, and went on to order sixty more straight off the production line from Canada for this operation. These locos were numbered 77001–060.

Thirty have since transferred to use in Germany, where they were given the Class 266 designation, although ECR actually renumbered them as Class 247s. The locos in Germany are 247011/016/020/026/029/031/034/035/ 038/039/041–060 and they retained their grey ECR livery, albeit with the addition of yellow warning panels, not actually a requirement in Germany!

Egyptian National Railways has also taken delivery of forty-one Class 66s, which work all manner of trains, including passenger duties, in the country. It also has a training loco AAST2 in its fleet.

A success story

The Class 66s delivered a reliability level better than anything previously seen before on Britain's railway and for lower maintenance costs.

In their early days, the EWS fleet – even when at full strength – was routinely delivering 97 per cent availability and when you consider the most reliable locos in the BR fleet were the Class 20s, which usually recorded 85–90 per cent availability on much lighter, short-distance work, this is an impressive figure. The heavy freight locos, Class 56s, 58s and 60s, were struggling to get above 70 per cent at times.

In fact, the poor reliability of the 56s was the catalyst for Foster Yeoman to take Class 59s in 1986, which ultimately led to the Class 66 order. If the 59s had not been built, would the 66s have seen the light of day? Probably, but you cannot say that definitely would have been the case.

Over their twenty-plus years, several Class 66s of all operators have been outshopped in customer liveries and one of the most striking was DRS's 66434 in the third, and most impressive, colours of Scottish logistic company W.H. Malcolm. It powers through Northway, near Ashchurch, with the 4V38 Daventry to Wentloog Tesco train on 5 March 2012. Sadly this livery has since been removed. *Jack Boskett*

The Class 66 story has been evolving for the last two decades and while the production line has finally ended, they will be part of the UK railfreight fabric for another two or three decades at least.

While EWS was the dominant railfreight player in 1996, twenty years later that is far from the case and by the start of 2019, of the 250 Class 66s it had ordered, sixty-four were in France, fifteen in Poland, ten had been sold to GBRf and 66048 was written off, leaving just 160, or 64 per cent of the original build, still in use in the UK with their original user.

Freightliner's UK's fleet has also contracted slightly, as has DRS's, but the GBRf fleet continues to grow and it is entirely plausible that it won't stop at 66799.

In short, the Class 66 is probably the biggest success of the privatised railway.

Opposite: Freightliner 66524 propels twenty HTA hoppers through the coal loading stage at Daw Mill Colliery in the West Midlands. This colliery has since closed and coal traffic is now relative rare on the UK railways as power stations switch to other fuels. *Jack Boskett*

Right: This loco started life as 66408 working for DRS and was then taken on by Advenza Freight and renumbered 66843. A short spell followed with Coals Rail before being taken on by GB Railfreight and renumbered 66744, later named *Crossrail*. It passes Melton Mowbray with 6L24, the 1034 Mountsorrel–Whitemoor, on 16 April 2012. *Paul Shannon*

3
The Class 67s
A Case of Promise Unfulfilled

The nationalised railway has had many stories to tell of locos that never fulfilled their true potential – the majority of the diesel hydraulic classes being the most obvious examples – but the privatised railway was meant to address that. Expensive decisions to acquire rolling stock would surely only be made on strong business cases and not on whims that would use taxpayers' money?

New rolling stock would really only be ordered for bespoke roles or routes, and while that is certainly true of the thirty General Motors/Alstom Class 67s – they were ordered essentially for mail traffic – the harsh reality is that the locos were little more than five years old when their main source of work was snatched from them when the Royal Mail ditched English Welsh and Scottish Railway – and rail in general – as one of its core transport suppliers in favour of cheaper, more reliable and generally more flexible road haulage.

RES: the first FOC sold

Rail Express Systems was the first of the five Railfreight businesses that Wisconsin Central bought, at the tail end of 1995. The company was then merged with the three Trainload Freight companies to form EWS in early 1996. While it grabbed the headlines in 1996 with its order for 250 Class 66s, these were 75mph freight locos with no train supply and not suitable for high-speed mail and charter trains that formed the bulk of the RES operation.

EWS worked with General Motors to devise a new loco to meet the RES brief and both improve it in terms of reliability and also in speed. In 1997 it placed a £43 million order for thirty brand new 125mph, ETH-fitted Bo-Bo locos, funded through Angel Trains. Unlike the Class 66s built in Canada, the Class 67 construction contract was awarded to Alstom in Valencia, Spain, due to a lack of capacity to build them in North America.

They had a new body-stressed monocoque body design compared with the 66s, albeit with obvious similarities in the bodyside, which shared the same corrugated style.

They used the same GM 12N-710G3B-EC two-stroke engine, but rated at 2,980hp. The locos also sported the same EWS livery as the 66s with the Z in the gold band.

The cab design was much different to the 66s, albeit based on a design built for the Spanish and Israeli markets. It had a single centre front window and a raked shape to give it a slightly better aerodynamic look.

The bogies were Alstom's H frame design, which EWS chose for its simplistic and proven reliability, and the new locos employed the same cab layout as the Class 66s to give drivers a familiar working environment. The 67s were not specified with cab air conditioning. They could only work in multiple with 66s and 59s using the AAR multiple working system.

Only having four axles, and an overall weight of 90 tonnes, meant the Class 67s had a heavy axle load of 22½ tonnes, and so had a high Route Availability rating of 8 that would – initially certainly – restrict them from operating over several lines. That was not an issue for their day-to-day mail traffic, but did present some problems for hauling charter trains.

The Class 67 will probably always be regarded as a class unfulfilled for a number of reasons, most notably changing traffic patterns and the loss of work by EWS to other operators.

Construction started in Valencia in 1998 and by September 1999 the first locos were available for EWS to show off to the press in Spain. 67001/003 were complete and undergoing testing while 67004–006 were very close to completion. No. 67002 had also been built but had been sent to the new high-speed AVE line at La Sagra, near Toledo, for testing. As much of the Spanish network was a wider, 5ft 3in, gauge than UK, the loco could not be tested on the RENFE network other than the high-speed lines that were built to standard gauge.

The factory was busy at work building the rest of the fleet, and the fabrication of the bodyshell of 67019 was complete, while the component parts for 67022 were in a pile ready for assembly. By late September

67001/003/004 had undergone testing on the small test track at Valencia with 67001 used for static testing. At the time of the press trip, EWS was claiming ten locos would be in traffic by 1 December, but it was to fall well short of that aspiration.

Arrival in the UK

The first loco to ship to the UK was 67003, which left Spain on 29 September 1999 and arrived at Newport docks on 6 October, the day after the fatal and tragic Ladbroke Grove rail crash – which somewhat glossed over the good news of the loco's arrival.

No. 67003 was delivered on its own, but the initial plan to send it to the Railway Technical Centre at Derby for bogie tests, gauge clearance and other weights and measurement checks was delayed when initial measurements suggested the loco was 5mm out of gauge.

No. 67003 was allocated to a new WAAN pool for the Class 67 fleet. The loco was moved to Cardiff Canton on 12 October by 60089 *Arcuil* and was then made good to be in gauge and duly moved to Derby on 2 November, by which time its programme of main-line testing was already three weeks behind schedule. The delays in commissioning 67003 saw shipping of more locos from Spain put on hold. The loco then moved to Toton on 22 November for commissioning and noise emission tests, plus checks to its AWS and radio systems.

In early November EWS admitted publicly that it would not have the 67s in traffic by 1 December, although also in November 67002 also reached a top speed of 140mph on test in Spain on the high-speed line.

The delays in commissioning had further impact as it threw the driver training programme behind schedule, a situation then further exacerbated by the onset of the busy Christmas period, meaning EWS could not release drivers as they were needed to handle the extra mail traffic that ran in December.

An initial main-line test run in the UK was planned for 22 November, but the loco was still not ready, and that aspirational date moved to 29 November. The first main-line tests were on to be on the Great Western Main Line from Old Oak Common in West London to Plymouth, running via Berks and Hants for 100mph and on the main line through Didcot for 125mph.

In mid-November, EWS was blaming Railtrack for deficiencies in its testing procedures that had precluded 67003 from taking to the network in anger, although Railtrack was still saying 67003 was fractionally too heavy on one axle.

On 26 November, 58019 *Shirebrook Colliery* hauled 67003 from Toton to Old Oak Common in readiness for main-line testing to start and finally, as hoped (second time around), on 29 November 1999, 67003 finally made its long-awaited debut, working from Old Oak Common to Taunton with a rake of NIA vans.

No. 67005 *Queen's Messenger* runs alongside the River Avon at Avoncliff on 18 April 2015 with 1Z74, the 0915 Victoria–Bath VSOE. *Martin Loader*

No. 67013 *Dyfrbont Pontcysyllte* propels a Wembley–Aylesbury ECS past Little Kimble on 24 May 2010. *Martin Loader*

With 67017 *Arrow* leading and 67022 on the rear, the 2U20, 1247 Paignton–Cardiff Central First Great Western train passes Pilning on 27 April 2010. *Martin Loader*

That test was deemed successful enough and the following night 67003 worked from Old Oak to Plymouth and back. On 2 and 3 December the loco underwent further testing on the route to Bristol.

By the end of the year the bodyshells of the last locos were completed in Spain and EWS faced the prospect of having several delivered even though nationwide clearance for the class had still to be granted. Meanwhile, rumours that the Class 67s were too heavy for use in Cornwall that were circulating in early 2000 were quickly dismissed by EWS.

In February ScotRail went public saying it was expecting to use 67s on the Edinburgh to Inverness and Aberdeen portions of its Highland 'sleeper' trains from May 2000, but EWS quickly issued a denial and said this was a premature announcement given only 67003 was in the UK at the time.

Crew training starts

By January 2000, 67003 was still only being used for test runs, which continued until 11 February, and it then moved back to Toton on 14 February, hauled by 66092, for tyre turning. This was very swift and later that afternoon the 66 hauled 67003 back to west London.

The prolonged testing period was to ensure the locos met all the current regulations, including vibration levels. It was hoped to have the loco certified for use on 21 February, although Railtrack had passed the loco for 95mph running – the same as the Class 47s it was to replace. By now Class 67 operation was already three months behind schedule.

On 20 February 2000, six more locos arrived when 67001/002/004/005/007/008 were unloaded off the *Arktis Meridian* at Newport. All six were taken to Toton for tyre turning as the correct tyre profile could not be achieved in Spain. No. 67004 was moved by 47306 *The Sapper* on 21 February and then 47798 *Prince William* collected 67001/002/007, returning them west with 67004 to Canton.

On 26 February there was a remarkable and unplanned passenger working by the new locos when 67005/008 rescued Virgin CrossCountry's 1V35, the 0636 Wolverhampton–Plymouth, at Wellington after 47766 *Resolute* – ironically one of three RES Class 47s hired by EWS to Virgin to meet a shortfall in Class 47 availability – failed with a main generator flashover. The 47 was never to work a train again.

No. 67021 brings up the rear of 1Z25, the 0928 Victoria–Worcester Shrub Hill 'Historic Worcester' Belmond Pullman VSOE charter at Cassington on 9 May 2018. The other Pullman Class 67, 67024, was leading the train. *Martin Loader*

No. 67023 passes Blackford, on the Highland Main Line, with 4D65, the 1512 Inverness–Mossend Safeway Intermodal train on 17 April 2003. *Martin Loader*

The 67s worked to Exeter, where the train was terminated. The 67s had been working 5Z57, the 0810 Bristol–Plymouth driver training run that was in front of 1V35. They stabled the vans in Newton Abbot and ran light to assist, taking the train to Exeter. No. 67008 then ran light to collect the vans while 67005 returned to Bristol.

With seven 67s now in the country, EWS could finally start crew training and the first depots to be instructed on driving the new locos were St Blazey, Margam and Old Oak Common.

No. 67003 was retained as the test loco and the other six locos were used for driver training. The 67s, now they were arriving, were starting to emulate their Class 66s cousins by being delivered to Newport, being unloaded and then put straight into traffic.

On 9 March another ten Class 67s arrived, with 67006/009–018 being unloaded from the MV *Jumbo Spirit*. The locos were shipped separated from their bogies, which were then fitted before the locos were craned onto the dockside.

Their arrival coincided with 67s finally starting to work booked mail trains. On 1 March 67001 worked 1V44, the previous day's 2320 Willesden Railnet–Swansea, from Bristol Temple Meads. The next day it worked 1M06, the 1425 Swansea–Willesden Railnet, back to Temple Meads.

Meanwhile, other 67s were being used on crew training, mainly in the West Country with 67008 running light to St Blazey on 26 February. On 13 March, 67013 was sent to Norwich to train EWS drivers in East Anglia on the new locos while 23 March saw 67016 visit Birmingham New Street, another first, when it arrived with 2S09, the 2005 Cardiff–Shieldmuir, which went forward behind AC electric 86401 *Hertfordshire Rail Tours*.

March saw EWS ramp up its Class 67 training massively, with 67012/017 moving to Doncaster on 24 March, and 67012 was sent to Tyne Yard, Newcastle, four days later, for crew training. On 29 March 67012 made the debut of the new class in Scotland when it took a rake of RES vans to Millerhill, although driver training was still to start in Scotland.

No. 67004 was sent to Bescot for training while late March saw the Norwich RES trains changed to Class 67 operation, allowing more Class 47s to be laid up. EWS had sixteen locos in traffic, with the first in the country, 67003, still not accepted into the operational fleet and the entry of 67011 also delayed due to minor derailment damage sustained at Cardiff Canton.

The blackthorn is in bloom, as 67027 *Charlotte* passes the recently cleared location at Cassington on 18 April 2018 with 1Z22, the 0814 Tyseley–Bristol High Level Siding Network Rail test train. No. 67023 *Stella* is on the rear. Martin *Loader*

On 5 April the second passenger working occurred, but only for those with fat wallets as 68011 replaced steam loco 35028 *Clan Line* on the VSOE luxury charter at Swindon. The loco only worked to Bath, but was used to recover some time on the heavily delayed train.

All Class 67s arrived and were immediately put in the WHPT pool for locos awaiting commissioning, and technically allocated to Toton, but as soon as they were accepted into traffic they were reallocated to Cardiff Canton in the WAAN pool.

On 14 April, 67002 reached Penzance, a first for the class, with a rake of Travelling Post Office (TPO) coaches from St Blazey, which then worked as the 1930 to Bristol. No. 67001 repeated the duty four days later. On 17 April, 67019–022 arrived at Newport on board MV *Stella Prima,* while WCML tests for 67s started the same month using 67017.

On 23 May, 67023–026 arrived on the *MV Fairload* and were soon unloaded, with all bar 67023 working their first trains on 31 May. Initially, Railtrack would only pass Class 67s for a maximum speed of 121mph, but the reality this was never exploited, let alone 125mph.

Railnet starts

Part of the modernisation of the movement of mail by rail didn't just centre on the introduction of the Class 67s, there was major investment in the new Railnet system in the late 1990s. This saw dedicated mail hubs, almost like 'freight stations' where mail in roller cages could be taken on and off the trains as they stopped for the shortest possible time so as to save costs.

The main Railnet hub was the Wembley Princess Royal Distribution Centre in London but there were also hubs at Shieldmuir, near Motherwell in Scotland, Low Fell, near Newcastle, Warrington, Doncaster, Bristol Parkway and Tonbridge, while there was also a dedicated mail platform at Stafford.

The idea was that mail could be brought in the roller cages to the hubs by road, easily transhipped with minimal fuss and materials handling equipment, and so saving manpower and time. It was a great intermodal logistics concept. Added into Railnet were the introduction of Class 325 mail EMUs – dedicated freight-only four-car dual voltage EMUs that had some obvious operating efficiencies compared with traditional loco-hauled mail trains.

It should also be remembered that the massive shift from loco-hauled passenger trains to multiple units in the late 1980s and early '90s had meant the ability to add mail vans to passenger trains was lost, hence the desire to create Railnet and make it cost-effective to still use rail for what was a logistics-style operation that was being very well delivered by the road hauliers.

Railnet also meant mail trains did not have to call at main stations, which themselves were usually in very congested parts of the cities they served. It was a very good concept.

Working one of the trains that the Class 67s were designed for, 67030 emerges from the bushes at Defford on 23 April 2002 with 1E43, the 1509 Plymouth–Low Fell Royal Mail train. Unfortunately within a couple of years this traffic would be lost to road and it would be a while before the class would find any further practical use. *Martin Loader*

On 11 May 2006, 67011 passes Achallader with 5Z07 crew training run in readiness for Class 67s taking over from Class 37s on the Fort William 'sleeper', which they did the following month. *Bill Atkinson*

Infrastructure monitoring trains that needed 100mph-plus running are normally undertaken by the New Measurement Train with its HST power cars but if it is unavailable then locos are substituted and this was usually Class 67s or later 68s before becoming a Colas operation with 67s again. On 17 April 2017, DBC's 67028 and 67005 *Queen's Messenger* work 1Q18, the 0856 Doncaster West Yard–Kings Cross–Doncaster West Yard with overhead line test car *Mentor* in the train, past Broad Fen Lane, near Claypole on the ECML. *Bill Atkinson*

On 15 May there was an important development that would affect the 67s, namely the opening of the new Railnet mail terminal adjacent to Bristol Parkway station. This meant mail trains no longer needed to used Bristol Temple Meads station. Whilst the first train to use the new facility was worked by a 47, earlier, on 1 May, 67005 had visited on a test train to the railhead for gauge clearances.

On 1 July, the first advertised charter for the new locos ran when 67014 set off with Hertfordshire Railtours' 'Spanish Inquisition' tour from Finsbury Park to Cornwall. No. 67014 worked to Westbury, where it was joined by 67010 to work in multiple to Plymouth Friary. No. 66199 worked the train to the short freight-only Cornish branch line from Lostwithiel to Carne Point, and then the 67s worked back to Newton Abbot and 67014 went forward back to north London.

The following day, 67011 worked 6Z59, the 1502 Tyne Yard–Milford Junction MGR train, thought to be the first time a 67 worked a train of these wagons. On 19 July 67022 was used for a buckeye training run.

On Friday, 21 July 2000, 67026 worked a 0930 Victoria–Bristol Parkway Royal Mail Terminal special. This was to take invited guests to see 67001 named *Night Mail*. The loco sported nameplates on its cabsides. After its naming, 67001 worked the 1410 Bristol Parkway RMT–Victoria and some of the press were treated to rides up front on the loco for stages of the trip back to London.

However, the naming event did see the Royal Mail stating that while it wanted to expand its use of rail to move its goods, it could only do so if the railway improved its service – both to retain its business, let alone increase it. EWS cited the 67s were a key development to address that issue as they were superior to Class 47s in terms of reliability. Sadly, a few weeks later, the crash at Hatfield was to set the rail industry back many years, and for the Royal Mail it was to be the start of a period of desperation in terms of using railways.

Finally, on 1 August, a few days after 67001's day in the limelight, the last four 67s, 67027–030, docked at Newport, also arriving on the *MV Fairload*, and EWS had the full fleet at its disposal. They arrived with a spare Class 67 cab shell.

This allowed more Class 47/7s to be laid up, although interestingly, EWS was not able to dispose of all the RES 47s in its fleet, and some would actually be retained and have light overhauls and repaints at Toton to prolong their lives a few months.

On 5 August, 67002 was named *Special Delivery* at the Old Oak Common open day.

Rumours of thirty or even fifty more 67s being ordered were quashed by EWS in August 2000 and while EWS only had 25 per cent of the Royal Mail traffic and was eyeing up more, it was unlikely it would win enough to warrant more Class 67 orders.

On 11 August 67027/030 entered traffic, while 67028 had entered use the day before.

No. 67029 and Driving Van Trailer 82146 work the DBS managers' on 29 May 2009 past at Ashwell. *Bill Atkinson*

EWS had long had the contract to supply Thunderbird locos for the East Coast Main Line and in 2004 it swapped the older Class 47s with Class 67s, of which four were stationed along the ECML at King's Cross, Doncaster, Newcastle and Edinburgh. They were used to rescue any failed train. On 7 June 2011, 67017 *Arrow* hauls East Coast's 43238/312 past Claypole on 5F05 King's Cross–Edinburgh Craigentinny ECS. *Bill Atkinson*

On 10 June 2006 a Class 67 worked a passenger train on the West Highland Line for the first time as 67008 handled 1Y11, the 0450 Edinburgh–Fort William ScotRail 'sleeper', seen passing Achallader. It was heavily delayed due to a number of issues. This was the only rime 67008 worked this train as it was not selected to be in the pool of regular locos for WHL work. *Bill Atkinson*

Full fleet operation

With the full fleet of thirty locos in traffic, the 67s settled down to working mail trains on the routes emanating from the Willesden Railnet terminal, especially on those lines that were not electrified. This saw the locos working a mix of mail trains and TPO trains to Swansea, Plymouth, Penzance, Norwich and Tyne Yard.

The first 47/7 laid up as a result of the impending arrival of the Class 67s was 47779 in August 1999, followed by 47765 *Ressalder* and 47766 *Resolute* in March 2000. Of these, 47766 was one of three locos – along with 47741 *Resilient* and 47747 *Res Publica* – that had been released to go on long-term hire to Virgin Trains.

Progressively through 2000, more RES 47s were withdrawn or moved to hire with Virgin CrossCountry, although remarkably at the end of the year, despite all 67s being in traffic, forty-one Class 47s were still in the RES fleet – including two dedicated Royal locomotives – and withdrawals were still relatively few and far between. However, they were used less and less on the lucrative mail traffic that depended so heavily on reliability of the traction to ensure they were not heavily delayed.

Charters started to be added to the Class 67s' portfolio in late 2000 and the locos soon became the default traction option by EWS for these trains unless a promoter requested specific traction or a Class 67 was barred from the route the train was taking. Notable route bans for 67s were the lines to Oban, Mallaig, Kyle of Lochalsh, Pwllheli and the Central Wales line.

An interesting charter working was on 17 February 2001 when 67003 and 66135 worked in multiple from Newport to Rugby, and back again from Birmingham International in the evening, on Pathfinder Tours' 'Merseyside Beat' special. This combination was at the request of the promoter as something different. Other 66/67 pairs have appeared on charters from time to time.

An unwelcomed crash

Early on the morning of 1 November 2000, at just gone 0330, 67002 was involved in a serious collision near Bristol. It had been a night of poor weather and the eight-van 1635 Shieldmuir–Bristol Parkway, hauled by 67012, was diverted via Severn Tunnel Junction. This meant when it arrived at its destination it was the wrong way round for the empty move to Barton Hill Depot for servicing, so 67002 was added to the rear to top-and-tail the train to the depot.

As the train approached Lawrence Hill in the Bristol suburbs, it was signalled to stop due to the 0230 Avonmouth–Didcot coal train, hauled by 60072 *Cairn Toul*, being held at a signal in front of it. However, when

Diverted from Marylebone to Paddington because of engineering work in the Northolt Park area, the 1505 Wrexham & Shropshire to Ruabon waits to depart on Sunday, 21 September 2008. EWS Class 67025 *Western Star* and 67013 are the locos. *Brian Morrison*

In 2009 DB Schenker tried out a novel way of reducing costs on one of its RHTT circuits by using a DVT instead of a second Class 67. A St Albans–Toton trip passes Wellingborough on its return run on 17 October 2009, with former WCML DVT 82146 leading and powered by 67029 *Royal Diamond*. *Brian Morrison*

the driver applied the brakes, the 67 failed to slow down and the train passed two red signals before it smashed into the rear of the rake of MGR wagons, which had just started to move as the coal train pulled away from its signal check at about 10mph, at 50mph. The impact caused 67002 to ride up and land on top of the wagons and then hit the road bridge over the railway.

Despite the ferocity of the accident, the loco stood up remarkably well and the damage to No. 2 end cab was – in the grand scheme of things – not too bad; a Class 47 would have been seriously damaged, possibly with fatalities. The driver of 67002 suffered a broken arm but both the drivers on 60072 and 67012 were unhurt.

No. 67002 was recovered and taken to Toton on 6 November for assessment, which revealed it had suffered relatively minor damage and the loco was duly moved to Crewe Works and rebuilt, returning to traffic in August 2002. The cause of the accident was identified as being due to the brake controls being incorrectly set when 67002 was coupled up at Bristol Parkway.

On 15 October 2000 there was the first use of a Class 67 by the InterCity East Coast franchise holder, Great North Eastern Railway (GNER) when 67011 hauled the 1010 King's Cross–Leeds from Retford and returned on the 1430 Leeds–King's Cross back to Retford due to an overhead line power isolation

On 17 October, the entire fleet changed pools from WAAN to WAAK, the change being to reflect the locos were allocated to Cardiff Canton and not Toton. A few weeks later, on 6 December, 67005 was named *Queen's Messenger* at Euston by Queen Elizabeth II and the loco sported a small plaque to commemorate its special naming.

A start on the 'sleepers'

From late September 2001, Class 67s replaced Class 47s on the first of the three diesel-hauled legs of the ScotRail 'sleepers'. The 67s were first used on the Edinburgh to Inverness portion of the 'Highlander' sleeper, which was typically eight coaches north of Edinburgh.

That was followed by them taking over the six-coach Edinburgh to Aberdeen portion from June 2002, albeit after several aborted starts. This allowed EWS to do away with three more RES Class 47 duties, as a third was stabled at Perth to assist either portion if it ran into trouble. With the improved reliability offered by Class 67 haulage, it was felt a Perth standby was no longer needed.

When GBRf took over as traction provider for the Caledonian Sleeper, it initially had to rely on hired Class 67s from DB Cargo. Two locos, 67004/010, were repainted into CS livery for a few months, only to then be repainted again into CS red, despite 67s still being used for the Inverness train into the summer of 2019! On 9 July 2015, 67004 *Cairn Gorm* passes Auchengray, between Carstairs and Midcalder Junction, hauling 1B26, the 0640 Carstairs–Edinburgh portion off 1S26, the 2340 Euston–Glasgow Central, in place of the booked Class 90. *Robin Ralston*

PLATFORM N°4

On 25 May 2012, 67013 *Dyfrbont Pontcysyllte* approaches Birmingham Moor Street with a Chiltern Railways train from Marylebone. *Jack Boskett*

While it was certainly true that the 67s were more reliable than the 47s, on the occasions one did fail north of Edinburgh then the delays could be very lengthy unless a rescue loco could be sourced quickly. And then there was always the risk it was 66 without any train supply, which then had repercussions for the return working unless another 67 could be sourced. More often than not a Class 37/4 would then be used to operate the train with ETS.

Although 67s took over the Aberdeen and Inverness legs, the Fort William portion – which was usually just four coaches from Edinburgh – remained hauled by an EWS Class 37/4 as the 67s were still banned from the West Highland Line.

However, the introduction of RA7 Class 66s on this route from mid-2000 did suggest it would only be a matter of time before RA8 67s were cleared as well and it was always an aspiration of ScotRail to do this.

As it transpired, it would not be until June 2006 that 67s finally took over the final piece of the Scottish 'sleeper' jigsaw. Whereas EWS provided drivers for the Aberdeen and Inverness 'sleepers', the Fort William portion was still worked by ScotRail's own drivers and several traincrew at Glasgow Queen Street and Fort William had to be trained on the 67s.

There were several speed restrictions placed on 67s over certain structures while working to Fort William. There was to be no double heading of any combination, although assistance from the rear by another loco was allowed. The speed restrictions enforced on 67s, so that the journey time could not be cut compared with a Class 37/4. They also had to be fitted with in-cab Radio Electronic Token Block (RETB) equipment to allow them to work north of Craigendoran Junction.

The first loco used to Fort William was 67008 on 10 June, although it suffered many issues on the trip north and was severely delayed arriving at its destination. After that early hiccup, the 67s settled down to work the train pretty reliably, although 67008 was duly not selected to be a regular on the route! Instead, those fitted with RETB were 67004/007/009/011/030 and only these could be used on the train.

It was discovered early on in their West Highland tenure that the curving nature of the WHL was playing havoc with the 67s' brake blocks and these were being replaced with alarming regularity. The solution was to fit cast iron brake blocks to 67004/007/009/011, which addressed the problem, albeit limiting them to 80mph.

DB Schenker 67013 accelerates away from Culloden Viaduct with the 2115 Euston–Inverness 'sleeper' on the morning of 2 May 2017. *Jack Boskett*

No. 67022 heads south through Spalding on 18 November 2017 with a Leeds–King's Cross train diverted due to engineering work on the ECML necessitating trains running via the Joint Line and so being diesel worked. *Pip Dunn*

Having lost lots of their passenger work, Class 67s have been relegated to freight work and ex-Chiltern Railways silver 67015 revisits its old regular stamping ground of Princes Risborough as it hauls 6A49, the 0732 Didcot–Bicester MoD train, on 28 May 2015. *Paul Shannon*

Now looking a little shabby, but still in its original EWS livery applied back in 1999, 67022 passes Manchester Oxford Road with a Holyhead–Manchester Piccadilly passenger train for Transport for Wales on 16 May 2018. *Paul Shannon*

Opposite: On 27 September 2015, 67029 *Royal Diamond* heads along the newly reopened Borders Railway and passes Galabank Stow working 1Z33, the 1456 Tweedbank–Edinburgh. On the other end of the train is A4 60009 *Union of South Africa*, which had worked south. *Rob France*

It allowed the same 67 to be used for lengthy periods; in fact it was not unknown for one loco to do as much as three months on the trot on the duty. If 67030 was used, it was restricted to a day or two as it did not have the brake modification. The locos were taken off the Fort William 'sleeper' in early 2016, when re-engined GBRf's Class 73s took over the duty following a franchise change leading to a change in traction supplier.

The Highlander 'sleeper' ran as sixteen coaches from Euston to Edinburgh and would be split on arrival at Waverley. The eight-coach Inverness and six-coach Aberdeen portions would go, leaving two 'sleeper' coaches for Fort William that would be coupled to a day coach and the lounge car.

The Aberdeen portion left Edinburgh at 0440 as 1A25 and came back as 1B16 at 2140 while the Inverness portion, which was actually the through train from and to London Euston, left Edinburgh at 0420 northbound as 1S25 and returned as 1M16 at 2038 from Inverness, typically leaving at 2025 on Sundays. There were occasional fluctuations in these times but as a rule this was the pattern for many years throughout the 67-operated years.

The West Highland 'sleeper' turns were 1Y11, the 0450 Edinburgh–Fort William, which ran Mondays to Saturdays and came back as 1B01, the 1950 from Fort William on Mondays to Fridays and at 1900 on Sundays; none of the 'sleepers' ran south on Saturday nights or went north on Sunday mornings.

On arrival back at Edinburgh from Fort William in the evening – well, the early hours of the following morning – the 67 would detach the two day coaches and stable them in the bay while the two 'sleeper' coaches would be joined to the portions that had arrived from Aberdeen and Inverness to go forward to London as another sixteen-coach train behind an EWS Class 90. All three 67s would lay over at Waverley until the morning departures, unless they needed to go for fuel or if a loco swap was being effected.

While the Fort William portion had to have an RETB Class 67, the Aberdeen and Inverness portions could be worked by any of the thirty-strong 67 fleet. There was one exception to that rule when, in 2004, there was a need for the northbound Inverness train on a Saturday morning to be worked by an RETB 67 as it was then used to work an oil train to Lairg on the Saturday lunchtime – the furthest north Class 67s have ever worked.

Arriva blue 67003 leads 1Q15, the 0910 Derby RTC–Derby RTC, via Oxford, Network Rail test train past Shorthampton on 12 August 2015. The rear loco is 67016. *Martin Loader*

There was an unfortunate start to the Wrexham & Shropshire Railway's passenger service on 28 April 2008. The inaugural train, 1P01, the 0542 Wrexham General–Marylebone, suffered loco problems only a short distance into the journey, and time was lost as the rear loco had to be transferred to the front of the train at Wellington. No. 67026 is pictured approaching Kings Sutton with the disgraced 67025 *Western Star*, running thirty-seven minutes late. *Martin Loader*

The first use of a Class 67 on the Lairg oils was 67004 on 26 April 2004, but this came direct from Motherwell and it was only later that the train was worked north from Inverness by the 'sleeper' 67. This duty soon reverted to a Class 66 turn.

Mail blow

In 2003 came a monumental blow for EWS as the Royal Mail announced it was pulling out of using rail as a means to move its goods. This was a huge blow for EWS, especially given the investment it had made with the 67s, not to mention the investment the Royal Mail itself had made with Class 325 mail EMUs and the Railnet network.

The first noises that RM may ditch rail came in late 2000 after the Hatfield derailment caused network meltdown, with a series of speed restrictions forcing mail traffic on to the roads. The railway was able to ride out that storm, but there was lasting damage on the freight side as the post-Hatfield fiasco allowed road haulage to prove its viability.

The TPO trains were axed in January 2004 and the last mail trains ended later that year. While a small number of mail trains did return to the network in 2005, initially operated by GB Railfreight and later EWS, these were worked by the Class 325s that the Royal Mail already owned. It was also a fraction of the rail operation that had been lost so dramatically.

Most of the Class 67s were now spare and looking for work, which led to EWS initially using them on general freight traffic alongside Class 66s. They still had their 'sleeper' work and some occasional, and very piecemeal, charter work, although even this was being seriously challenged by the likes of new TOCs such as West Coast Railways and FM Rail, with the former slowly eroding and eventually eliminating EWS's monopoly in this field.

EWS also sought more work – especially passenger duties – for the now grossly underworked Class 67 fleet. In the summer of 2003, the 67s replaced Class 47s as East Coast Main Line Thunderbird rescue locos with GNER. This led to locos being stabled at King's Cross, Doncaster, Newcastle and Edinburgh to assist any failed GNER train, or indeed any incapacitated train in the route to minimise delays.

EWS already had this contract but still used Class 47s, and the switch to 67s did mean some – but not all – GNER drivers had to be trained on 67s. It was hardly taxing work, but did provide a steady income while not resulting in massive mileages.

The sun has only just risen as 67030 passes Elliot, near Arbroath, with 1A25, the 0440 Edinburgh–Aberdeen ScotRail 'sleeper' on 6 May 2008. *Martin Loader*

With no more Cornish mail trains, Class 67s no longer visited St Blazey for maintenance and any exams in the West Country that might be needed were now carried out at Tavistock Yard near Plymouth.

High speed, but too late

Ironically, on 12 September 2003, 67023 was finally allowed to run at 125mph to start testing of the class's true capacity when it was used with a rake of Virgin Mk 3 coaches between Plymouth and Old Oak Common. The reality is that 125mph running by 67s was never going to be needed.

EWS continued to pick up some extra work for the Class 67s, but still not enough. An interesting development came in the summer of 2004 when Virgin CrossCountry hired 67s and eleven-vehicle rakes of Riviera Trains' Mk 2 coaches – ironically still in Virgin livery after their disposal by VXC – to work summer Saturday holiday extra trains after receiving justified criticism the previous year when trying to use four and five-car Voyager DEMUs on these holidaymaker trains.

DBC has held the contact to work most VSOE operations of the British Pullman for many years and Class 67s are the booked loco. Before 67021/024 were repainted to match the train any 67 was used, ideally a clean one and reserve royal loco 67026 *Diamond Jubilee* was in action on 7 December 2012 passing Sleaford on 1Z84, the 0827 Victoria–Lincoln VSOE for the city's annual Christmas market. *Bill Atkinson*

DB Cargo 67013 passes Beningbrough, near York, hauling Virgin East Coast HST power car, 43238, with National Railway Museum branding as 0Z43, the 0515 Craigentinny–Neville Hill on 31 July 2017. The power car was being returned to Neville Hill following attention at Craigentinny. *Ian Horner*

The trains worked by 67s were, southbound, 1V15, the 0708 York–Paignton, and 1V19, the 0951 Preston–Paignton, while northbound the trains were 1M89, the 0843 Paignton–Preston, and 1E99, the 0905 Paignton–Newcastle.

The trains were, however, expensive to operate – hiring the locos from EWS and the coaches from Riviera Trains, plus there was a lot of empty stock mileage as well, and so it was no surprise the turns only lasted one season before cost-cutting led to passengers being forced to return to the inadequate Class 220/221 units.

Another development in 2004 was the creation of the EWS Manager's train. This was a train formed of three Mk 3 coaches and Driving Van Trailer (DVT) 82146 and operated in push-pull mode by 67029.

The 67 was repainted into a new silver livery with full-height 'three beasties' logos, while the coaches were painted into a deep maroon not too dissimilar to the Royal Scotsman train. The coaches were used to entertain customers and undertake meetings for senior EWS staff, especially when taking them to site visits or events.

By the end of 2019, Class 67s had little work of any kind, especially passenger jobs with just two hired locos a day needed for weekday Transport for Wales duties. No. 67022 passes heads out of Deganwy working 1D31, the 1650 Manchester Piccadilly–Llandudno on 4 June 2018. *Robin Ralston*

In early 2017, Colas acquired two Class 67s from DB Cargo, which has a surplus of locos in its fleet, and had them repainted into its striking orange, yellow and dark brown livery. They were acquired specifically for running 100mph test trains. On 28 February 2018, 67027 *Charlotte* and 67023 *Stella* cross Arnside Viaduct with 1Q90 heading to Preston. *Rob France*

The train was kept at Toton when not in use and 67029 was used for other duties when not working this train. Occasionally, another 67s could be used if required, assuming they were modified to work in push-pull mode.

Other work that was given to some 67s was the annual autumn Railhead Treatment trains (RHTTs), which run from October to late November or early December. These trains cover the network spraying high-pressure water jets on to the railheads to removed leaves and other causes of poor railhead conditions.

RHTTs are typically two wagons, top-and-tailed by locomotives to give the operational flexibility of a Multi-Purpose Vehicle (MPV) which is the preferred RHTT tool, but of which Network Rail had insufficient units. While some RHTTs operated used older ex-BR locos such as 20s, 37s, 47s or 56s, EWS having modernised its fleets provided 66s and 67s.

EWS also tried the 2008 RHTT season by using 67029 and the DVT from the managers' train on a Midland Main Line circuit. While this was a sensible solution given RHTTs tied up two Type 5 locos on such a light load, and the DVT operation could return it to operating with just one loco, it was not an operating practice that was pursued.

Other areas where 67s were used were in the Bristol area and East Yorkshire while a single loco was employed on the Inverness circuit that covered the HML and other routes as there was no need to reverse with this operation.

More passenger work

A big addition to the passenger diagrams for the Class 67s came in 2008 when Open Access Operator Wrexham, Shropshire and Marylebone Railway (WSMR) started running trains from 28 April. Using hired Mk 3 coaches from Cargo-D, the trains started initially with top-and-tail Class 67s but when Mk 3 DVTs came on stream, the trains changed to their intended push-pull operation with the 67 on the country end of the stock.

Opposite: The Thunderbirds stationed on the ECML are often used to haul diverted trains during engineering work, and that has regularly brought them to the Newcastle–Carlisle Tyne Valley line. On 15 September 2012, 67008 hauls East Coast's 91103 past Whitchester with 1S13 from King's Cross to Edinburgh. *Rob France*

By Royal appointment

Since 1995, the Royal Train had been operated using two dedicated Class 47s, but EWS, the operator for this exclusive train, had concerns over their reliability and so in late 2003 it announced that the train would start to be operated by Class 67s. No. 67005, already named *Queen's Messenger*, was unveiled at Toton on 18 February 2004 in the deep plum Royal Train livery to match the coaches. In January 2005, 67006 was also repainted, and named *Royal Sovereign*.

From 2007, 67029 was adopted as the official standby loco for Royal Train should either 67005/006 be unavailable, and it was duly named *Royal Diamond* in October 2007. It was the first 67 to have proper style nameplates mounted on its bodyside. In 2012, 67026 was outshopped in another silver livery – with Union Flag graphics – and named *Diamond Jubilee* to commemorate the Queen's sixty years on the throne, and this too has found use on the Royal Train. However, at the time of writing, 67026 had been withdrawn from traffic since June 2016.

Both 67005/006 sport plaques denoting 'By Royal Appointment', although they have had three different sets for three different owners – EWS, DBC and currently DBC.

For a couple of years Class 67s were used to top-and-tail four coaches on FGW services between Cardiff, Taunton and – briefly – Paignton. On 19 August 2009, 67005 *Queen's Messenger* and 67025 *Western Star* pass East Usk Junction near Newport with the 1400 Cardiff–Taunton. 67025 was withdrawn in April 2015 but a return to traffic with DBC was imminent in late 2019. *Paul Shannon*

The initial turns saw one loco work the 0645 Marylebone–Wrexham, 1110 Wrexham–Marylebone and the 1610 Marylebone–Wrexham, the second loco worked the 0542 Wrexham–Marylebone, 1017 Marylebone–Wrexham, 1510 Wrexham–Marylebone and finally the 2003 Marylebone–Wrexham, while the third loco was in charge of the 0725 Wrexham–Marylebone, 1317 Marylebone–Wrexham and 1810 Wrexham-Marylebone.

The service settled down to having three diagrams and four dedicated 67s, 67012–015, although a fifth loco, 67010, was soon added to the pool to give added contingency. The locos were repainted into W&S livery and named, while 67010 actually lost its *Unicorn* names when repainted.

The service ran from Marylebone to Wrexham via Leamington Spa, Coventry, Aston and Shrewsbury, although a couple of trains were routed via Solihull, Birmingham New Street and Soho. They could not call at Birmingham New Street due to contractual issues surrounding Virgin Trains, but they did serve Tame Bridge Parkway. Occasionally the trains took different routes due to engineering.

Diversionary routes for the WSMR Class 67s included running from Wrexham to Chester, then on to Crewe and south to Shrewsbury to take their booked routes, while sometimes the trains started at Shrewsbury, went north to Crewe and reversed and then went south via Stafford and Wolverhampton.

There were other diversions in the West Midlands as well via Smethwick Galton Bridge and Stechford, calling at Smethwick instead of Tame Bridge Parkway.

The WCML also occasionally welcomed a WSMR train, running from Coventry to Willesden then on to Acton Canal Wharf and reversing at either South Ruislip or Neasden Junction prior to reversing and heading into Marylebone. One train also ran via the Trent Valley from Rugby to Crewe to reverse and another also ran via the Oxley Chord, avoiding Wolverhampton and another went via Duddeston and Aston on one Sunday. WSMR certainly endeavoured to run its trains via whatever route was open rather than use buses instead!

Later diagrams saw one loco work 1P01, the 0510 Wrexham–Marylebone, 1J82, the 1120 back to Wrexham, and finally 1P33, the 1525 to the capital. The second loco worked 1P03, the 0723 Wrexham–Marylebone, and 1J83, 1630 return, and the third loco started in London to work 1J80, the 0733 to Wrexham, and then worked 1P13, the 1127 Wrexham–Marylebone, and 1J84, the 1833 back to North Wales.

The service never made money, despite backing from DB Regio, and sadly it ended in January 2011, the last trains being on 28 January, with 67013 working the 1328 Wrexham–Marylebone and 1830 return.

All was not lost for the 67s and the stock, however, as from 2011 they started to work for Chiltern Railways from Marylebone to Kidderminster via Bicester and Solihull. Before they became regulars with Chiltern Railways, on 9 June 2010, 67010 and a WSMR set worked 1G55, the 1830 Marylebone–Birmingham Snow Hill, calling at Hatton and Lapworth.

In December 2007, new Open Access operator Grand Central started running trains between Sunderland and King's Cross using three HST sets, but issues with these sets led to some trains being worked by DB Schenker Mk 2 coaches top-and-tailed by Class 67s, with 67003/020 provided. This lasted only for a few weeks until its HSTs could take over.

In the Class 67s' final few weeks of operation on the Chiltern Line, 67008 speeds past Launton on 21 April 2015 with 1K57, the 1715 Marylebone–Kidderminster.
Martin Loader

No. 67012 was named *A Shropshire Lad* when used by the now defunct Wrexham, Shropshire & Marylebone Railway, but it has since been de-named. On 1 February 2012, it speeds past Hatton with Chiltern Railways' 1H32, the 1055 Birmingham Moor Street–Marylebone. *Martin Loader*

As well as the 'sleeper' trains, from December 2008 EWS provided two Class 67s and two sets of six Mk 2 coaches to ScotRail to work two peak-hour turns on the Fife Circle. The locos and stock would stable at Millerhill during the day.

The first loco would work 2K01, the 0632 Edinburgh to Edinburgh via the Fife Circle, and then come out to play in the evening for 2G13, the 1708 departure from Edinburgh for a second run via Fife Circle.

The other loco would work 2K18, the 0729 Glenrothes with Thornton–Edinburgh, and then later work 2L69, the 1721 Edinburgh–Cardenden. No specific locos were needed to work these trains, but it was often the case it would be one of the RETB locos as they were more often than not in Scotland anyway.

The turns ended in 2015 when DRS won the contract and started to run the trains using new Class 68s, for which 68006/007 were re-liveried into ScotRail Saltire livery.

Western passenger work

Later in 2008, in December, a new turn for Class 67s started with First Great Western. Two 67s would top-and-tail 2D04,

the 0732 Taunton–Bristol Parkway, then work 2Y10, the 0913 Bristol Parkway to Weston-super-Mare. The rest of the turn was then 2U14, the 1102 Taunton–Cardiff Central, 2C79, the 1400 back to Taunton, 2U24, the 1616 Taunton–Cardiff, and finally 2C89, the 1900 Cardiff–Taunton. The sets were serviced at Bristol Barton Hill.

A second daily passenger turn for Class 67s with FGW was introduced from December 2009 and included a run to Paignton. This turn was 2U02, the 0619 Bristol TM–Cardiff; 2C67, the 0800 Cardiff–Paignton; 2U20, the 1247 Paignton–Cardiff; 2C85, the 1700 Cardiff–Taunton; and finishing on 2M68, the 1917 Taunton–Bristol TM. This turn only ran for ten months, finishing in October 2010, but provided the enjoyable sight of a loco-hauled train in the day along the Dawlish sea wall.

In 2010, the traction provider for these two FGW turns was changed to GBRf, which hired in Class 57/3s from Virgin Trains to work the first turn. In 2012 it ended as a loco-hauled job and reverted to a DMU turn.

In the summer of 2007–10 a Saturdays-only turn from Bristol TM to Weymouth started to run with Class 67s in charge. This was 2O72, the 0906 Bristol TM–Weymouth, and 2V67, 1655 return, which was usually four coaches top-and-tailed by two 67s to save running round at Weymouth. There were some differences in times in some timetables, and sometime the train ran from Cardiff Central.

The train ended as a Class 67 job in 2010, but on 3 June 2017, 67010 made a return to the service – which was by then an HST turn – working 1O72, the 0906 Bristol TM–Weymouth, and 1655 return. On this occasion a full rake of eleven Mk 2 air cons – some in retro BR Blue and grey livery – was used. From 2010 the turn was worked by FGW Class 57s and then became an HST turn in 2011.

In 2015, 67s took over from 57/3s on the daily Holyhead–Cardiff loco-hauled train and 67001–003 were painted in the Arriva turquoise livery to match the Mk 3 coaches. The reality is any 67 that has been modified for push pull operation is used on the train, namely 67001–003/008/010/012–018/020/022/026/029.

This train is 1V91, the 0533 Holyhead–Cardiff via Wrexham General, and 1W96, the 1716 return also via Wrexham General. In December 2014 a second loco-hauled diagram for Transport for Wales was introduced and this was 1D11, 0711 Crewe–Chester; 1H82, the 0738 Chester–Manchester Piccadilly; 1D34, the 0950 Manchester Piccadilly–Holyhead; 1H89, the 1301 return; then 1D31, the 1650 Manchester Piccadilly–Llandudno; and finally 1K96, the 1934 Llandudno–Crewe.

Other work

The spare 67s were also used for other work, and one notable job was working on high-speed test trains, usually when the bespoke New Measurement Train – which uses HST power cars and Mk 3 trailers – was unavailable, in such instances top-and-tail Class 67s were provided before giving way to Class 68s briefly.

Class 67s are also often used for rolling stock moves, especially taking DMUs and EMUs to works for overhaul or collecting those that have been treated to a refresh, and frequently these moves are top-and-tailed.

In a similar vein, DB Cargo also has been quite successful in winning contracts for the delivery of new-build trains when they arrive via the Channel Tunnel, although it has competition in these lucrative market from GBRf, Rail Operations Group and Freightliner. However, Class 67s are often used to work these trains, which usually run with barrier vehicles between the locos and the new train.

The crest applied to the bodysides of both 67005 and 67006 to acknowledge their use as Royal locos. Three sets of plaques have been fitted, denoting when the company was EWS and DBS, and currently they carry plates that say DB Cargo. *Pip Dunn*

After GBRf took over as traction provider for the Scottish sleepers in 2015, initially it kept Class 67 on some of the trains, hiring them from DBC June 2019 until rebuilt Class 73/9s were delivered from Brush to take over as planned.

The inevitable teething issues with the new MTU-engine 73s led to a need to keep 67s on some trains, mostly the Inverness leg, but the introduction of Mk 5 coaches on the Highlander 'sleeper' in late 2019 ended any use by 67s as these coaches have Dellner couplers, so they have to be hauled by compatible 73/9s. Thus Class 67s could no longer be used, and that has led to loss of the class's last 'sleeper' work.

Thereafter, DBC's requirement for Class 67 reached an all-time low. Four a day are needed as LNER Thunderbirds, two are used for passenger jobs with Transport for Wales, and the remaining locos are used for freight and occasional charters, including the ad hoc appearances by the Royal Train (which itself is used far less these days) and VSOE British Pullman turns – for which repainted 67021/024 are meant to be the dedicated locos.

Colas

In November 2016 DB Cargo surprisingly offered two Class 67s for sale by tender. The truth was a deal had already been agreed for Colas Rail to buy two of the locos from DBC. However, as a legacy from ORR intervention over EWS's disposal policy, the locos had to be 'offered for sale'.

The two locos selected were 67023 and 67027 – the latter surprisingly one of the few that had recently been repainted in to DBC livery.

The deal was concluded in early 2017 and the two locos were taken to Toton for light overhauls and repaints into Colas livery, entering traffic shortly afterwards.

The locos had been acquired because Colas had taken over the Infrastructure Monitoring train haulage contract for Network Rail – ironically from DBC – and needed two locos with 100mph capability. Class 50s had been considered but were ruled out because of their age and perceived reliability risk.

Nos 67023/027, named *Stella* and *Charlotte* respectively after Colas staff, occasionally work other freight jobs for Colas when spare.

No. 67002 *Special Delivery* heads west at Baulking on 10 December 2008 hauling a single EWS Mk 2 coach. Power of 2,980hp might seem a little excessive to move one coach, but the Class 67s became underemployed within five years of being delivered. *Martin Loader*

Liveries

All thirty locos were delivered in the then standard EWS livery with the three beasties logo and the Z in the gold band. By mid-2019, twenty years after their construction, just over a third of the original build still carried this livery, namely 67007–009/011/016/017/019/020/022/025/030, of which 67019/025 were withdrawn from traffic.

The first variation from this came in February 2004 when 67005 was repainted into Royal Train Livery, which was then applied to 67006 the following January. The livery was the all-over dark plum with a thin yellow stripe just above the solebar. Numbers were fitted on cast plates above the nameplates.

These two locos have since sported two other versions of the livery, first with a thin red and gold band at the solebar added in 2007 and cast EWS logos added. In 2016 this solebar stripe was changed to just red and red and white DB logos were added to the cab ends. Then in 2018 both locos had a full repaint with a thin white stripe at the solebar, cast DB crests on the cabsides and DB logos on the front.

They also sport cast Royal coats of arms and cast plaques highlighting that EWS, and more recently DB, is the approved haulier of the Royal Train.

Unless clean – which in fairness the two locos usually are – or hauling the Royal Train – the livery otherwise is quite drab. And when it gets dirty, which it does if there are no Royal Train commitments, then it can look positively awful.

In 2006, 67029 was repainted into a striking all-over silver with full-height three beastie logos for its role as the preferred loco for the EWS Managers' train. In 2012 the logo was changed to the DB badge to acknowledge the loco's new owner.

In 2008, four locos, 67012–015, were repainted into the silver and grey livery of WSMR. In 2010 67010 was added to the pool and received this livery. Initially W&S branding was applied to the bodysides, and the locos were all named.

When WSMR folded, the locos and stock were taken over by Chiltern Railways and the branding removed. The locos then worked from Marylebone to Kidderminster until 2015, when they were replaced by

Class 68s. Nos 67012/014 still carried this livery in mid-2019.

In 2010 67018 received a coat of DB Schenker red with a maple leaf logo. It was duly named *Keith Heller*, after the outgoing DBS chief executive officer, who left the company in 2011. The red was actually a lighter shade than DB red.

Proper DB red has been seen on 67004/010/013/015/027/028, of which 67027 has since been sold to Colas and duly repainted.

From 2015, Class 67s started to work the Arriva Trains Wales Holyhead–Cardiff 'Welsh Assembly' train and for this, 67001–003 were all repainted into unbranded Arriva turquoise, which all three still retained in mid-2019.

As mentioned, in 2012, a special Diamond Jubilee silver livery was bestowed on 67026 complete with a fluttering Union Flag on the bodyside.

In 2015, GBRf hired Class 67s from DB Cargo to operate some legs of the Caledonian Sleeper trains to help launch the service until Class 73/9s came on stream. No. 67004 was repainted in the company's Midnight Teal livery and named *Carin Gorm* in March 2015, and 67010 followed shortly afterwards. Interestingly, the locos only carried this livery for a matter of months before being repainted into DB red in 2017 and 2016 respectively, even though Class 67s continued to work these trains until late May 2019!

Two repaints into DB Cargo red had branding applied – 67028 sported 'Leading the next generation of rail freight', while 67010 carried 'First choice for rail freight in the UK'. This was 67010's fourth livery.

In early 2017, when Colas acquired 67023/027, it lost no time in having them repainted into its yellow and orange livery. No. 67027 had had a short spell in DB red beforehand.

On 1 September 2010, 67002 sets back towards Ashchurch MoD depot, having arrived with 7X36, the 0455 Didcot–Ashchurch. The scar on the side is where is Royal Mail-inspired *Special Delivery* nameplates have been removed – they were fitted with a strong glue rather than bolts. This loco has since been repainted into Arriva turquoise. *Paul Shannon*

The most recent new livery seen on the 67s was the umber and cream Pullman livery bestowed on 67021/024 in 2018 for their role as the preferred locos for the British Pullman VSOE operation.

Names

When EWS took the press to Spain to see the 67s being built, the project engineer suggested that it would be unlikely that any be named due to concerns that fitting nameplates would make the locos out of gauge.

He was not correct in saying none would be named, but initial concern over the gauge clearance should any of the class sport standard nameplates was addressed by naming the first locomotives with thinner plates – only 6mm thick – and they were fixed on the cabsides, and by using adhesive rather than the traditional bolts.

The nameplates were made using cast aluminium plates, which then had material ground out to leave the required letters.

The first ten 67s to be named would have these plates but from the naming of 67029 in October 2007 standard-style nameplates were fitted to the bodysides of some locos.

No. 67001 was named *Night Mail* in July 2000 and was followed by 67002 being christened *Special Delivery* the following month and 67004 *Post Haste* in December. The theme of mail-related names was obvious, but it turned out to be short-lived.

No. 67005 was named *Queen's Messenger* in December 2000, and in July 2001 67010 was named *Unicorn* at Bristol Barton Hill. *Western Star* nameplates were fitted to 67025 in September 2001 and then in January 2002 67017 was named *Arrow* and 67018 became *Rapid*. The next naming was 67027, named *Rising Star* in September 2002, and then there was lull until February 2005, when 67006's new-found Royal Train status was honoured with it being named *Royal Sovereign*. This was the last 67 to have the thinner nameplates fitted.

One of three DB Cargo Class 67s repainted in Arriva Trains Wales Turquoise, but not given any branding, 67003 passes Hargrave, between Crewe and Chester, with 1W91, the 1615 Cardiff–Holyhead on 11 July 2012. *Paul Shannon*

By this time, the first 67s has started to lose their names, mainly because of the loss of the Royal Mail work, with 67001/004 being shorn of their plates in July 2004. No. 67002 hung onto its plates until July 2010. The *Unicorn* plates from 67010 were removed in February 2010 when it was repainted into W&S livery.

When 67029 was named *Royal Diamond* in July 2007, the loco was the first to sport proper-style nameplates affixed to the bodyside as opposed to the cabside as was the case on all the previously named locos.

The four Wrexham and Shropshire locos were all named in quick succession in the summer of 2008. They were 67015, named *David J Lloyd* at Gobowen station on 16 May 2008, followed by 67012 named *A Shropshire Lad* at Shrewsbury station on 3 July, 67013 *Dyfrbont Pontcysyllte* at Wrexham station on 9 July and finally 67014 named *Thomas Telford* at Wellington station on 15 July.

No. 67018 lost its *Rapid* nameplates in March 2009 and it was duly repainted and renamed *Keith Heller* in January 2010. The new nameplates for 67018 were again mounted on the cabsides and were a smaller size to that used on a standard nameplate but were in the same font.

The next 67 named was 67026 on 23 March 2012 at Manchester Piccadilly, when *Diamond Jubilee* plates were unveiled along with its new livery. This was to celebrate Queen Elizabeth II's sixty years on the throne.

Following the end of W&S work, 67012–015 lost their plates, with 67013 the first in December 2014 and the other three in April to June 2015.

An unusual naming took place three years later, on 23 March 2015, when 67004 was named *Cairn Gorm* at Inverness station and the loco was outshopped in new Caledonian Sleeper livery. This was strange because the contract to hauling this train had switched to GBRf, which duly had to hire in 67s to cover certain legs until its 73/9s were delivered.

The loco only sported this name for a few months and in 2017 it lost its plates when repainted into DB red. The most recent Class 67s namings – by mid-2019 – were the Colas pair 67023/027 being named *Stella* and *Charlotte* in June 2017.

Withdrawals and the future for the 67s

Several Class 67s have spent periods in store, sometimes for short periods, but ever since the loss of the Royal Mail traffic, and then the switch of much of their passenger work to other operators, some locos have been laid up for in excess of four years.

No. 67019 was stopped in March 2015 to Toton and has been slowly stripped of some parts to keep other 67s running. A month later, 67025 was laid up at Crewe Electric depot. It was joined by 67017 in December 2015, 67011/026 in June 2016 and 67009 in October 2016.

More recently, 67008 was stopped in June 2019 at Toton and 67018 was stopped in March 2019 at Crewe. All these locos could be returned to traffic relatively easily, and indeed any loco in the WQAA pool is effectively in warm store and so could soon be put back to work. For those in the WQBA pool – 67009/011/017/019/026 – however, their future is less assured – certainly with DBC.

It remains indisputable that there simply is not enough work to go round for the 67s and unless DBC can regain some traffic or win some new contracts then the remaining 67s will remain underutilised on freight trains.

However, in August 2019, long-time withdrawn 67025 was taken to Toton for repairs to return it to traffic, and was seen sporting freshly overhauled bogies prior to being repainted into Transport for Wales' predominately white livery – with a red band at cant rail height. It was close to returning to traffic in November 2019 and is the first of seven locos to be dedicated to the TfW TOC to work with ex-LNER Mk 4 coaches on trains between Cardiff and Holyhead.

With the advent of Class 800 Azuma IEP EMUs on the ECML, then there is every chance they could soon lose their Thunderbird duties and with this added to all the other contract losses that DB has lost in recent years for the locos then the demand for 67s could be minimal indeed.

The Colas deal shows DBC is not averse to selling the locos, and it is possible DBC could offload some more locos, either by agreeing deals or simply putting them out to the market and seeing if there are any takers. The issue is that DBC has sometimes sold locos and then duly lost work to operators using its old locos!

One thing is for sure, the 67s are not even halfway through their realistic lifespan so would be of appeal to other operators, either in the UK or abroad. Whatever happens, overall the story of the 67s so far is one of them having lots of promise, sadly not fulfilled. And that is through no design flaw in the locos themselves, just the change in traffic patterns.

4

The Class 70s

General Electric Enters the UK Market

Freightliner did a very good job in keeping the impending arrival of a totally brand new class of locomotive, the Class 70 PowerHauls, a secret from the railway press in the build-up to them being ordered.

Unlike EWS, which went all out and announced it was ordering 66s and 67s, Freightliner did no such thing. And unlike the DRS Class 68s, which were widely rumoured for up to a year before the company actually confirmed something was happening, the birth of the Class 70s somewhat slipped under the radar.

That said, Freightliner always liked to keep its business as regards major investment under wraps until it was in a position to make an official announcement, but the fact the plan to order the first of a wholly new class of loco was kept out of the media until a press release was issued is remarkable nevertheless, especially in the internet age with its forums discussing every topic under the sun.

So the company definitely caught the railway world by surprise with a press release on 19 November 2007 that announced it was ordering a fleet of thirty brand new Type 5 diesel locos for its nationwide operations under the name Project Genesis. This was also the date the order was signed. They were also the first locos ordered from General Electric and thus broke the EMD domination of the new loco market in the UK.

The Class 70s were GE's first dabble in the UK market and came on the back of a few, ultimately unsuccessful, attempts to crack the European market. Perhaps buoyed by the success GM/EMD was having with its Class 66s, which were now seen far and wide within Europe and not just restricted to the UK, the company tried again with its new PowerHaul platform.

It had built the Blue Tiger Co-Co loco for demonstration and hoped to sell the type in Germany and other European countries, but only a few orders were received and mostly for Asian markets.

In 2006 the company started the first talks with Freightliner over offering its PH37ACmi design for the UK loading gauge – and this would morph into the Class 70 design we know today.

What was said

The press release announced that: 'The Freightliner Group has placed an order for 30 freight locomotives of a new design giving even greater hauling capacity and a significant improvement in fuel economy than currently seen on the UK network. Project Genesis, which is being developed in partnership with General Electric (GE), will bring new technology to the UK railfreight market, enabling Freightliner to move longer and heavier trains whilst reducing CO_2 emissions per tonne moved.

'This development comes at a time when the government is making large investments in the rail network and Freightliner must continue to mirror this to meet the rising demand for delivery of products throughout the UK. The tonnages moved have been increasing each year.

'This substantial investment, the largest loco order ever placed by Freightliner, fits perfectly with the Department for Transport's recently published strategy document *Towards a sustainable future* which sets out the transport system's role in supporting continued economic growth and making a key contribution to the government aim of a 60 per cent CO_2 emissions reduction by 2050, The new locomotives enable both economic growth and lower emissions.

'The diesel locomotives will have an array of new features, including AC traction technology and dynamic brake which helps to generate 10% fuel efficiency when compared with previous diesel locos. In addition the cabs will bring new standards of comfort to freight train drivers, with air-conditioning as standard. Freightliner has kept its recognised Trade Unions involved (including RMT and ASLEF) and will involve groups of drivers for input into the design and build of the cab.'

Working a Freightliner Heavy Haul duty, 70003 passes Gossington, between Gloucester and Bristol Parkway, on 5 March 2010 with 4Z70, the 0853 Rugeley Power Station–Stoke Gifford coal empties. *Martin Loader*

The locos were financed via Lloyds TSB but were later sold to Macquarie in December 2012 when it bought all Lloyds' rail operations. While they had been announced as Project Genesis, the locos were known as PowerHauls.

The story didn't quite work out as well as Freightliner or GE had hoped and ten years on the jury is definitely out when it comes to deciding if the Class 70s have been a success.

The new locos

Inside the new Co-Co loco was General Electric's P616LDA1 V16 engine, set to deliver 3,820hp, so making it more powerful than a Class 66 and indeed the most powerful diesel loco to run in the UK apart from the Brush trial loco HS4000 *Kestrel* of the late 1960s.

With a maximum tractive effort capability of 544kN and a continuous tractive effort of 427kN they had better pulling power than a Class 66 – even a regeared 66/6 of which Freightliner had ordered twenty-five locos tailor-made for heavy haulage. This meant Freightliner could use them on its Heavy Haul flows.

They had six GE AC 5GEB30 traction motors and a GTA alternator. Their multiple working was the same AAR system used on the Class 59/66/67s, so at least some commonality and forethought went into that aspect of the design.

Fitted with a 6,000-litre fuel tank, which should in theory give them a range of at least 1,000 miles between fills, the locos tipped the scale at 129 tonnes, making them an RA7 machine and comparable with a 66.

The Class 70 used a body design not to dissimilar in set-up to the BR Class 58s of the early 1980s. It had a thin body with two full-width cabs. There was no engine room as such and instead access to the engine and other internal equipment was made via a set of doors accessed by standing on a solebar platform.

To meet the crashworthiness standards required the 70s had rather unsightly metal anti-climbers in which were incorporated the headlights and running/tail lights. The locos were no lookers, that is for sure and they were labeled 'ugly', 'unsightly' and 'industrial' as their cab fronts were a mass of slats, groves and blocks. Of course, locos are not there to look pretty, they are they to do a job, but compared with the 66s, these looked pretty hideous and they were soon nicknamed 'Bettys' due to the cult US programme *Ugly Betty* that was on TV at the time. This name soon died a death, although they we also called Fuglys (Freightliner Uglies!), and it is true to say there was little praise whatsoever for their design. The question that Freightliner needed answering though was how good would they be at hauling heavy freight trains.

The Class 70s are also used on intermodal container trains and on 23 July 2012, 70007 passes Uffington with 4O51, the 0958 Wentloog–Southampton. *Martin Loader*

Colas Rail's 70801 and 66846 pass Bourton in slightly hazy light on 9 April 2015 with 6M50, the 0755 Westbury–Bescot engineers' train. This train is a regular duty for 70s and is often double-headed. *Martin Loader*

Main-line passenger work for Class 70s is very rare and is mostly on charters at the request of promoters, and even then workings have been few and far between. The first trip was on 17 April 2010 when 70003 – piloting 66154 – was used for Pathfinder Tours' 'Yorkshire Dalesman' trip from Crewe to Leeds. *Bill Atkinson*

At the time of the order the railway press was quick to try to predict the new loco's classification, with Class 68 or 69 thought to be the most likely, However Freightliner opted for the Class 70.

The first arrivals

At the delivery of the first two locos in November 2009 at Newport, Freightliner explained that it had decided against the Class 68 as 'that's what everyone thought it would be', and added that Class 69 was also ruled out 'for obvious reasons!'

This was the second time the Class 70 classification had been used, although the previous 70s, a fleet of three trial third-rail DC electric locos, had been retired by January 1969 just after TOPS had been introduced and none had carried 70xxx numbers. There was no chance of the two types being confused!

The locos were built at GE's Erie factory in Pennsylvania and by June 2009 70001/002 were ready for testing, which occurred the following month. On 3 October the two locos were hauled to Lamberts Point Docks in Norfolk, Virginia, and then sailed to the UK on board *MV BBC Kusan*. They docked at Newport on 7 November, were unloaded the following day and shown off to the press that day.

After weighing and initial testing, the first loco to haul a train for its new operator was on 2 December when 70002 set off from Stoke Gifford, near Bristol, hauling 1,330 tonnes of coal to Rugeley Power Station before discharging and running back with the nineteen empty hopper wagons. On 24 November, 70001 was named *Powerhaul* at Leeds Midland Road, with the nameplates fitted to its solebars as had been the case with some Class 20s in the BR era. No. 70004 was named *The Coal Industry Society* on 9 February 2011 at the National Railway Museum at York.

The next day, 3 December, 70001 worked 4L93, the 1008 Lawley Street–Felixstowe intermodal train, running via North London as opposed to Peterborough, and the loco continued to work containers trains between Port of Felixstowe and Birmingham that week.

Getting the first two locos into traffic in less than a month was a great effort by all involved, and a lead time that can only be dreamed of by the Train Operating Companies taking new passenger rolling stock fleets into traffic for a first time.

While 70002 was making history working the first train, the same day, 2 December, 70003–006 docked at Newport on board the *MV Beluga Fortune*, having sailed from Norfolk. They were unloaded and added to the fleet on 4 December.

No. 70002 passes Cossington with 6U77, the 1348 Mountsorrel–Crewe, conveying ballast in IOA wagons on 9 April 2011. *Bill Atkinson*

No. 70007 took a different route to the rest of the fleet. It was taken by the MV *Tirranna* from Norfolk to Bremerhaven in Germany, arriving on 27 August 2010, and was immediately taken to Berlin for displaying at the Innotrans trade show in the city on 21–24 September. Once this was completed it was taken by rail – hauled dead in train – through the Channel Tunnel and arrived at Dollands Moor on 10 October. Once in the UK it was taken to Warrington the same day and after a check over was put into traffic straightaway.

A costly drop

The next batch of locos were 70008–012, which arrived at Newport on the *MV Beluga Endurance* on 4 January 2011 and were unloaded the next day. However, when the last loco, 70012, was being unloaded, part of the lifting gear failed, causing it to be dropped approximately 5 metres from the crane, and it landed back in the hold of the ship.

The caused the loco's frame to be bent quite dramatically. It was eventually unloaded on to the dock on 8 January and put on to a road trailer for accident assessment to take place.

The damage was so severe the loco was understandably not accepted into traffic and was duly left at Newport for some months. In June 2011 it was taken by road to Seaforth, near Liverpool, and shipped back to America on board *MV Atlantic Concert* on 25 June. It docked at Norfolk on 12 July 2011 and was taken by road to Erie on 22 July. Remarkably, the loco was repaired to a degree and is used as a test bed and shunting loco at GE's plant. No replacement loco was ever built to replace it.

Delivery of the Class 70s was relatively slow, and there was another prolonged gap until the next four locos,

Opposite top: Colas 70817 passes the delightful scenery of Freshford working 6C36, the 1145 Westbury–Aberthaw cement tanks, on 19 February 2019. This was the final loco of a second batch of seven Class 70s for Colas. *Glen Batten*

Bottom: The Colas locos work the length and breadth of the country, and on 9 September 2017 70802 passes Benhar, between Shotts and Fauldhouse, working the 1222 Viewpark–Oxwellmains empty cement train. *Robin Ralston*

70013–016, arrived. They were shipped on the *MV BBC Colorado*, docked at Newport on 17 December and were unloaded the following day. The final four locos were 70017–020 and these arrived via Seaforth Docks in Liverpool. The first was 70017, which docked on the *MV Atlantic Companion* on 10 January 2012 and was unloaded the same day. Next was 70018, which arrived a few days later on 20 January on the *MV Atlantic Cartier*, and then the final two locos, 70019/020, arrived on 16 February on the *Companion*.

That left the option for ten more locos 70021–030 to be fulfilled, but clearly, without any announcement, this order was quietly cancelled and with damaged 70012 not going to be replaced the Freightliner fleet stood at just nineteen – 70001–011/013–020. The works numbers for the locos were 58781–800.

Operations

Freightliner started as a management buyout in 1996 and was solely concentrating on its core business – moving containers from ports to terminals. In 2000, however, it set up the new trainload sector Heavy Haul, which would compete with English Welsh & Scottish Railway for bulk

trainload traffic of coal, oils, metals and aggregates. For this it used Class 66s – including regeared Class 66/6s. Because the haulage capabilities of the Class 70s was superior to all 66s, they were seen as suitable for Heavy Haul work as well.

No. 70001 was initially added to the DFGI intermodal pool, but 70002–006 were added to the DFGH Heavy Haul pool. The later deliveries were split between the two fleets, namely 70007–009/017–020 being added to the intermodal fleet while 70010/011/013–016 were allocated to the Heavy Haul business. Later, 70013–016 were added or the intermodal fleet in 2014, joined by 70002/006/010/011 in 2015. That left just 70003–005 in the Heavy Haul pool. Nos 70002/006 returned to this sector in 2016 but in 2017 all locos were allocated to the intermodal sector, although by this time they had started to be placed in storage.

The intermodal locos worked across the sector's entire portfolio, with only those trains that could be electrically hauled throughout, or for the vast majority of their journeys, only seeing occasional Class 70 haulage from time to time as Class 86s and 90s were – obviously – preferred for those operations. Class 70s sometimes appeared on the Coatbridge to Crewe working.

Almost brand new 70019 departs Eastleigh with 4O14, the 0536 Garston–Southampton Maritime container train on 22 March 2012. Freightliner's experience with the Class 70s has not been perfect, resulting in it not taking up the option for ten extra locos. *Mark Pike*

On 4/5 January 2011, 70008–012 were unloaded from the *Beluga Endurance* at Newport Docks. During the lifting of the final loco, 70012, on the Wednesday morning, an issue with the unloading crane saw the loco dropped about 20ft back into the hold of the ship, seriously damaging its frame and writing off the locomotive. *Mel Holley*

A close-up of the damage sustained by 70012. It was finally unloaded on 8 January and left on the quayside for accident assessment to take place, which saw it remain at Newport for five months. In June 2011 it was taken by road to Seaforth, shipped back to America on 25 June and returned by road to Erie on 22 July. *Mel Holley*

Key routes were from Southampton Maritime to the likes of Birmingham Lawley Street; Wentloog, near Cardiff; Garston, Liverpool; Birch Coppice, near Birmingham; Trafford Park, Manchester; Leeds and Daventry. They also worked from Felixstowe, Coatbridge and London Gateway to the same terminals.

The Heavy Haul locos were used on infrastructure trains, delivering ballast and materials to Network Rail for infrastructure enhancements and repairs. These would be nationwide, and 70s would be used where suitable drivers were available – not all Freightliner drivers were trained on Class 70s.

Other work was coal, when it was still transported in bulk by rail, a market that has now sadly declined due to changes in power generation. Coal trains ran to several power stations across the UK, but given most pits had closed by the mid-2010s, much of it was collected at ports.

The power stations FHH served in the main were Rugeley, Drax and Longannet, with coal from Immingham and Hunterston ports plus Ravenstruther colliery. Sometimes the trains would stable at Stoke Gifford (near Bristol Parkway), Hunslet Leeds and York.

Other work was cement and aggregates, and flows in this sector included traffic from Earles and Tunstead to West Thurrock, Seaham, Moorswater and Drax.

A demonstrator loco

The PowerHaul was a loco GE felt it could sell to other markets and in late 2010 a Class 70 in kit form, manufactured at GE Transportation's plant in Erie, was shipped to Turkish loco manufacturer Tülomsaş at its Eskişehir plant. The loco, with works number GE-2011, was assembled and unveiled on 28 February 2011.

To say the Class 70s have failed to live up to expectations can be summed up in this image of ten of the nineteen-strong Freightliner feet stored at Leeds Midland Road on 14 June 2019. Leading the line are 70013/016, while also laid up are in this line are 70001/004/009/011/014/017–019. For a fleet that is less than eight years' old, this is not a good advert for GE. *Anthony Hicks*

In late 2010 a Class 70 in kit form – manufactured in Erie – was shipped to Turkish loco manufacturer Tülomsaş and assembled and unveiled in February 2011. It undertook some trials on the Turkish network before eventually shipping to the UK in September 2012. On 17 October the loco was unloaded at Newport bearing the number DE37001, but that was soon changed, rather crudely, to 70099. Later it was taken on by Colas and repainted and renumbered 70801. *John Patston*

The locomotive undertook some trials on the Turkish state railways network (TCDD) for testing and demonstration over the year but it was a speculative build and not part of any order. GE Transportation had signed a memorandum of understanding with Tülomsaş in 2008 covering a collaboration to supply PowerHaul locomotives for the European, Middle East and North African markets. GE undertook a number of negotiations' with several potential customers in Europe at the time.

The loco, painted in all-over dark green, was due to ship to the UK in September 2012 – having been registered on TOPS as 70099 in the MBDL pool in June. As it transpired, it was the following month before the loco actually arrived in the UK when on 16 October the ship carrying it arrived at Newport and it was unloaded the following morning bearing the number DE37001, which was soon changed to 70099.

The loco was taken first to Crewe Basford Hall Yard that evening by 66561 and then on 23 October it was moved to Brush Traction at Loughborough by 66504 to be prepared for UK operation. It was swapped to the DHLT Freightliner holding pool for stored locos.

At this time GB Railfreight started to confirm its interest in testing the loco, while Colas was also considering the Class 70s for its fleet. However, the delays in getting the loco available for trials saw GBRf cool its interest in evaluating the class.

No. 70099 stayed at Brush for some six months, and indeed was robbed of some components to aid the return of 70014/018 to traffic after they had arrived for fire damage repairs. It was 30 April 2013 when 70099 finally escaped from Brush, but it was still not able to leave working under its own power; instead 66536 was provided to collect it and return it to Crewe. It was then taken to LNWR for tyre turning on 7 May by 66513 and 70002, an interesting development considering it hadn't even worked a train!

Overnight on 4/5 May, 70099 finally left Crewe and was hauled dead in train to Southampton Maritime terminal. On 7 June it was taken to the DB Cargo depot at Eastleigh pending developments but by this time Colas was in advanced negotiations about taking the loco plus nine more machines – basically the ten locos that Freightliner had an option for but chose not to take on.

No. 70099 was still pretty inactive and it was 5 August when it was collected by 47727 and taken to Cardiff Canton – Colas Rail's main engineering base.

Colas takes ten 70

Colas Rail Freight had a varied fleet of locos and was always seeking new traction to boost its fleet. The inability to order any more 66s – it had five in its fleet – saw it opt to turn to the PowerHaul design and it agreed to take ten Class 70s acquired through Lombard Finance. One of that ten would be 70099 and the loco's arrival at Cardiff saw a start on driver training. Meanwhile, over in Erie, 70802–810 were under construction, with works numbers 61859–867.

The first two Class 70s were delivered to Newport on 7 November 2009 and are unveiled to the waiting press, who were then able to have a walk around the locomotives. *Jack Boskett*

However, 70099 never turned a wheel on its own in its deep green livery and was soon repainted into Colas colours and renumbered 70801 – the official renumbering taking place in late August 2013.

In February 2014, the loco was unveiled in its new livery and finally, on 17 February, it worked on the network when it ran light from Eastleigh LNWR depot to Eastleigh Yard and then took 56302 to Westbury before continuing to Bristol Barton Hill. Its first freight job was later that day, from Westbury to Eastleigh.

Before 70801 appeared, 70803/805 arrived in the UK, being unloaded at Seaforth on 4 January, followed by 70804 on 30 January. However, these locos did not leave the Liverpool dockside until 20 February, so three days after 70801 made its debut, when they ran light from Seaforth to Eastleigh.

The Colas 70s arrived piecemeal for such a small production run, and also because they were coming from America. No. 70802 docked on 27 February, followed by 70806/807 on 23 April, 70808/809 on 16 May and finally 70810 ten days later on 26 May. All locos were put into traffic relatively quickly.

In 2015, Colas ordered a further seven locos, 70811–817 (64243–249 were their works numbers) and these also shipped from the States in small batches. No. 70812 arrived on 24 February 2017, followed by 70811/813 on 29 March, and then finally 70814–817 on 18 April.

Colas operations

The Colas locos are mainly used for trainload freight work and infrastructure support operations. Duties have included cement from Aberthaw to Moorswater in Cornwall and Westbury, from Oxwellmains to Aberdeen and timber traffic to Chirk from Carlisle, Baglan Bay and Heathfield in Devon.

Coal traffic has also been handled by Colas and its Class 70s, with flows from Leeds to Briton Ferry and Aberthaw to Avonmouth, and the locos have also been used on oil trains from Grangemouth to Dalston, Lindsey to Colnbrook, Kingsbury and Long Marston. Other freight flows have been taking car parts from Bridgend to Dagenham for Ford.

Opposite: Several Class 70s caught fire early on in their careers, resulting in some modifications being necessary to address the issue. The worst damage was to 70018, which ignited on 5 April 2012 between Basingstoke and Winchester and required the fire brigade to attend. The loco was taken to Southampton Millbrook, where the extent of the damage is obvious in this image taken that day. *James Mayl*

Freightliner's new General Electric Class 70s got off to an awkward start with a number of loco fires and by 2019 half the fleet was stored and the rest woefully underutilised. No. 70002 passes Ellesmere Port with a Fiddlers Ferry–Ellesmere Port coal empties on 11 June 2010. *Paul Shannon*

The infrastructure work is nationwide depending on what Network Rail wants and where there are major engineering possessions. Colas 70s are often seen stabled at Westbury, Eastleigh and Cardiff Canton. In 2018 GBRf did finally borrow a Class 70 to assess the class's performance up the incline from Liverpool Docks to Tuebrook with the company's Biomass train.

The loco was set again GBRf's sole Class 59, 59003, a Class 66/7 and a Class 60. The 59 topped the hill at 7mph, the 66 slipped to a stand and had to be banked, the Class 70 achieved 11mph, whilst the 60 was the best at 12mph. This led to GBRf buying ten ex-DB Cargo Class 60s from Colas Rail.

Problems with the 70s

It would be a lie to say the Class 70s have been a roaring success, and a number of fires on the Freightliner locos in their early days did not enhance the type's reputation.

Nos 70014 and 70018 both suffered serious fires in 2012, and 70005 had a minor fire the following year. In the case of 70018, the fire was quite serious and happened on 5 April 2012 between Basingstoke and Winchester, requiring the fire brigade to attend to put out the flames. The stricken loco was later taken to Southampton Millbrook and then on to Maritime, where the extent of the damage was obvious. The loco was then taken to Brush at Loughborough for repairs and modifications that saw it out of traffic for a year.

No. 70014 caught fire in November 2012 and it too was taken to Loughborough. It was also incapacitated for over a year, returning to traffic on 27 November 2013.

No. 70005 had a small engine fire on 14 July 2013 near Wigan North Western, although it was extinguished by the train crew.

On 27 February 2016, 70803 sustained damage to its No. 1 end cab when it collided with an engineers' train at Ivybridge in Devon and derailed. It was rerailed and taken to nearby Tavistock Junction Yard, later moving to Laira where repairs were undertaken. A less serious incident befell Colas Rail's 70804 on 30 October the same year, when it derailed at Toton, but the damage was negligible.

Opposite: No. 70004 *The Coal Industry Society* passes Lowgill near Tebay with an Up infrastructure train conveying sleepers on 19 April 2014. *Rob France*

Class 70s rarely work passenger trains but the third railtour engagement for one of the General Electric locos was on 21 June 2014 when 70002 led DB Cargo's 66135 on a Pathfinder charter to Carlisle. The return train passes Kitchenhill near Penrith on its way back to Eastleigh. *Rob France*

Powerhaul Class 70s are used on all manner of Freightliner traffic and on 29 August 2016, 70003 was climbing the Shap incline with 4S44 intermodal train. *Rob France*

Above: The horse in the field next to Circourt Bridge, Denchworth, watches 70802 as it ambles along the Up relief line on 27 April 2016 with the well-loaded 6M50, 0755 Westbury–Bescot engineers' train. *Martin Loader*

Right: No. 70802 passes Oaksey on 25 March 2019 with 6L39, the 0500 Bridgend Ford Sidings–Dagenham vans, containing automotive engines. *Martin Loader*

Below: An orange and yellow convoy adds a splash of colour to the green summer landscape at Purton on 17 June 2017 as Colas Rail's 70805, 70814, 70813, 70812 and 70803 run alongside the River Severn as 0Z98, the 0730 Cardiff Canton–Bescot, taking the locos to their weekend engineering duties. *Martin Loader*

Colas has made big gains in the infrastructure support market, providing locos and drivers to operate trains to, during and from worksites when upgrades are ongoing. On 16 April 2016, 70806 was at Northway on an overnight possession. *Jack Boskett*

The nineteen Class 70/0s were also subjected to a number of technical modifications to make them comparable with the later 70/8. These included a new cooling arrangement. The work was undertaken at Brush Loughborough and 70010 was the first to be upgraded. There were also some bogie modifications undertaken to the original locos during 2013.

However, more interestingly had been the decision by Freightliner to store several of its Class 70s for considerable periods and a line of ten of the locos dumped in a siding at Leeds Midland Road depot did not paint a very good picture for a type less than ten years' old.

By mid-May 2019, ten of the nineteen-strong Class 70/0s fleet were stopped, with 70009/013/016/018 all having been stopped in excess of two years. Those laid up were 70001/004/009/011/013/014/016–019.

Class 70 passenger workings

By mid-June 2019, just five Class 70s had worked passenger trains. The first trip was on 17 April 2010 when 70003 worked Pathfinder Tours' 'Yorkshire Dalesman' tour. The thirteen-coach train started at Swindon with DB Cargo 66154 in charge and it worked at Crewe. Here the Freightliner loco was added to the train, with the 66 retained as a 'buffer' as it was unclear if a Class 70 could couple with Mk 1 stock.

No. 70003 worked north to Carnforth and then the train headed east via Hellifield and Keighley to Leeds. It then continued via the Hambleton Junctions and Joan Croft Junction to Hatfield & Stainforth, where the train reversed, returned to Leeds and then followed the same route back to Swindon with the 70 being detached at Crewe.

The second working was on 23 March 2013, again with Pathfinder Tours as the promoter. This train was the 'Scenic Settler' and started with 66089 working from Eastleigh to Crewe via Coventry. The Class 70 Freightliner provided this time was 70004 *The Coal Industry Society* and it worked to Carlisle via the WCML. The return was due to be via Dent and the Settle & Carlisle line but that route was blocked due to snow drifts near Kirkby Stephen, so the train came back via the WCML as per the outward. A year later, on 21 June 2014, this train was rerun with 70002 piloting 66135 and working out via the Settle and Carlisle line, then returning via the WCML.

The next two workings were by Colas locos, both on the same day. Throughout the summer of 2018, West Coast Railways ran its 'Jorvik & Scarborough Spa Express' every Thursday. This was diesel-hauled to York with a steam loco working forward to the seaside resort, and for the first leg WCR tried wherever possible to use locos from its fleet that did not enjoy as much passenger work as its 47/57s, so mostly its 37s, 47/0s and sometimes 33s.

On 7 June 2018, the train started at Dumfries with 47804 and at Carlisle 70811 was provided to pilot the 47, running via the WCML, Copy Pit, Hebden Bridge and Leeds. The return was with 70805 coming on the train at York and working back to Carlisle.

By late-2019, there had been just one example of Class 70 working a scheduled timetabled passenger train and that happened on 6 May 2019. No. 68009 *Titan* failed at Fenny Compton on 1H37, the 1355 Birmingham Moor Street–Marylebone. Colas's 70805, ironically one of the two used by WCR a year before, was in the area and able to rescue the train and drag it to Banbury, where it was cancelled.

5

The Class 68s

The New Cat on the Block

As mentioned in Chapter 1, Direct Rail Services was, like so many other FOCs, a reliant user of the Class 66s, ordering its first batch of ten locos in 2003 and later taking more locos. It had a fleet high of thirty locos, later reduced to twenty-nine then nineteen machines, which it still retained in 2019.

DRS operates all the nuclear fuels trains in the UK and accordingly, due to the sensitive nature of this cargo, requires unrivalled reliability. All trains are double-headed so if a loco does fail, the other should be able to get the train to a position of safety where it can be rescued by another loco or two.

It started its operation with second-hand, refurbished ex-BR Class 20s dating from the late 1950s, before taking on Class 37s – themselves a design dating from the early 1960s – as its core locos. It also dabbled with fleets of Class 33s, also dating from 1960, and Class 47s dating from 1962, the latter aimed at winning passenger work. It has since dispensed with its 33 and 47s while slowly cutting it back its 37 fleet and virtually eliminating its Class 20s.

Even with old locos that had been rebuilt, the fact there were always two locos on the train meant there were few instances of a train being a complete, line-blocking, failure.

Finite lives

However, there was still a finite life in the old ex-BR machines, plus they were not the most environmentally friendly of locos, and the Class 66s were seen as a sensible solution with which to update the fleet.

At the time the 66s were ordered, they were the only real option for off-the-shelf traction for UK hauliers. They were actually ordered with intermodal traffic in mind, but they did occasionally work nuclear trains, remarkably, also always in pairs.

But even the Class 66s were only ever seen as a short-term option, and indeed the first ten locos were only taken on a five-year lease. While other locos joined the fleet, DRS was also quick to give up those 66s that were at the end of their initial lease periods.

The DRS fleet engineers wanted something more modern and up-to-date than the rather basic Class 66s. That desire led it them talking to German loco builder Vossloh, which had been enjoying success with its designs in mainland Europe.

Of course, any new loco for the UK could not be an off-the-shelf model due to the loading gauge issues that had dogged the UK for decades, even centuries, compared with the rest of Europe.

The story of the new loco fleet – what we now know as Class 68s – can be traced back to the summer of 2010 when the first rumours started to 'do the rounds' suggesting that DRS was looking to order a fleet of brand new locos to boost its traction. DRS wanted a mixed traffic loco as it looked to win more work in the passenger sector, for which it only had elderly Class 37/4s and 47/4s, and later 57/3s.

DRS initially confirmed the rumours 'off the record' that indeed it was talking to Vossloh for a Caterpillar-engined Bo-Bo mixed traffic loco with a top speed of 100mph, electric train supply and one that it claimed would have a 30 per cent lower fuel consumption than a Class 66, as well as better emissions. They weren't, officially, known as 68s back then, although that was the obvious class number from the outset.

It was to be April 2011 when *Railways Illustrated* magazine broke the story that DRS was indeed looking at Vossloh locos and the company finally went public with its intention, saying it wanted to acquire fifteen funded through Beacon Rail, although no deal was actually signed off at that point. Eventually an order was indeed placed in January 2012 for that initial batch of fifteen. A new shed for the 68s was also built at Crewe Gresty Bridge depot to maintain them.

With a paltry load of just two nuclear wagons, 68001 *Evolution* and 68023 *Achilles* pass Defford on 21 June 2017 with 6M63, the 1158 Bridgwater–Crewe nuclear flasks train. BNFL, DRS's parent company, stipulates all trains are double-headed even if Class 68s are used. *Martin Loader*

A short-term contract for 68s on Northern Rail's Cumbrian Coast operations was placed in 2018. No. 68004 *Rapid* passes Nethertown, between Whitehaven and Sellafield, on 14 April 2018 as it leads 2C34, the 1433 Carlisle–Barrow-in-Furness Northern train. No. 68017 *Hornet* is bringing up the rear but is not powering the train. *Martin Loader*

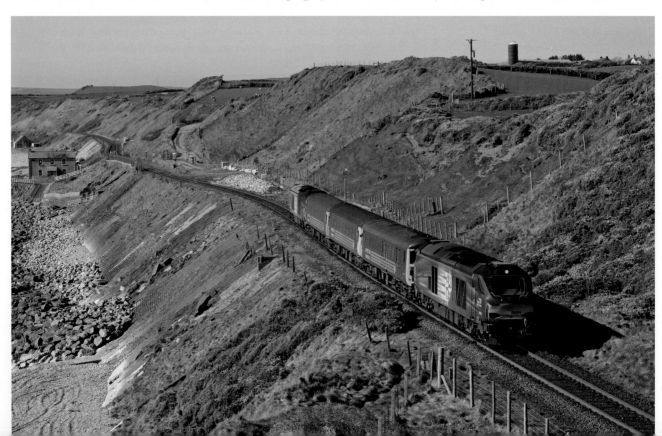

Charter work was one key demand on Class 68s and the high-power locos can handle heavy loads at high speeds for long distances. No. 68004 *Rapid* passes Tredington on 22 July 2017 with Pathfinder Tours' 1Z07, 0543 Bristol Temple Meads–Carlisle 'Lakeland Explorer' railtour. *Martin Loader*

Construction

The Class 68 was a UK version of the existing Vossloh Eurolight platform and looked very similar, but obviously scaled down to meet the UK loading gauge. The Eurolight was available as Bo-Bo and Co-Co versions but the 68s were the former.

Construction started in autumn 2012 in Valencia in Spain, in the same factory that had built the Class 67s for EWS in 1998. The first loco, in plain white and unnumbered, was seen on test within the confines of the factory a year later in autumn 2013. In December that year, 68001 finally broke cover when it moved to Velim in the Czech Republic for testing. The loco was still in white undercoat but with large Vossloh logos on its bodysides.

No. 68001 undertook several months of testing at Velim, working loaded trains and sometimes working with a full-size Eurolight. While 68001 was busy being tested, construction was continuing in Spain for the other locos. The first finished loco to arrive in the UK was 68002, which landed in the country on 18 January 2014, sporting the name *Intrepid*, a name once carried by Class 42 Warship D825. It arrived at Southampton via the *MV Autostar* and was taken by road to Carlisle Kingmoor for acceptance and initial staff training.

On 15 April, 68003 *Astute*, 68004 *Rapid* and 68005 *Defiant* – all sporting their nameplates, affixed in Spain – docked at Liverpool, followed by 68006 *Daring*, 68007

Valiant and 68008 *Avenger* on 10 June. The next batch of locos, docking in Liverpool on 31 July, saw a change for as well as 68009 *Titan*, the other two locos in the batch were 68010/011, both unnamed but also in the Chiltern Railways silver and grey livery.

That was because in late 2013 came confirmation of one of the worst-kept secrets in the industry: that Chiltern Railways was to replace its DB Schenker Class 67s with hired DRS Class 68s on its Marylebone–Birmingham/Kidderminster circuit, and six Class 68s would be delivered in the TOC's livery.

Nos 68012–014 also arrived in Liverpool, on 29 August, also in Chiltern livery and unnamed. With them was 68001 *Evolution*, but its stay in the UK was, initially, very short as it was then taken by road to Berlin for display at the 2014 Innotrans exhibition in September. It returned to the UK on 10 October, by which time the last of the original batch of locos, 68015, had arrived, on 23 September. This, like 68002 before it, came in via Southampton.

The locos were put into traffic slowly, and initially used for crew training and test runs. Carlisle drivers were the first to be trained but slowly more DRS depots had their drivers familiar with driving the 'Cats'.

Initial workings were all on freight trains but the first passenger working came on 23 September 2014, when 68006 worked 1Z25, the 0623 Glasgow Central–Gleneagles additional train for a golf tournament. No. 68005 was on the rear and this later worked 1Z56, the 1829 return.

No. 68008 *Avenger* rounds the curve at Hatton North Junction, between Leamington and Solihull, on 19 April 2018 with 1K45, the 1615 Marylebone–Kidderminster. Chiltern Railways prefers to use its own dedicated silver locos on these trains to provide a corporate image, but DRS blue 68008/009 still see regular use. *Martin Loader*

No. 68022 *Resolution* approaches Acle on 26 May 2017 with 2P10, the 0809 Norwich–Great Yarmouth Abellio Greater Anglia train. No. 68003 *Astute* is on the rear. The 68s and Mk 2 coaches were provided on a short-term contract to cover while AGA DMUs were undergoing repairs after accidents. The 68s were hired for about a year and were crewed by DRS drivers. *Martin Loader*

Stop
Look
Listen

Beware
Of Trains

Trains run either way
on each line

Warning
Do not trespass
on the Railway
Penalty £1000

Above: At high speed, 68015 approaches the footpath crossing near Launton on 15 August 2016 with 1K45, the 1615 Marylebone–Kidderminster Chiltern Railways' train, which later terminated at Leamington Spa due to a fatality near Solihull. *Martin Loader*

Right: The relatively rare sight of a Chiltern silver 68 on an infrastructure train as 68011 works the 6U77 Crewe–Mountsorrel past Castle Donington. This duty is often worked by a Class 68 and is frequently used to test locos after repairs at Crewe Gresty Bridge, hence the use of a Chiltern loco. *Bill Atkinson*

DRS hired Class 68s to Colas for a short period to operate any 100mph loco-operated test trains. On 25 July 2016, 68022 *Resolution* and 68005 *Defiant* work 1Q19, the 1512 Selby Canal Junction–King's Cross past Cromwell, between Retford and Newark. *Bill Atkinson*

No. 68030 is unloaded at Workington on 22 May 2017. The 68s were delivered via four ports: 68002/015 came through Southampton, 68001/003–014 via Liverpool, 68016–034 via Workington and when 68001 came back from display at the Berlin Innotrans show in 2014 it docked at Immingham.
Willy Ward

The next passenger working was the first charter working for the class when, on 6 December, 68014 handled Pathfinder Tours' 'Yuletide Yorkshire Explorer' from Newport to Leeds. This has since proved to be a rare use of one of the Chiltern sextet on a passenger train away from the Chiltern lines. The route it took was via Bristol Parkway, Birmingham Crewe, Manchester Victoria, Preston, Carnforth, Hellifield and Keighley.

More locos

In September 2014, DRS ordered a second batch of Class 68s, 68016–025, and their construction continued the production line at Valencia. Deliveries of these were made in the second half of 2015 and early 2016, and all came through Workington Docks. Nos 68016/017 arrived on 24 October, followed by 68018/019 on 15 November, 68020–022 on 23 March 2016 and 68023–025 on 14 April.

These locos arrived in DRS livery and unnamed, and had their nameplates fitted at Carlisle Kingmoor depot. They were christened, in order, *Fearless, Hornet, Vigilant, Brutus, Reliance, Tireless, Resolution, Achilles, Centaur* and *Superb.*

A third order was placed in July 2015 for another seven locos, 68026–032, and this was soon increased by two more, 68033/034. The latter two were bought outright by DRS, unlike the previous thirty-two, which were all sourced through leasing company Beacon Rail. Locos built from 68026 onwards were built by Stadler, which acquired Vossloh in late 2015 and accordingly had Stadler worksplates rather than Vossloh. The works numbers, which had been 2680–2703 for the Vossloh locos, started at 2944 and ran to 2950 for the next seven locos, while the last two had works numbers 3038/39.

Nos 68026/027 arrived in on 30 March 2017, again at Workington, but came in a plain blue livery to which simple white DRS logos were added by staff at Carlisle Kingmoor. They also had no names, and would not have for some time. They arrived with four Class 88s, 88006/007/009/010 (see Chapter 6).

Nos 68028–031 arrived on 22 May, again in plain blue, and finally 68032–034 on 20 July. Of these, 68033/034 were delivered, unnamed, in the same DRS livery applied to 68001–009/016–025.

No. 68008 *Avenger* passes Stafford on 4 March 2015 with the 6U77 Mountsorrel–Crewe infrastructure train. The orange socket on the left of the ETS jumper shows this loco is one of the eight modified for push-pull work on Chiltern Railways duties. *Ian Nightingale*

To meet a bizarre franchise commitment, TransPennine Express had to run a Class 68-hauled passenger service before the end of December 2017, so on the 30th of the month, 68003 *Astute* and 68030 top-and-tailed a rake of ex-Virgin Mk 3 coaches to work 1Z68, the 2038 Manchester Piccadilly–Manchester Airport, and 1Z69 2112 return. *Ian Nightingale*

Rumours abound that the production line may not end at 68034 – indeed locos up to 68044 or even 68047 have been mentioned. In 2017 DRS invited tenders for ten more locos, which many think may be on the same 'Class 68' platform, albeit with a lighter axle load to have a lower Route Availability, and a modified engine type to meet newer stringent emission regulations. But by late-2019, no order had been confirmed and it remains to be seen if any more 68s – or modified versions of the locos – will be built for any UK operators.

Unlike many new-build locos, the 66s and 67s especially, the 68s have been warmly welcomed by enthusiasts. That is because they have a decent sound, work regular passenger trains and have good names. The fact that some names had been seen on Class 42s, 43s, 47s and 50s perhaps enhanced their appeal. DRS says they are not actually named after warships, as some believe, and the names chosen are meant to 'invoke a feeling of power and bravery'.

Chiltern workings

As mentioned, a deal was struck in 2014 for six locos a day to be provided to Chiltern Railways to replace Class 67s on loco-hauled turns from Marylebone to Birmingham Moor Street and Kidderminster.

The dedicated Class 68s were 68010–015, delivered in CR silver livery, and they have been modified to allow them to work in push-pull mode with Mk 3 coaches. The locos are always on the country, north, end of the train, so leading northbound, so should a loco swap be needed at the terminus station at Marylebone then it is easy to do so. One of six ex-Virgin Trains West Coast Mk 3 Driving Van Trailers (DVT) is on the other end of the train.

The modified locos are recognisable by the fitting of an extra orange socket to the left of the ETH jumper. However, to give DRS extra flexibility in its loco supply, the company also modified 68008 *Avenger* and 68009 *Titan* to work with the Mk 3 coaches, and the truth is that in the last three years there has usually been one of the blue locos in traffic. Quite why CR didn't ask for these to be re-liveried is baffling.

The six silver locos were not named unlike their DRS blue counterparts, although 68010 was later named *Oxford Flyer* in December 2016. This was to commemorate the instigation of a new Marylebone–Oxford service via a new chord at Bicester.

The first Class 68 working for Chiltern was on 15 December 2014 when 68012 worked the 0744 Banbury–Marylebone and 1750 Marylebone–Banbury, which was the first timetabled passenger working by the new locos. These trains became the first booked for a 68 and used a rake of ex-BR Mk 3 coaches, still in BR blue and grey livery, and still with droplight windows.

No. 68002 *Intrepid* crosses the River Tilt at Blair Atholl working 4D47, the 1319 Inverness–Mossend intermodal train. This is the return working of 4H47, the 0505 Mossend–Inverness, and was regularly worked by a Class 68 when this image was taken on 8 July 2016. *Glen Batten*

On 30 June 2016, 68004 *Rapid* arrives at Honiton with 1Q23, the 0456 Old Oak Common–Salisbury, via Exeter, test train. This is the one and only time to date that Class 68s have worked on the Salisbury–Exeter line; in fact on this day they were given special permission to run as they are not even passed for the line! On the rear is 68020 *Reliance*. *Mark Pike*

A deal for DRS Class 68s working for Transpennine Express was signed off in 2017, and during 2018-19 TPE was training drivers on handling Class 68s and the new CAF Mk 5 coaches. However, their entry into traffic was many months late and did not start until August 24 2019. One of 14 locos relieveried in to TPE livery, 68024 *Centaur* passes Colton Junction, near York, with 3Q62, the 0755 Scarborough-Manchester International depot trial run on 26 February 2019. *Ian Horner*

Although allocated to Carlisle Kingmoor, much of the maintenance on the Class 68s is undertaken at Crewe Gresty Bridge. No. 68007 *Valiant* stands inside depot on 19 July 2014. This loco was later re-liveried – along with 68006 *Daring* – into ScotRail's Saltire livery for use on the Fife Circle trains. *Jack Boskett*

In the stunning Scottish Highland scenery 68023 *Achilles* heads north over Culloden Viaduct with a Mossend–Inverness intermodal train on 2 May 2017 for Stobart Rail. The trains reverted to being worked mostly by Class 66s. *Jack Boskett*

Unnamed 68033 and 88002 *Prometheus* top-and-tail a special nuclear flask train from Carlisle Kingmoor to Bicester, pictured leaving Oxford Hinksey yard on 15 February 2019. The coaches aside the wagon are barrier vehicles and also convey security staff. *Paul Shannon*

Showing its ScotRail Saltire livery to good effect, 68007 *Valiant* works 5L70, the 1824 Cardenden–Mossend, past Burntisland on 6 May 2019. Because the Fife Circle trains serving Edinburgh are based in Motherwell, and return there during the day, these trains cover more empty stock mileage than they do in passenger use. *Anthony Hicks*

Before the first locos moved to the UK, both the Class 68s and 88s were sent to the Velim test track in the Czech Republic for extended testing. In 2014, 68001 was stood next to a Vossloh Eurolight loco showing the obvious similarities in design. *Neil Bennett*

During 2015 five turns a day went over to Class 68 operation and demanded plenty of high-speed running throughout the day. The locos are maintained by DRS at Crewe, but routine exams are undertaken at Wembley. Three sets a night stable at Stourbridge Junction, having arrived at Kidderminster.

As the locos return to Crewe for major exams and any unplanned maintenance, there are of course occasions when they appear on other duties, they are especially used on a freight or infrastructure trip from Crewe Basford Hall Yard, which is a good way of testing a loco after repairs.

When there was a shortage of serviceable push-pull 68s, for a couple of weeks in February 2017 DRS provided 68002/018 to work top-and-tail on Marylebone–Banbury services. Another unusual working was on 4 November 2018, when 68010 worked from Marylebone to Stratford-on-Avon due to engineering working closing the line to Birmingham.

Other passenger work

Another passenger turn the locos picked up from an early date was from 1 April 2015 when two turns for ScotRail on the Fife Circle started. Two dedicated locos, 68006/007, were re-liveried in the Scottish Saltire livery, although they kept their names. But these two locos by no means had exclusivity on these turns and in the intervening two years all locos apart from Chiltern 68009–015, have appeared on the trains.

Two sets of Mk 2 coaches are stabled at Motherwell and are taken empty every morning to work 2K01, the 0635 Edinburgh Waverley–Glenrothes with Thornton, which then returns as 2G02, the 0743 back to Edinburgh. The other set runs empty to Cardenden to work 2K18, the 0735 to Edinburgh. The locos then take the stock back to Motherwell, where they are stabled. They return in the afternoon to Edinburgh to work 2G13, the 1711 to Glenrothes with Thornton, and 2K14, the 1822 back to Edinburgh, while the second loco is used for 2L69, the 1719 Edinburgh–Cardenden, and then both sets return to Motherwell. They cover as much ECS mileage as they do working passenger trains! The turns do not run on weekends.

The nature of the trains that do a return trip is they do not actually reverse, they simply go round in a big loop. It means there are six passages by 68s over the iconic Forth Bridge every weekday. There is constant talk that these Class 68 turns will be ending soon as more DMUs are freed up by new electric multiple units entering traffic with ScotRail.

The next passenger trains to come the way of the new locos started in the summer of 2016. When Abellio Greater Anglia (AGA) lost yet another DMU due to accident, an additional loco-hauled turn was introduced. DRS already supplied two Class 37/4s for use by AGA, but could not spare any more Type 3s, so instead two Class 68s were supplied, top-and-tailing a set of three Mk 2 coaches sourced through Riviera Trains. These trains were crewed by DRS drivers rather than AGA men.

Two Class 68s, 68019/021, returned to Velim in the spring of 2018 to undertake tests with the new CAF Mk 5 coaches for Transpennine Express. No. 68021 *Tireless* is with a Nova 3 set on 12 April 2018. *Keith Fender*

Unlike the 37s, which work in multiple via through wiring, the rear 68 was left idling on the rear. The service started on 11 July 2016 with 68016 *Fearless* and 68023 *Achilles*, and over the forthcoming months regular swaps saw most of the fleet appear. Nos 68001–005/009/016–019/021–025/027/028 all worked, although 68009 only worked for a day – with 68016 on 2 September 2016 – as its push-pull capability was needed on the Chiltern lines, while 68027 only worked once – on 21 June 2017 – but was removed from the set that date after it developed a TPWS fault. That, and 68028, were the only two plain blue, unnamed, 68s to work on the set.

The locos worked to both Lowestoft and Great Yarmouth during the day. The turn was split in two halves, with the morning turns being 2P06, the 0652 Norwich–Great Yarmouth, and 2P07, 0732 return, 2P10, the 0809 Norwich–Great Yarmouth, and 2P11, 0845 return and then 2J70, the 1005 Norwich–Lowestoft and 2J73, the 1057 return.

The set then took a break and came out in the afternoon to work 2P28, the 1640 Norwich–Great Yarmouth, and 2P29, 1717 return, followed by 2P34, the 1806 Norwich–Great Yarmouth; 2C35, the 1847 Great Yarmouth–Norwich; 2P40, the 2040 Norwich–Great Yarmouth; 2P41, the 2117 Great Yarmouth–Norwich; and

finishing on 2J94, the 2205 Norwich–Lowestoft, before returning back to Norwich Crown Point depot empty for the locos to be refuelled and the coaches to be cleaned.

However, the set was regularly used for two extra turns in the middle of the day if required and if DRS could crew it. Those trains were 2J74, the 1205 Norwich–Lowestoft; 2J77, the 1257 Lowestoft–Norwich; 2J78, the 1405 Norwich–Lowestoft; and 2J81, the 1457 Lowestoft–Norwich; before taking up the rest of its booked turn at 1640.

The contract for the 68s and Mk 2s was frequently extended, but finally came to an end in September 2017, by which time seventeen locos had been used. To commemorate the end of the operation, on 16 September AGA ran a charity charter train from Norwich, which ran first to Ely and back and then to London Liverpool Street and back. The train used a full AGA set of Mk 3s, complete with a DVT, and for this trip DRS provided the first and last of the class, 68001 and 68034, with 68034 working its first passenger train in the process.

In spring 2018 a Class 68 turn was introduced on the Cumbrian Coast line. In 2015, DRS took over two turns on the Carlisle to Barrow route for Northern Rail. The plan was for 37/4s to work with DBSOs, although due to the delays with the latter coming into traffic, top-and-tail Class 37s were initially used.

However, there were many complaints over the poor delivery of these trains, some in part to the coaches, some due to the 37s themselves and some due to driver error or a training issue for the staff.

After local MPs got involved, it was agreed to turn one of the sets over to Class 68s. This meant Northern had to hire in DRS drivers and the trains had to be top-and-tailed by two 68s as they could not work with the ex-Edinburgh–Glasgow DBSOs. The diagrams meant one set ended up at Carlisle and the other at Barrow, and this alternated throughout the week.

The use of 68s on this turn did not really achieve much and was nothing more than political. In late 2018 the 68s were quietly removed from the duties due to increased demand for locos on RHTTs, and both turns went back to 37s for the final three months before the trains went back to DMU operation in late December 2018. The 68s used tended to stay on the set for lengthy periods but during the use of the locos for their few months 68003–005/017/018/033 all appeared.

The Pennines

In 2017 it was announced DRS had signed a deal with Train Operating Company TransPennine Express to provide Class 68s working in push-pull mode with new Mk 5 CAF coaches and DVTs. The coaches were acquired from Beacon Rail and would run in fixed formations of five vehicles.

Nos 68019–032 were to be dedicated for this work and were progressively re-liveried into TPE's new silver with light blue and purple scheme. The first repainted were 68019 and 68021 in 2017, and both retained their DRS names. They appeared without any yellow warning panels, the first diesel locos to run on the main line like this for decades.

The locos were moved initially into a XHTP pool while modifications were undertaken to allow them to work with the Mk 5s. In late 2017, 68019/021 were moved to the dedicated Velim test track in the Czech Republic to undertake tests with the new Spanish-built coaches, but the two locos returned to the UK in early 2018.

Some locos spent periods in warm store at Barrow Hill pending their conversions and re-liverying. By early 2019 all fourteen locos had been modified as well as 68033/034, which are – like Chiltern – the designated contingency locos.

In between their standing down from day-to-day traffic and their return in TPE livery, some of the 68s had their DRS decals removed and were left in plain blue. A few operated in traffic like this, such as 68022 in late 2017.

The push-pull modifications are different to those on 68008–015, so the two fleets will not be interchangeable. The planned introduction of the sets on the Liverpool Lime Street to Scarborough and Middlesbrough routes has been delayed and delayed again, and the planned December 2018 and May 2019 introductions did not happen. In early

Unpainted 68003 and an Israel Railways Euro 3000 loco undergo static tests at the Vossloh Albuixech site on 10 February 2014. *Keith Fender*

On 3 June 2016, 68025 *Superb* approaches North Queensferry as it comes off the Forth Bridge working 2L69, the 1721 Edinburgh–Cardenden. *Rob France*

April the first set of Mk 5s was passed for use, so training could be ramped up. Locos started to be moved in to the TPEX pool in early 2019 and a planned, staged, introduction from July 2019 was expected. In the fullness of time, thirteen loco-hauled sets should be in traffic working eleven diagrams a day replacing three-car Class 185 DMUs.

Testing of the Mk 5s has been on the WCML from Manchester and Crewe to Bletchley, then on the Pennine route itself, with 25 January 2019 the first day one of the new trains was used in daylight on their intended route.

Prior to the arrival of the Mk 5s, TPE hired the redundant ex-Virgin Mk 3 'Pretendolino' set of coaches with a view to using these on Pennine trains as a stopgap. On 27 November, 68027 was used to take these coaches from Crewe to Plymouth Laira for work to be undertaken to return them to a usable condition. On arrival, 68027 failed and a couple of days later debranded 68022 was sent to collect it and return it to Crewe.

After the work on the coaches was completed, on 16 January 2018, 68011 – itself taking a break from its usual Chiltern duties – was sent to Laira to collect the coaches and take them to Crewe. However, the set never entered traffic and apart from being used for a few training runs, saw limited use with TPE.

However, to meet a franchise commitment, TPE had to run a Class 68-hauled passenger service before the end of 2017 so on 30 December, 68003 *Astute* and 68030 top-and-tailed 1Z68, the 2038 Manchester Piccadilly–Manchester Airport and 1Z69 2112 return, with the Mk 3 coaches as a public passenger train.

In early July 2019, rumours circulated that TPE was so annoyed with CAF and the coaches that it was looking to pull out of the contract altogether, and so shelve the use of loco hauled trains on the Pennine route, but this did not prove to be and on August 24 the service finally started when 68027 *Splendid*, hauling Mk 5 coaches 11509, 12725-727 and 12809, appeared on 1F48, the 0555 Manchester Victoria-Liverpool Lime Street. With the loco on the Liverpool end of the train, it then worked 1E25, the 0656 Liverpool-Scarborough, 1F62, the 1041 return, then 1E39, the 1356 back to Scarborough, 1F76, the 1744 from Scarborough and finally 1J63, the 2056 Liverpool-Stalybridge.

Since then, 68s and Mk 5s were slowly introduced onto more services on the TPE route.

The unnamed 68s have been named since re-liverying. Initially a set of proposed names was 'leaked', including *Nautilus*, *Endeavour*, *Excelsior* and

Patriot, but these did not materialise and instead 68028 gained the name *Lord President*, that being the same as 87028 carried in BR days, while 68030 was named *Black Douglas*, again 87030 bore this name in the 1980s. However, 68026 *Enterprise*, 68027 *Splendid*, 68029 *Courageous* and 68032 *Destroyer* were more in keeping with the DRS theme, while 68031 was named *Felix* after a 'celebrity' cat who 'works' at Huddersfield station!

It has been suggested that 68033/034 were to be named *Courageous* and *Victorious* but the first of these names was applied to 68029 in June 2019 and accordingly the last two 68s had not received any nameplates as of early-November 2019.

Charter workings

One of the reasons for acquiring 68s with ETH and 100mph capability was to use them on charter trains, which has been a growing part of the DRS portfolio over the years.

After that aforementioned first run in December 2014, Class 68s soon became the default traction for any charter booked to be operated by DRS, unless the promoters specifically requested other loco types, or a 68 was not cleared for the route intended to be taken.

Promoters including Pathfinder, UK Railtours, Nenta Traintours and Retro Railtours have all used Class 68s many times, while when the locos came in to traffic DRS was still operating the Northern Belle luxury Pullman train. This train was sold to West Coast Railways in late 2017

but it continued to be operated by DRS until a contract termination was agreed between its new owners and DRS to allow WCR to operate the train itself with its own traction – usually Class 57s.

When worked by top-and-tail 68s, the Northern Belle has taken locos to Carmarthen (68016/017), Alnmouth (68001/017), Edinburgh (68005/022), Winchester (68016/017), Leeds (68016/017) and Plymouth (68003/019).

On 13 February 2015, 68005 worked from Carmarthen to Carlisle, where it was swapped for 68002 for the run to Edinburgh for Pathfinder on its regular biennial trip to Scotland for the Six Nations rugby. The same locos worked in reverse on the 16th.

An unusual working occurred on 28 February 2015 when 68003 was hired by West Coast Railways for a Euston to Carnforth leg of its 'Winter Cumbrian Mountain Express' for Railway Touring Company. Four weeks later, Chiltern silver 68011 worked the same leg, with 47746 *Chris Fudge* tucked in behind. On 18 July 68004 worked from Newport to Carlisle and back for Pathfinder.

On 23 June 2016, 68023 – making its passenger debut – worked from Crewe to Wembley Central for the Branch Line Society on a charter that would have otherwise been an ECS move, and a few weeks later, on 9 July, Retro used 68005/018 from Leeds to Canterbury. A week later, 68021 worked from Taunton to Carlisle for 68003 to work back to Somerset. On 27 August 68022 worked a day excursion from Gloucester to Alnmouth with 68005 handling the return, again for Pathfinder.

The superb scenery of the Cumbrian Coast is demonstrated to great effect as 68017 *Hornet* passes Coulderton with 2C40, the 0842 Carlisle–Barrow. 68003 *Astute* is on the rear on 19 May 2018. *Rob France*

Chiltern 68011 passes Oddington, between Bicester and Oxford, on 16 August 2016 with 1T54, the 1818 Marylebone–Oxford Parkway, running 'wrong line' on this bi-directionally signalled line. *Martin Loader*

Class 68s have good haulage capability on heavy freight trains, as shown by 68004 *Rapid* passing Barrow-on-Trent on 12 August 2015 with the 6U77 Mountsorrel–Crewe ballast train. *Bill Atkinson*

Nos 68026–032 were delivered in a plain blue livery to which white DRS logos were added temporarily. No. 68030 shows off this variation to good effect on 4 July 2018 as it passes Stenson Junction with 6U77 Mountsorrel to Crewe. All these locos are now in Transpennine livery. *Ian Nightingale*

Class 68s took over two passenger turns on the Fife Circle for ScotRail from DB Cargo Class 67s in 2015. On 29 March 2017, 68017 *Hornet* waits to leave Edinburgh with the 1707 to Glenrothes with Thornton. This is not one of the two preferred and re-liveried locos, these being 68006/007. *Pip Dunn*

The first passenger working by a TPE-liveried 68 was on 11 March 2019 when 68019 took over a returning Edinburgh–Carmarthen rugby special from 68016 at Carlisle. There have been other notable charter trips, with ScotRail 68007 working 9 February 2019's Newport to Blackpool 'Blue Boys' Ribble Rouser' charter to Chaddesden; its first passenger working outside Scotland on the national network.

Freight

And it's not just passenger work that has occupied the 68s, which were conceived and designed to be a truly mixed traffic loco.

They have been used to work intermodal duties on pairs from Daventry to Mossend, and as single locos from Grangemouth to Aberdeen and Inverness. The WCML workings now tend to be worked by Class 88s.

As mentioned, given only five of the eight push-pull modified 68s are needed every day, and a sixth as a spare,

there can sometimes be a spare Chiltern silver 68 available for DRS to use on other work.

They have also been used on infrastructure trains from Crewe Basford Hall to Mountsorrel, Carlisle to Shap, Crewe to Toton and from Carlisle to Crewe. They have also seen infrequent use on RHTT trains in the autumn months, although Class 37/57/66s tend to be favoured for these duties.

While nuclear traffic is usually more likely to be in the hands of 37s, 57s or 66s, nevertheless Class 68s will be used as required, especially in Cumbria, and the turn to Bridgwater is a favourite for using the locos. Despite their improved reliability compared with other classes, the trains are still double-headed. Sometimes mixed 68/88 pairs are used on these trains.

The Class 68s were also – briefly – used on some test trains where 100mph locos were needed. Colas had just taken over the trains from DB Cargo and until it arranged to acquire two Class 67s from DBC, Colas turned to DRS to hire 68s.

On 2 June 2017, sporting its ScotRail Saltire colours, 68007 *Valiant* has arrived at Edinburgh with the 1814 from Glenrothes with Thornton. Many of the Class 68 names were previously carried by Class 42/43 Warships, 47s or Class 50s, and this loco's name was carried by 50015, which is now preserved. *Pip Dunn*

On 23 June 2017, 68002 *Intrepid* arrives at Brundall with the 1005 Norwich–Lowestoft AGA train. No. 68024 *Centaur* is on the rear. Both these names were carried by Class 42 Warships, D825 and D808 respectively. *Pip Dunn*

No. 68003 *Astute* passes Bardrill, just south of Gleneagles, on 31 August 2016 with 4A13, the 1223 Grangemouth–Aberdeen Craiginches Tesco intermodal train. *Martin Loader*

No. 68003 *Astute* passes Stracey Arms on 26 May 2017 with 2P29, the 1717 Great Yarmouth–Norwich Greater Anglia service. No. 68022 *Resolution* is on the rear, but not under power. *Martin Loader*

The locos worked top-and-tail in place of the normal 125mph HST New Measurement. This brought 68s to Plymouth, Penzance, Paignton, and other routes. However, since 67023/027 joined the Colas fleet these workings have ended.

However, as DRS is once again providing traction for some Network Rail Infrastructure Monitoring trains, so 68s could appear from time to time if required, although Class 37s tend to be favoured for this work.

Class 68s have also occasionally been guest locos at heritage railways, for example on 29 December 2014 68007 *Valiant* visited the Mid Norfolk Railway diesel gala and it worked passenger trains alongside preserved locomotives. It even came to the rescue of a failed train during the day!

During 19–21 May 2016, 68025 *Superb* – then brand new and making its debut on passenger trains – starred at the Severn Valley Railway's diesel gala. Sadly, during the event, the loco's worksplate was stolen, but thankfully it was rapidly recovered.

One for the future

The Class 68s have been an undoubted success, although they are certainly not cheap locos to acquire. But they have proved themselves to be reliable on Chiltern workings and look set, along with the Mk 5 coaches, to revolutionise the trans-Pennine line that suffers from severe overcrowding.

They are also the first new locomotive in the UK in decades to actually have a bit of character, something that is quite rare in this day and age! It's possible more orders could be possible, not just with DRS, and only time will tell if that proves to be the case.

By 14 November 2018, 68030 has been re-liveried into TransPennine Express colours but as the use of the 68s on the Liverpool–Scarborough route had still to start the TPE locos were sometimes used on other work. The loco, before it was named *Black Douglas*, leaves Bescot with an infrastructure train for Toton. *Ian Nightingale*

DRS's new 68005 *Defiant* stands on display at the Birmingham NEC at the Multimodal event in April 2014, where it was showed off to the Princess Royal and many other dignitaries. *Jack Boskett*

6
The Class 88s
Underused but with Great Potential

In September 2013, *Railways Illustrated* magazine broken the news that DRS was ordering ten electro-diesel versions of the Vossloh Class 68, and like their diesel stablemates, they would also be built in Valencia.

The locos, which would be the first Vossloh electric locos in the UK, would use the same bodyshell at the 68s, with obvious changes to the grille and roofs, but as much of the running gear as possible would be the same to maintain some commonality.

The locos, which were to be Class 88 on the Rolling Stock Library, would be able to run off the 25kV AC overhead power lines but have a small 950hp Caterpillar C27 12-cylinder diesel engine inside to allow them to run on non-electrified lines. The diesel engine would allow the locos to work 'last mile' operations on branch lines, yards or railheads, thus avoiding the need to switch to a diesel loco for the final leg or employ a diesel shunter in a yard.

The diesel engine would also enable the train to keep moving if the overhead power lines had to be isolated in an emergency – or even planned – situation, such as if the wires were brought down by another train's pantograph or bad weather, or if there was a planned isolation of a short section of the track's OLE on the train's route. Likewise, if there was an issue with the loco running on electric power, the diesel engine could prevent the train from coming to a halt and blocking a line.

Like the 68s, the Class 88s would have a top speed of 100mph and run on a Bo-Bo wheel arrangement. They would also have electric train supply with an index of 96 – ideal for provide hotel power to a long train, including a 'sleeper' train.

The locos would be the first electro-diesels for the UK since the ten Class 74s were built from Class 71 straight DC electric locos in 1967–68. The Class 88s were the first bespoke, purpose-built EDs since the Class 73/0s in 1962 and the Class 73/1s in 1966–67. They are also the first EDs with 25kV AC as their source for electric running.

First new electrics for twenty years

The Class 88s, which would be numbered 88001–010, were the first new electric locos ordered in the UK for more than twenty years, when the forty-six-strong Class 92 was built by Brush in 1993–95. Like the Class 68s, the Class 88s would be financed via Beacon Rail and DRS would lease the locos. Their works numbers were Stadler 2851–60.

The locos were ordered for WCML intermodal work and DRS was expecting growth in this market. They could also have been suitable for the Caledonian Sleeper haulage contract, which DRS was bidding for. The two Anglo–Scottish 'sleeper' trains were part of the ScotRail franchise, but on 31 March 2015 they were separated into a standalone franchise and the new operator, Serco, was looking for a traction provider.

The two trains ran from Euston – one to Edinburgh and Glasgow Central and the other to Aberdeen, Inverness and Fort William. They were operated using DB Cargo traction and drivers (apart from the West Highland leg, which was still crewed by ScotRail drivers). DBC Class 90s worked south of Edinburgh and 67s north, and five 90s and three 67s a day were needed each day to work the service.

However, despite DRS bidding for the haulage contract, the work was won by GB Railfreight. Therefore any hope that Class 68s and 88s would be hauling 'sleeper' trains was not to be. However, while some observers assumed the Class 88s were ordered solely for this work, this was not the case and, besides, the construction of the 88s did not even start until well after it was announced that the 'sleeper' haulage contract had been awarded to GBRf.

DRS maintained that the reasoning for ordering the 88s was unchanged – they would be employed in intermodal trains on the West Coast Main Line – and the logic was that their diesel engines would be useful in the unwired railhead at Daventry and also if the trains worked to Grangemouth.

A rare picture of an unnamed Class as 88003 was on display at the Berlin Innotrans show in September 2016 before its *Genesis* nameplates were fitted. This was the first time the press got to look and see inside the locomotive. *Pip Dunn*

No. 88005 *Minerva* heads north near Carstairs working 4S43, the 0616 Daventry–Mossend Tesco intermodal train, on 3 December 2018. This is a regular turn for a Class 88. All seven names once carried by the EM2 Class 77 DC electric locos in the 1960s have been used on 88004–010. *Robin Ralston*

No. 88007 *Electra* passes Dinwoodie, between Beattock and Lockerbie on the ECML, working 4M48, the 1443 Mossend–Daventry intermodal train for Tesco on 25 February 2018. *Robin Ralston*

Construction of the 88s therefore started in spring 2015, with the first loco ready later that year. The first 88 off the production line was 88001, which was named *Revolution*, and, like 68001, it also visited Velim in the Czech Republic in late 2016 for extensive testing and as such was not the first to arrive in the UK. That claim to fame befell 88002, which arrived in the UK on 21 January 2017. It sported *Prometheus* nameplates; a name previously carried by long-scrapped Woodhead electric Class 76 E26055.

No. 88002 came to the UK via road – and ferry – but later deliveries would arrive by sea at Workington. The deliveries of 68s and 88s via Workington was seen by DRS as a way of supporting local Cumbrian businesses.

The next batch of 88s to dock in the UK was on 1 March 2017, specifically 88001, 88003 *Genesis*, 88004 *Pandora*, 88005 *Minerva* and 88008 *Ariadne*. All the locos had their nameplates fitted in Spain. This left the final four to arrive on 30 March, with 88006 *Juno*, 88007 *Electra*, 88009 *Diana* and 88010 *Aurora,* all docking at Workington along with 68026/027.

As well as ex-EM1 Class 76 name *Prometheus*, seven of the ten names chosen for the Class 88s were those previously carried by the seven EM2 Class 77 Woodhead electric locos that operated from 1954 to 1968 before being sold to the Netherlands. Only 88001/003 had names not previously used.

Prior to its arrival in the UK, 88003 had been sent to the Innotrans trade show in Berlin on 20–24 September 2016, and this presented the first chance for the press to see the loco. It was possible to walk through it and see the internal layout of the locomotive. The small Caterpillar diesel engine was ticked away in a 'cupboard' and was not easy to see on an initial look inside the locomotive. After its visit to Innotrans, 88003 returned to Valencia before shipping to the UK.

Physically, the 88s look very similar to the 68s, which is fairly obvious as they share the same body design, but there are fewer bodyside grilles on an 88, with three on one side and four on the other – and they are smaller than those on a 68.

Opposite: No. 88008 *Ariadne* heads north from York while hauling 6S31, the retimed 1508 Doncaster Up Decoy–Millerhill Network train, running on behalf of Network Rail. The train is conveying new sleepers, for use on track renewal work in Scotland. The Class 88s were not ordered with this work in mind! *Ian Horner*

On 30 March 2017, the last four of Direct Rail Services' Class 88s were unloaded at Workington along with two Class 68s. That afternoon, 66421 hauled the new locos through Carlisle on their way to Kingmoor depot for acceptance. In order they are 68026, 88007 *Electra*, 68027, 88010 *Aurora*, 88009 *Diana* and 88006 *Juno*. *Pip Dunn*

The Class 88s were not ordered with the intention that they would work nuclear fuels trains, but they are occasionally used on them. Running off their 940hp diesel engines, 88002 *Prometheus* and 88009 *Diana* pass Dunnerholme near Askham-in-Furness with the 6K73 Sellafield–Crewe trip on 21 August 2018. At Carnforth they can switch to electric power. *Rob France*

No. 88006 *Juno* heads south at Rowell, near Carnforth, with the partially loaded 4M48 intermodal train for Daventry on 16 July 2017. *Rob France*

More flask work for Class 88s was on 30 June 2018 as 88002 *Prometheus* and 88008 *Ariadne* power 6C52, the 0625 Crewe Coal Sidings Sellafield flasks, and pass Silverdale, between Carnforth and Arnside. Although this might seem mundane work, it is the most profitable work in the DRS portfolio and the reason the company was created; also BNFL is its priority customer. *Rob France*

No. 88007 *Electra* heads south at Rowell, near Carnforth, with the partially loaded 4M48 intermodal train for Daventry on 16 September 2018. *Rob France*

The driver's desk inside 88003. *Pip Dunn*

Class 88 workings

The first working by an 88 in the UK was on 3 April 2017 when 88002 piloted 68025 *Superb* on a Carlisle to Crewe loaded test run with a train of bogie wagons. The next few months saw extensive test runs with the class to train drivers and allow the locos to accumulate mileage before being accepted into traffic.

With a failure to win increased WCML intermodal work, added to the fact the Scottish 'sleeper' contract did not land on the desks of Carlisle Kingmoor managers, DRS was left with ten expensive-to-lease Class 88s for which it had to find other work.

While the Class 88s have taken over most of the key intermodal trains on the WCML that DRS retained, replacing Class 66s, growth – certainly in the DRS portfolio – has not been as expected and there can be no denying there is not really enough core work to have warranted ten Class 88s being ordered.

Other work for the fleet has seen them working in pairs on Cumbrian nuclear traffic, and sometimes working in multiple with a Class 68, while there has been some use of the class on East Coast Main Line infrastructure workings. In April 2019, 88003/007 were sent to Norwich or clear the class for working in East Anglia, and they also visited King's Lynn. By late 2019 there had not been any other workings by 88s in the area.

The 88s have worked occasional charters, mainly at the request of promoters, with the first being on 9 May 2017 when 88002 worked from Euston to Carlisle and back. No. 68022 *Resolution* was on the rear for insurance and stock moves. A few days later, on 18/19 May, 88003 was a star attraction at the Severn Valley Railway's diesel gala, working, of course, using its small diesel engine.

On 20 May, 88002 was in charter action again, this time for Pathfinder and working with 68025 in multiple on the WCML from Crewe to Carlisle and then heading south via the Settle and Carlisle line – again working in multiple, both on diesel. At Farington Junction, 68025 was switched

off and the 88 worked solo back to Crewe. This train was initially planned to be a pair of Class 88s. Another mixed 88/68 combination was on 12 August, when 88004 *Pandora* and 68016 repeated the same train as on 20 May.

On 10 February 2018 88001 worked from Nuneaton to Crewe on a Pathfinder tour and it returned later in the day, but in multiple with 68004. On 18 May 2018 88010 *Aurora* was in action at the Severn Valley Railway. On 21 July 2018, 88005 worked Euston to Crewe for UK Railtours, taking passengers to a DRS open day at Crewe, while 88002/007/009 all worked legs of a Branch Line Society charter on April 27, while 88006 *Juno* was a guest at the SVR in May 2019 – and in doing so it became the final loco of the ten to work a passenger train of some description.

The Class 88s are a complex, but versatile machine, and it remains to be seen if they will prove to be a 'costly mistake' or 'one for the future'. They certainly have great potential; it's a question if that potential will ever truly be realised.

The small Caterpillar engine is tucked inside a 'cupboard' inside a Class 88. This is the inside of 88003 as seen at Innotrans in 2016. *Pip Dunn*

As both pantographs are up, this pair of Class 88s has 10,720hp at its disposal to move 4S43, the 0616 Daventry–Mossend, as it glides past Docker, between Oxenholme and Tebay, on 15 November 2017. The locos are **88009** *Diana* and **88008** *Ariadne*. *Paul Shannon*

When Rebuilding Can Be the Answer

Re-engineering locos has been a feature of British main-line diesels and electric for decades, and indeed some locos were delivered from construction with alterative engines. Most of these were for evaluation purposes but on some occasions, BR re-engined entire fleets after the original engines proved problematic and new engines were seen as an option for improving reliability. That said, it didn't always work!

Locos built with trial – non-standard – engines include Class 42 Warship D830 *Majestic*, which had two Paxman 12YJXL engines instead of the Maybach MD650 engines its classmates had fitted. Two Class 17 Claytons, D8586/87, had Rolls Royce 'D' engines instead of Paxman 6ZHXL units.

Other engines were tweaked to see if more power could be gained, and if so at what cost. Class 45 Peak D57 was an example, having its 2,500hp Sulzer 12LDA-B engine boosted to 2,750hp for a period in the 1960s, and 37292, uprated to 2,000hp in 1981–85.

Sometimes locos were downrated for a variety of reasons, such as all the Class 47s, which had their Sulzer 12LDA-C engines permanently downrated from 2,750hp to 2,580hp after reliability issues.

Other fleets were totally re-engined, none more notable than the Mirrlees-engined Class 30 Type 2s, all 263 of which were rebuilt with English Electric 12SVT 1,470hp powerplants in the late 1960s. Interestingly, the Class 30s, which had 1,250hp JVS12T Mirrlees engines for the first twenty pilot scheme locos and 1,365hp engines for the 243 production series locos, also had several locos subjected to trial engine tweaks; D5545, D5655–70 were uprated to 1,600hp – thus making them Type 3s – while D5835 was boosted to a Type 4 rating of 2,000hp.

Other projects were mooted: Class 23 D5901 was prepared for fitting with an EE unit to replace the troublesome Napier units that had dogged the ten Class 23s from construction. This project was shelved after some of the preparatory work had been undertaken.

Likewise, proposals were drawn up to re-engineer the twenty Class 28 Co-Bo Type 2s, only for the project to be stillborn on the grounds of cost.

DRS's fledgling operation started in 1995 using five ex-BR Class 20s that it had refurbished. It then went on to acquire more of the elderly Type 1s, and had ten more rebuilt, but in recent times has all but done away with the class, retaining just three for autumnal RHTT work. Back on 6 May 2008, 20302/306 lead 20307/310 past Brock with 6K73, the 1538 Sellafield–Crewe nuclear flasks. The use of four locomotives is because the train splits into two portions at Crewe, serving individual power stations, each going forward with two Class 20s. *Martin Loader*

In 1985 BR started a refurbishment programme on its Class 37s that included fitting six locos with trial engines – four Mirrlees and two Ruston – to evaluate possible replacements for the old English Electric units. However, neither company won any order to supply engines for any production series rebuilding programme. Mirrlees 37903 and Ruston 37906 pass Washwood Heath on 21 August 1994 with a rare passenger outing – working Pathfinder Tours' 1Z27, 0821 Bristol Temple Meads–Crewe 'Crewe Cruiser' railtour. *Martin Loader*

Twenty of the Class 21s – D6100-03/06–08/12–14/16/19/21/23/24/29/30/32/33/37 – had their MAN L12V18/21 engines replaced with Paxman 12YJXL engines in the mid-1960s, turning them into Class 29s, although this costly refurbishment did nothing to extend their lives.

In 1976, 47046 was rebuilt with a Ruston Paxman 16RK3CT engine as a test bed for the new Class 56s. Ironically, it never proved itself as the first 56s had been built and delivered, from Romania, before 47601 took to the rails! The loco did a few months' work but was obsolete before it started as such. It was then re-engined again in 1979 with another design of Ruston Paxman engine, the 12RK3CT, as a test bed for the Class 58s and this time it did return to traffic before the Class 58 production run started. Remarkably, despite being non-standard, it lasted in traffic until 1990, some three years after the fiftieth and final 58 was delivered.

In 1986, six Class 37s were also re-engined, four, 37125/148/150/249, had Mirrlees MB275T engines fitted, while 37136/206 received Ruston RK270Tt engines. These test bed engines were never developed further into any re-engineering project but did stay with the locos until their withdrawals in the late 1990s.

In 1991, three Class 56s, 56083/084/086, had their Ruston engines downrated to 2,800hp from the 3,250hp output and another three locos, 56069/077/107, were similarly downrated to 2,400hp. Both these trials were to see if cost savings could be made by lengthening the times between engine overhauls. The locos retained these ratings until the mid-1990, when they returned to their designed outputs.

No. 50049 *Defiance*, when converted to Railfreight test bed loco 50149 in 1987, was also downrated from 2,700hp to 2,400hp.

Ruston-engined 37906 passes Marshfield on 27 August 1998 with 6Z52, the 1105 Cardiff Docks–Llanwern slag empties. These workings turned out to be the swansong for the 37/9s, with the locos being withdrawn shortly afterwards. The 37/9s gained a reputation for being very loud and after spells preserved, 37901/905/906 survive today pending returns to traffic with main-line operators. *Martin Loader*

Private era re-engineering

While the MTU HST, Class 57 and 73/9s rebuilding programmes have proved on the whole successful, and GBRf hopes the Class 69s will do likewise, there have also been several privatisation era re-engineering plans that never got beyond the discussion stage.

In mid-2000, Direct Rail Services confirmed it had contemplated fitting new engines to its Class 20s, while fifteen years later it was investigating the feasibility of fitting Caterpillar engines to Class 37s. Both projects never got off the ground.

EWS considered the options of rebuilding Class 60s with new engines, but again it was soon ruled out, presumably on cost grounds.

One refurbishment programme that did get off the ground was the Class 91 upgrade programme instigated by GNER in 2000, which saw 91027 as the first to enter Doncaster Works for a complete rebuild.

To differentiate between an original and a refurbished loco, the overhauled examples have 100 added to their numbers, so 91027 emerges as 91127. The last loco to be rebuilt was 91024, emerging as 91124 in April 2003.

One quirk of the plan saw 91023 renumbered as 91132. This loco had been involved in both the Hatfield and Heck collision, which had fatal consequences, and so its identity was changed.

Other locos rebuilt have been four Class 37s for Network Rail in 2007. They were fitted with ERTMS equipment for a trial on the Cambrian lines. This meant any train working west of Shrewsbury to Aberystwyth or Pwllheli had to have ERTMS fitted. To accommodate charter, infrastructure and freight traffic on the line, four 37/0s were acquired and overhauled by HNRC at Barrow Hill.

The locos chosen were 37100/170/178/217, of which 37217 had been withdrawn way back in 1995. The locos were renumbered as 97301–304 respectively. Whilst these overhauls did not see any major changes to the fleet, they are nevertheless worth mentioning.

In 2005, EWS was giving consideration to re-engineering Class 60s with new GM engines, but the project never came to fruition. Despite the locos only dating from the early 1990s, in 2004 the first of the 100-strong fleet were withdrawn and one point the company had just four operational examples. Today, about twenty locos remain with DB Cargo, all of which have had light overhauls, while ten went to Colas – and are now with GBRf – and four are being refurbished for DC Rail. Still in its old Mainline Freight Aircraft blue livery but with a full height EWS 'three beasties' logo, nameless 60044 leans into the curve at Kintbury with 6Z20, the 0945 Whatley–St Pancras stone train, on 2 April 2007. The train is a rake of ex National Power hoppers! No. 60044 remained in the DB Cargo active fleet as of mid-2019. *Martin Loader*

8
The Class 57s
The Low-Cost 'New' Loco

Like anything in the world, new-build equipment inevitably costs more than second-hand or refurbished alternatives. That is especially true where the capital cost of new build is very expensive and it is most certainly the case with locomotives.

The price of brand new locomotives is hard to quantify, but in 1996 when English Welsh & Scottish Railway ordered its Class 66s, it's probably a fair assumption that each cost about £1.5 million each – and that is taking the economies of scale and bulk buying into account.

EWS was able to place such a big order for locos as it had the traffic to occupy them. It needed the reliability Class 66s would bring over the elderly ex-BR locos – most of which dated from the 1960s – that they would replace.

A fine display of vintage semaphore signals at Fenny Compton, pictured on the glorious sunny evening of 19 June 2000. Two upper quadrant, and three lower quadrant arms are clearly visible. No. 57001 *Freightliner Pioneer* heads northwards with 4S59, the 1513 Millbrook–Coatbridge container train. No. 57001 was the first of Freightliner's General Motors conversions, being rolled out of the Brush Works at Loughborough on 21 July 1998. It used the bodyshell from 47356. *Martin Loader*

In superb evening light on 21 April 2010, DRS's 57003/009 pull slowly out of the Daventry International Railfreight Terminal (DIRFT) with 4S47, the 1849 Daventry–Coatbridge 'Sugarliner', and pass Barby Nortoft. *Martin Loader*

In early 2008 Cotswold Advenza acquired two Class 57/0s from Freightliner, and on 22 January 57005 leaves Long Marston with 6Z98, the 1230 to Bescot, on conveying a rake of fifteen TDA tanks. Note the patch on the loco's bodywork at the far end showing where the *Freightliner Excellence* nameplate has been removed, prior to sale to Cotswold Rail. *Martin Loader*

Now painted in Advenza Freight blue, 57006 passes Claydon with 6Z72, the 1025 Stockton-on-Tees-Cardiff Tidal scrap train, on 13 May 2008. *Martin Loader*

Although EWS acquired five ex-BR freight businesses, the one operation it did not take on was the container business Freightliner. This was the brand name tagged on to the intermodal operation of moving International Standard Organisation (ISO) containers by rail and was one of – many will argue – the few good things to come out of Dr Richard Beeching's *Reshaping the Railways* report of 1963.

Freightliner flourished throughout the 1970s and was a good, cost-effective business. It bridged that gap between loss-making wagonload and profitable trainload freight operations. A container could be lifted off a ship at the docks, placed on the train, held in place by simple but effective twistlocks, taken to a railhead and, using an overhead crane, transhipped on to a lorry, which had a skeletal trailer with twistlocks, and then taken for final delivery.

Unloading was effortless, quick and simple. It alleviated the biggest costs: shunting, excessive manpower and 'branch line' working. The lorries acted as shunters and trip 'engines' so to speak and their drivers were 'guard', 'driver' and 'shunter' for that operation.

Management buyout

The Freightliner operation was acquired by a management buyout on 25 May 1996 and it immediately set about making the business profitable. It had inherited a mixed bag of elderly ex-BR locos, of which only its ten Class 90s, 90141–150, which dated from 1990, could be deemed to be relatively new.

The rest of the fleet was thirty Class 86 AC electric locos dating from 1965–66 and forty very well-worked Class 47s, some of which were stored, others of which were very high on engine hours. In preparation for the sell-off, various 47s were moved between the shadow freight operations and it is fair to say Freightliner got the roughest locos in the fleet.

Freightliner also started its operations still hiring pairs of Class 37s and single Class 56s from EWS. But as EWS rationalised its fleet, several more 47s were made available to Freightliner although, again, they were not the best. Put it this way, EWS was not going to get rid of its better locos; it would be the worst ones, those longest out of works, which would be made available.

Over the next two years, Freightliner acquired twenty-six other second-hand Class 47s; again, some were stored and were only used for spare parts.

So given the Class 47s Freightliner acquired were – generally – those with some of the highest engine hours and the longest out of works, it was clear quite early on, despite some overhauls being undertaken on the locos, they would only ever be a stopgap solution to running the existing business, let alone growing it.

When the MBO was completed, Freightliner was initially not in the position to acquire new locos. As a result, the company looked at the concept of completely re-engineering some of its Class 47s. Rebuilding existing locos would be cheaper and – theoretically – quicker, and so allow it to gain a fleet of 'new' locos at lower cost and a shorter lead time.

No. 57302 *Virgil Tracy* climbs out of the Severn Tunnel and approaches Pilning on 27 April 2010 with 2C79, the 1400 Cardiff Central–Taunton First Great Western service. Classmate 57309 *Brains* brings up the rear. The locos were on hire to GBRf to work this train. *Martin Loader*

The biggest issue with the Class 47 design was the unreliability of their ageing Sulzer 12-LDA-C engines, which were lucky to give 75 per cent availability for any sustained periods. General Motors engines, however, were routinely achieving 95 per cent availability.

Freightliner was now in a competitive world. If it let its customers down with repeated train failures, then they could go to EWS or – pretty soon – one of the other new freight companies. And then there was the other issue – a failure of a Freightliner train could cause delays to other operators who would all be seeking compensation. The Nationalised BR concept of 'oh dear, these things happen' wouldn't wash any more.

Therefore running with failure-prone Class 47s was not a long-term solution for a reliable and sustainable business. Some Freightliner 47s did have overhauls, but these were costly and was really only a 'sticking plaster' over a bigger problem.

Aware that its 47s could not last forever, and that acquiring new locomotives, such as Class 66s, was not – yet – an option, Freightliner Management were soon in dialogue with Brush, which was offering the market the low-cost Class 57 option and looking for a suitable customer.

Better reliability

It was late 1997 when Brush officially announced it was offering the Class 57. This was not the first time the concept of re-engineering Class 47s had been mooted, as Railfreight Distribution had discussed the idea in the early 1990s, but the plan came to nothing, in part due to the privatisation process getting under way.

Brush claimed the Class 57 would give better reliability and the GM 645-12E3 two-stroke 12-cylinder engines it used were widely regarded as being less prone to failure than Sulzer units – and so Freightliner could have all the benefits of new locos but at a fraction of the price. By not having to build new bodyshells, the cost of a 'new' loco was probably a quarter of that of a Class 66, plus the lead-time for construction was quicker.

The replacement engines were 5 tonnes lighter than the Sulzer unit they replaced, and so the locos had additional ballast weights fitted to keep them the same weight as a 47.

Still wearing Pullman livery, but with the Northern Belle branding painted out, and on long-term hire to Rail Operations Group, 57305 *Northern Princess* passes Challow on 15 November 2018 with 5Q32, the 0941 Portbury Automotive Terminal–Manchester International Depot (Longsight) ECS, conveying a set of Spanish-built Mk 5 coaches for the forthcoming Trans Pennine loco-hauled services. *Martin Loader*

In bright all-over Network Rail yellow, 57312 passes Compton Beauchamp on 23 February 2012 with 5D66, the 1144 Bristol St Philips Marsh–Eastleigh Network Rail snow train. GBRf's BR blue 73208 *Kirsten* is on the rear – extremely unusual traction for the former Great Western Main Line. *Martin Loader*

The bogies and traction motors from the donor Class 47 would also be reused and the DC generators replaced by a refurbished Brush BA1101A AC main alternator retrieved from withdrawn Class 56s.

The locos would have superior pulling power over a 47: 1,600 tonnes was their capacity, while a single 47 could haul 960 tonnes. To aid this impressive pulling power, the locos were fitted with automatic sanders and wheel-slip control. Overall, the 57s would have a top speed of 75mph, necessary for hauling Class 4 intermodal trains.

The locos only had one set of field diverts – set at 55mph, unlike the three on a Class 47. Unlike many Class 47s, the 57s were initially not fitted with additional fuel tanks.

Freightliner initially agreed a deal with Brush for six locos to be rebuilt at a cost of £3 million, with the option for twenty-four more conversions and the possibility of as many as sixty. Of course, Brush would have happily entertained as many conversions as was possible.

The first donors

On 11 March 1998, 47187/317/322/347/350/356 were moved into the DFHZ pool from the DHLT pool, the 'holding pool' for Freightliner locos that had been withdrawn from traffic. The new pool code had a level of humour attached to it; HZ being Heinz, famous for its '57 varieties' marketing moniker! These locos had all been withdrawn from traffic and were stood down but not disposed of as they had already been identified for rebuilding.

Their Sulzer engines had the highest accumulated hours and were the longest out of works. Engine hours is a measure to dictate when a loco is due overhaul – typically anything between 8,000 and 10,000 hours is the trigger to send a loco for overhaul. However, they are also misleading, as the engine itself may not have accumulated those hours and in fact an engine may be in a loco run for 500 hours and then be replaced by another engine, yet the loco has still only accumulated 500 hours even if the replacement unit has zero or 5,000 hours on it. But it acts as a guide to the fleet engineers as to when a loco is likely to need works overhaul.

Freightliner envisaged the 57s running between 25,000 and 30,000 hours – or six years – between overhauls compared with the 10,000 to 12,000 hours the company made a Class 47 operate for between overhauls.

The first of the six locos selected for conversion, 47356, was last overhauled way back in August 1986 at Crewe Works. Second in line for conversion was 47322, which was last through works in July 1987. Both these locos were still in shabby versions of the original Railfreight livery first seen on a Class 47 in 1985. The former was in the original version while the latter had the later 'red stripe' version with a red solebar.

These locos would become 57001 and 57002 respectively, while the third loco converted, to become 57003, was two-tone grey 47317, a former Railfreight Distribution machine. The donor for 57004 was two-tone grey 47347, while 57005 used Railfreight grey 47350 as its

Still showing the scars of its Arriva Trains livery, despite an attempt to debrand it, West Coast Railways' recently acquired 57314 brings up the rear of the Railway Touring Company's 1Z39, 0502 Cardiff Central–Llandrindod Wells 'Heart of Wales' railtour, at Rousham, between Oxford and Banbury, on 13 April 2013. The lead locomotive, 57601, can just be seen disappearing behind the bushes. *Martin Loader*

Following the failure of the previous evening's 1A40, 2145 Penzance–Paddington GWR 'sleeper', with loss of air, the empty stock had to be worked to London on 12 July 2018 in order to work that evening's Down train. As the Berks & Hants line was closed for engineering works, the train was diverted via Swindon. No. 57605 *Totnes Castle* passes Grove with 5C99, the 1001 Laira–Reading Traincare Depot ECS. *Martin Loader*

donor. The final loco of the first half dozen conversions was two-tone grey 47187, which was to become 57006. The locos were moved to Brush at Loughborough in 1997 – with 47356 arriving on 3 March, and the rebuilding started.

Although the initial contract was for just six locos, in October 1998 the company hinted it would be looking to order twenty-four more Class 57/0s. However, Freightliner's policy for loco ordering was small batches at a time, and accordingly it only went on to authorise another six Class 57 conversions – in July 1999. The six donor locos for 57007–012 were, in order: 47332, 47060, 47079, 47231, 47329 and 47204. Of these, 47332 was in the 'Dutch' grey and yellow livery and the others were in two-tone grey, some with Railfreight Distribution logos.

However, the proposal for the other eighteen mooted conversions was soon scuppered and instead Freightliner soon switched its acquisition policy to new-build Class 66s, so killing off the Class 57 production line for the FOC pretty much as soon as the first locos appeared from Loughborough.

Stripping for rebuild

When a loco arrived at Brush, it would be stripped down. The Sulzer engine would be removed for disposal, or even possible reuse in another Class 47, and the other major components removed for overhaul or replacement. Any corrosion on the bodywork – usually not a major issue on the main superstructure of a Class 47, but a big issue on some of the roof panels – would be attended to.

The engine inside 57001 was fitted on 16 March 1998. All engines were second-hand and reconditioned by VMH in Kentucky. A spare engine was also acquired for parts. The engines were the smaller version of the 16-cylinder units used in the GM Class 59s that had been in use in the UK since 1986. Silencers were also fitted to the engines.

Freightliner was keen to keep the cost of the rebuilds to a minimum, so there was no redesigning of the exteriors of the locos. The locos arrived with a mix of front ends where the four-character train reporting display headcode panels had been fitted. Some had flush fronts where the panel had been removed and plated over and two white marker lights fitted – and this modification was usually done as a result of a collision. Others had opaque lenses, and some had the white marker lights on their indented panels.

The engines were rated at just 2,500hp – 80hp less than a Class 47 – but Freightliner initially classed them as Type 5s based on their increased pulling power. Freightliner had such faith in the tractive effort of the 57s that it did not specify multiple working.

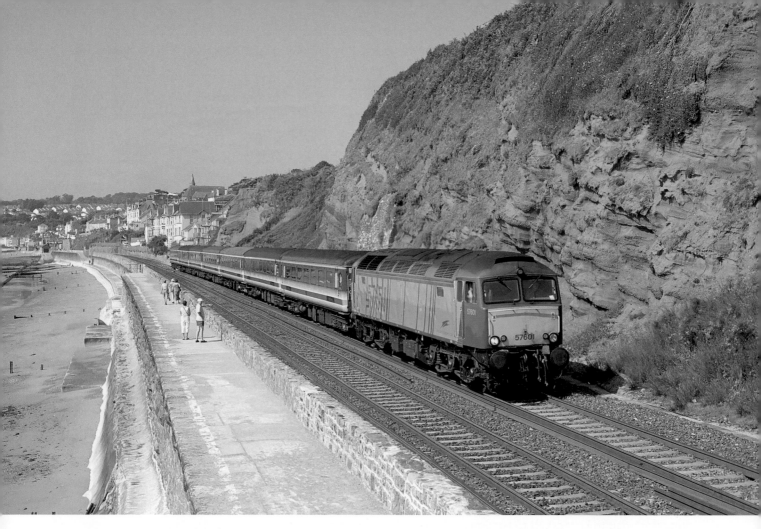

When 57601 was released from Brush it went on hire to FGW for extended trials. It hauls 1A43, the 0920 Plymouth–Paddington, past the famous Dawlish sea wall on a glorious sunny morning on 2 July 2001. *Bill Atkinson*

An interesting duty for a Virgin Class 57/3s was hauling Pendolino EMUs from Crewe to Holyhead and back on passenger trains. No. 57301 *Scott Tracy* hauls 390053 *Mission Accomplished* on 1A78, the 1414 Holyhead–Euston, at Rhosneigr on 2 November 2006. *Bill Atkinson*

The Virgin Class 57/3s came into their own when diversions were in force and Pendolino units needed dragging over non-electrified routes. On 5 May 2007 57305 *John Tracy* hauls 390020 *Virgin Cavalier* on 1M87, the 1310 Glasgow Central–Euston, past Ais Gill. *Bill Atkinson*

After sale to West Coast Railways, 57601 was repainted in the company's first version of maroon livery with a black band. It heads 1Z81, the 1432 Carlisle–Hellifield private charter, past Ais Gill on 4 October 2007. This loco is now in Pullman livery. *Bill Atkinson*

If the loco arrived with indented panels, it left with them after conversion. Only the opaque lenses were changed in favour of the white lights. Those with flush fronts were 57001/004/012 at No. 1 end and 57009 was likewise at No. 2 end. All other panels were the old indented style

The same folding red tail light lenses, as fitted when the locos were constructed in the mid-1960s, were also retained. Unlike the Class 47s in the Freightliner fleet, the 57/0s were not equipped with multiple working at conversion and indeed, if it was fitted, as was the case on 47204, it was removed.

However, if the loco arrived with bufferbeam skirting, this was removed. This had been a source of draughts for drivers for many years and was progressively removed by Railfreight Distribution and InterCity from their Class 47 fleets. Those that arrived with skirts were 47060/079/187, 47317/322/329/332/347/350/356, while 47079/204/231 had already had them removed.

Externally, the main changes were to the top roof grilles, and even these were not easy to spot. No. 57001 was unveiled in its new Freightliner green livery with yellow wrap round cabs and green roof at a ceremony at Brush Loughborough on 21 July 1998. To all intents and purposes, it looked every inch a Class 47, but it certainly didn't sound like one.

There were changes inside the cabs. A new cab interior had already been developed and fitted to Freightliner's 47270 in early 1997 aimed at improving the comfort for drivers. Class 47s had been notorious for draughts throughout their careers, and masses of masking tape sealing up the drivers' desks was commonly seen on the locos. The new cab on 47270, showcased in January 1998, addressed these issues and was rolled out on the 57/0s. In truth it wasn't a major change.

The six Class 57s leased to Network Rail were later transferred to DRS and their first duties were RHTTs, for which they were needed straight away and so there was no time to repaint them into DRS livery. Therefore, shots such as those of 57306 and 57310 on 6Z30, the 1100 Stowmarket–King's Lynn-Stowmarket RHTT, on 12 October 2012 at Soham Coates, between Ely and Soham, are quite rare. *Bill Atkinson*

No. 57605 *Totnes Castle* hauls 43144 and a full failed HST set past Oxford as 5Z70, the 1445 Oxford Up Carriage Sidings–Old Oak Common HSTD on 28 September 2015. The four FGW Class 57/6s are occasionally used for ad hoc fill-in jobs such as this in between their normal 'sleeper' duties. *Mark Pike*

On 4 September 2010, GWR 57604 *Pendennis Castle* is seen at Thornford on the Yeovil to Weymouth line with 2V67, the 1655 Weymouth–Bristol TM; the final loco-hauled service on the Bristol–Weymouth line. *Mark Pike*

New names

No. 57001 was unveiled sporting the name *Freightliner Pioneer*. After a competition among the company's staff it had been decided to name all the locos with the Freightliner prefix, rather like the Class 52 Westerns had been some twenty-five years earlier.

The names chosen, in loco order, were 57001 *Freightliner Pioneer*, 57002 *Freightliner Phoenix*, 57003 *Freightliner Evolution*, 57004 *Freightliner Quality*, 57005 *Freightliner Excellence*, 57006 *Freightliner Reliance*, 57007 *Freightliner Bond*, 57008 *Freightliner Explorer*, 57009 *Freightliner Venturer*, 57010 *Freightliner Crusader*, 57011 *Freightliner Challenger* and 57012 *Freightliner Envoy*.

The nameplates were in the standard BR Corporate style and fitted behind the cabs at mid-height. Large Freightliner decals were added slap bang in the middle of the bodyshell. Numbers were on all four cabsides just above the solebar and repeated in full at the same size on the front of the loco to the left of the BR-style standard high-intensity headlights. Smaller Freightliner logos were added on all four cabsides under the driver/secondman's windows and also on the front, either on the recessed headcode panel or above the marker lights depending on each loco's style.

When Freightliner painted its first Class 47 in the new livery – 47193 in April 1999 – it became very hard to different to tell it apart from a 57 other than the numbers.

It was soon apparent during the building of the second batch of Class 57/0s that production would end at 57012. The Class 66s had been performing well for EWS and offered levels of reliability never before see in the British diesel loco fleet. There was no getting away from it, the brand new 66s were a better long-term bet than the 57s, and the project was pretty much killed off as soon as it started.

Of the sixteen ex-Virgin Class 57/3s, twelve are now with DRS – of which three were stored in mid-2019, and four had been sold to West Coast Railways. No. 57310 *Pride of Cumbria*, passes Fauldhouse, on the Shotts line, with 1Z72, the 1347 Edinburgh–Edinburgh via Shotts and Carstairs, Northern Belle charter on 10 September 2015. On the rear out of sight is 57305 *Northern Princess*. Robin Ralston

On 19 June 2014, DRS 57302 *Chad Varah* stands at the buffer stops at Euston. Just four 57/3s are stabled on the WCML for rescue duties if required. *Jack Boskett*

The last of the 57/0s, 57012, was taken into the Freightliner fleet in February 2000, by which time 66501–505 were already in traffic and other orders for 66/5s had been placed.

The reason the company never took up the full option was simple – its business had grown to the point that it was able to acquire new Class 66s leased through the established ROSCOs, with Porterbrook supplying the first locos.

We will never know which other 47s could have been added to the 57/0 project to become 57/0s but the likes of 47142/147/150/152/193, 47224/258/283/287/292/295, 47323/339/340/345/353/376/377 and even 47473 could have been contenders.

Where the 57/0s worked

When the 57s were ordered by Freightliner, the company was only active in the intermodal market, and it would not be until 1999 that it started branching out into the Trainload freight sector with operations first for Railtrack and then later other bulk contracts, which led to the birth of its Heavy Haul business in 2001.

However, this new business did not really affect its Class 57s, which were to remain part of the intermodal business for their entire, albeit short, working lives with the company.

The locos were initially maintained under contract by EWS. Their first duties saw them working out of Felixstowe and Southampton on container trains – especially the heavier loads – to Leeds, Birmingham Lawley Street, Crewe Basford Hall, Garston, Trafford Park, Ripple Lane and Wilton.

There were some oddball occasional jobs by Freightliner's 57/0s and sometimes they went off route – either planned or otherwise. For example, in 2002 the Wentloog–Millbrook intermodal train would run via Swindon to allow Freightliner drivers to retain the route knowledge, and this was often worked by a 57/0.

Occasionally, they worked charter trains as well, at the request of promoters. The first working was 57001 *Freightliner Pioneer* on 7 November 1998 on Pathfinder Tours' 'Cheshire Mole' trip, which the new loco worked from Chester to Stafford. Nos. 57002/005/006/010 all also worked charters for this promoter.

After conversion, 57003 was moved by road to the nearby Great Central Railway GCR for some tests and running in, and during its stay, on 19 December 1998, it worked some passenger trains at the line.

Other Freightliner Class 57/0s have visited heritage railways to work passenger trains for visitors, and they include 57002 and 57012 at the Severn Valley Railway in October 1999 and October 2000 respectively and 57011 at the Mid Hants Railway in March 2000, while visitors to the East Lancashire Railway have included 57009 in July 2000, 57008 in September 2000 and 57004 in July 2003.

A demonstrator passenger loco

While the Class 57/0 project was pretty much killed off as soon as it had started as Freightliner changed its traction policy and started to order Class 66s, for sensible business reasons, 57012 was not to mark the end of 57 conversions.

Instead, Porterbrook, which had financed the Class 57/0 project and leased the new locomotives to Freightliner, saw the concept of re-engineering Class 47s had other possible applications.

With that in mind, the Class 57 was still seen by Brush and Porterbrook as an attractive 'new' build solution for other, especially passenger, operators.

At the turn of the millennium, both First Great Western and Virgin Cross Country were still using Class 47s in front-line passenger service. While the latter had ordered new Class 220/221 DEMUs to replace its loco-hauled operations, and so that would eliminate its 47s, FGW still needed locos solely for its 'Night Riviera' Paddington–Penzance sleeper train operation.

ScotRail had just changed its Edinburgh–Aberdeen and Inverness 'sleeper' operations from hired EWS Class 47s to new Class 67s, and while this might have been an option for FGW, no deals were agreed.

So for the foreseeable future FGW was 'stuck' with its 47s, and again, their reliability was not ideal. In fact, seven locos were needed to cover two trains and one ECS shunt release loco at Paddington.

FGW's 'sleeper' trains did not make any profit, so moving to hiring in, or even acquiring, its own Class 67s was not seen as a viable financial option, but like Freightliner, the Class 47s were well-worked and tired, and could not last forever.

Porterbrook speculated that if it built a Class 57 demonstrator fitted with electric train supply (ETS, sometimes called electric train heat, ETH) and put it in the 'shop window', orders could well follow. It had active 47825 in its fleet, but it was not leased to any train operator, although VXC and Anglia Railways had used it on a spot hire basis.

No. 57310 *Kyrano* couples to 390019 *Virgin Warrior* at Crewe on 30 January 2008. The 57 will then haul the Pendolino unit dead to Holyhead on the 0900 ex-Euston. The retractable Dellner coupler made attaching a 57 to a 221 or 390 unit so much easier. *Pip Dunn*

Spare from a reduced requirement as WCML Thunderbirds, Virgin Class 57/3s, were hired to other operators and Amec Spie started its freight haulage business by exploiting their availability. On 13 August 2007, 6J37, the 1327 Carlisle–Chirk, passes Helsby behind 57313 *Tracy Island*. *Paul Shannon*

On 28 January 2000, 47825 worked the 1830 Liverpool St–Norwich in place of a Class 86/2 and that was the last time it hauled a train. On 28 March it was hauled dead from Ipswich to Crewe and then ran light to Loughborough the following day, its working life – with a Sulzer engine – over.

No. 47825 already had ETS, so that was one less expense to incur. It would differ to the 57/0s because the reconditioned GM engine that would be put inside it would be the slightly more powerful 2,750hp General Motors 645-12F3B version of the same unit inside the Freightliner locos.

Originally the number 57401 was mooted, but this series wasn't vacant on the rolling stock library as it was used by a Class 156 DMU, so 57601 was chosen.

At Loughborough, 47825 was stripped down and work started, on turning it into an ETS 57. The conversion process was very similar to the 57/0s, although there were some minor changes. A week short of a year after it arrived at Brush, on 24 March 2001, 57601 was unveiled in a striking silver livery with purple cabs and full body-height italicised numbers – with its number repeated on the cabsides in white.

Unlike the Freightliner locos, and with no customer order, Porterbrook decided to smarten up their external appearance. Brush had made the front ends completely flush with the headcode panels and marker lights removed.

New light clusters were fitted above the bufferbeam with large headlights and smaller white lights/red tail lights next to them on the inside. A cab roof headlight was fitted in front of the horn grille, but there was no mistaking that this was still a Class 47 bodyshell. No. 47825 had arrived with its skirts removed, so this modification was not needed.

The loco emerged from the works and after a few initial tests on the Great Central Railway (Nottingham) – on the East Leake branch – it went on lease to FGW, which had agreed with Porterbrook to test it on its loco-hauled trains between Paddington and Plymouth or Penzance.

It initially started work on one of the few daytime loco-hauled turns that FGW had introduced recently. It would typically work the 0920 Plymouth–Paddington, via Bristol Temple Meads, and then return on the 1542 Paddington–Exeter, which also ran via Bristol, and then take the ECS to Laira.

In the summer of 2018, due to industrial action on Northern, West Coast Railways stepped in to provide a free shuttle service on the Oxenholme–Windermere branch. On 24 June 57316 passes Burneside with 33029 on the rear. *Rob France*

These trains were typically seven Mk 2 coaches, although sometimes two Motorail vans were added to give the loco a slightly heavier workload, but the loads were never really going to tax it beyond its capabilities.

No. 57601 later started to see use on the Paddington–Penzance 'sleeper' trains working alongside FGW's Class 47s – 47811/813/815/816/832/832/846. It stayed on hire with FGW until November 2003, although in April 2003 it was sold to West Coast Railways, albeit initially remaining with FGW.

Virgin opts for 57 Thunderbirds

Porterbrook deemed 57601 to be a success and offered the concept to the wider market. First to take up an order was Virgin West Coast, which agreed a deal for twelve locos in 2002.

Virgin West Coast had started to replace its Class 86/87/90-hauled Mk 3 sets with Class 390 Pendolino units from 2002 but they presented a problem – how these new trains could be rescued if one broke down.

These were to be 'Thunderbird' locos strategically stabled on the VWC operation between Euston and Glasgow Central. Locos would be stabled at Willesden, Rugby, Stafford, Preston, Carlisle and Polmadie. Thunderbirds were the railway's equivalent of the tow

trucks you see on the motorway. They are stabled at strategic locations to rescue any failures to get trains moving and so as not to block the railway for any longer than necessary. They got their Thunderbirds name from the TV puppet show of the 1960s.

Why twelve locos were needed was intriguing, why it was later extended to sixteen locos was baffling and why Virgin at one stage wanted twenty Thunderbirds was positively ludicrous!

Initially, the donor locos would be Class 47/8s still in use with Virgin's sister franchise CrossCountry, and all owned by Porterbrook. As the new Class 220 DEMUs started to be delivered and accepted into traffic, loco-hauled sets could be stood down and 47/8s could be released for conversion.

No. 47845 *County of Kent* was the first Class 47 stood down by VXC and selected for rebuilding. On 11 October 2001 it worked its last passenger train and ran light to Brush for stripping and conversion.

The Virgin locos would be identical to 57601, with the same flush front ends with the new light arrangement. Originally the Virgin locos were going to be numbered from 57611 through to 57622, and in a bizarre twist given what an image-conscious company Virgin was, they were to be painted in what Virgin described as a neutral colour – green.

On 4 May 2016, 6C52, the 1619 Heysham–Sellafield flasks passes Millom Marsh top-and-tailed by 57301 *Goliath* and 57306 *Her Majesty's Railway Inspectorate 175*. Rob France

Indeed, during the rebuilding of 57611, the bodyshell was repainted in all-over green, and it was only after this was completed that a policy change saw both the numbers and livery changed. Virgin wanted a number series starting in 01, so the 57301 number series was chosen. It also decided to repaint 57301 in the same red and silver livery the Pendolinos were appearing in, so the loco had a full repaint! It made sense to adopt the Virgin livery and indeed the number series, but it was surprising it had taken the time for '57611' to reach the paint shop for this to be implemented.

But either way, 57301–312 were to be the new numbers for the Virgin locos and 57301 appeared in June 2002 sporting a predominately silver bodyside with sweeping red curves at both cabs and likewise the mandatory full yellow fronts were also applied to sweep around to the sides. The roof was red, albeit with the new cooler group grilles being bare silver metal. The Virgin logos were applied full height on the bodyside, while Virgin logo plaques were applied to the front end.

No. 47827 was the next loco released from VXC for conversion and its planned 57612 number was naturally changed to become 57302. The third loco in line for rebuilding was 47849 *Cadeirlan Bangor Cathedral* and this was released from traffic in December 2001. The loco had jumped the queue for conversion; it wasn't originally planned to be used, but after catching fire on 8 December 2001 at Kenilworth, it moved to Brush and it was decided rather than repair it, it would become 57303.

However, during the work – 47849 had progressed to the stage that its front end headlights had been fitted and its headcode panels plated over – it was discovered that repairs to collision damage it sustained in 1972 as 1630 meant it was deemed to be unsuitable for conversion. It was duly dropped from the programme and sold for scrap. Instead, ex-Glasgow-Edinburgh push-pull loco 47705 was acquired from Riviera Trains and was converted to 57303.

Next in line were 47807 *The Lion of Vienna*, sent to Brush for rebuilding as 57304, followed by 47822 *Pride in*

Shrewsbury, which was to become 57305, while 47814 *Totnes Castle* became 57306.

However, when 47844 *Derby and Derbyshire Chamber of Commerce & Industry* was sent to Loughborough for conversion as 57307 it too was found to have sustained serious damage after a derailment at Southall in an earlier life as 1583 in 1969 (and it later crashed again as 47844 at Bournemouth West Depot when it collided with a departmental de-icing unit on 14 February 1991) and it too was dropped from the programme. Ex-Freightliner 47225 was duly selected to replace it. It became the first of the 57/3 conversions to use a no-heat freight loco as the donor and so needed fitting with ETH.

There was a plan for the body of 47844 to be taken to Crewe and cosmetically restored to be a 'gate guardian' static exhibit at Crewe Works, but this plan was never executed.

After the conversions of 47844/849 had both been shelved, the latter at some cost, Porterbrook changed its conversion policy. Firstly, it started to delve further into the histories of its locos to see if any other potential donor locos had been involved in accidents. If they had, they were rejected for consideration.

This led to a reprieve for 47826, which had been a candidate for rebuilding after it was clear it had suffered a major smash in its days as 47274. Instead the loco was given a 'Super-E exam' to extend its life as a Virgin Class 47 instead of conversion. The loco remains in traffic today with West Coast Railways.

Up to 57307, donors had either been ex-VXC locos – or at least intended to be ex-VXC locos! However, the donor for 57308 came from the FGW pool as 47846 *Thor* was released from traffic. Firstly, 57601 was available to take its place in the FGW fleet, plus 47846 was due for major overhaul so was simply retired and sent to Brush. The next loco was 47806, which became 57309, followed by 47831 *Bolton Wanderer* becoming 57310 and 47817 *The Institution of Mechanical Engineers* selected to become 57311.

Now owned by West Coast Railways, 57001 leads Statesman Rail's 1Z91 0620 Preston–Bristol Temple Meads 'Bath & Bristol Christmas Statesman' Pullman past Heyford on 10 December 2011. *Martin Loader*

No. 57005 *Freightliner Excellence* approaches the site of Ashbury Crossing at Shrivenham on 8 August 2006 with 4O51, the 1002 Wentloog–Southampton intermodal train. *Martin Loader*

Still part of the Virgin fleet, but on hire to Amec Spie, 57311 *Parker* passes Brock with 6J37, the 1327 Carlisle-Chirk timber train, on 8 May 2008. *Martin Loader*

However, the conversion of 47225 also highlighted that it was possible to convert a 47/0 or a 47/3 to a 57/3, albeit with a degree of extra cost. So after 47831 was chosen for conversion to 57311 respectively, Porterbrook decided to stop using ETH 47s. This was because the remaining 47/8s were now becoming popular assets to sell or lease to other companies – especially spot hire companies. Therefore, all conversions from 57312 used ex-Freightliner no-heat 47s instead.

The last of the initial batch of 57/3s for Virgin, 57312, was built using the body of ex-Freightliner 47330. In 2003, Virgin had ordered another four Class 57/3s, and actually had an option for four more as Virgin deemed it needed twenty Thunderbird locos on its route.

Four more ex-Freightliner locos were added to the programme and 57313–316 were rebuilt using the remains of, in order: 47371, 47372, 47234 and 47290. The plan to build 57317–320 was shelved and instead the extra four locos Virgin deemed it needed were made up by retaining 47/8s for a short period.

Of these additions to the 57/3 programme, 47705 arrived with its bufferbeam skirting still in place but the others did not, while 47234/290/330 arrived with Green Circle multiple working equipment that would then be removed.

Names

Given their role as Thunderbird locos, all the 57/3s were named after characters from the hit TV show *Thunderbirds* and featured nameplates with the programme's logo. For this Virgin had to pay a copyright fee.

The first six locos were named after the Tracy family and while 57301 *Scott Tracy* was named with all the typical Virgin pomp and ceremony at an event at Euston on 17 June, with Thunderbirds creator Gerry Anderson performing the unveiling, the rest had their plates affixed at Brush when the locos were built.

No. 57305 erroneously had the *Alan Tracy* nameplates fitted at first but they were soon swapped with its correct loco – 57303, with 57305 gaining its correct *John Tracy* nameplates. Of the other first half a dozen, 57302 was named *Virgil Tracy*, 57304 *Gordon Tracy* and 57306 *Jeff Tracy*.

Nos 57307–316 had other names from the series, with 57307 being named *Lady Penelope* and having its nameplates painted pink rather than black like the other locos. No. 57308 was *Tin*, 57309 was *Brains*, 57310 *Kyrano*, 57311 *Parker* and 57312 *The Hood*. The final four were 57313 *Tracy Island*, 57314 *Firefly*, 57315 *The Mole* and 57316 *FAB1*. All were upper case lettering under the logo, while all had separate plaques with the International Rescue logo on them.

161

Not just Thunderbirds

The 57/3s were used for a variety of duties with Virgin, not just rescue missions, and they were also used to haul trains diverted via routes where there was no overhead wires. Common examples were Birmingham New Street to Nuneaton, over the Settle and Carlisle line, from Carlisle to Glasgow via Dumfries and from Crewe to Preston via Manchester and Bolton.

One unusual duty in the late 2000s was Virgin's decision to run a Euston–Holyhead train each day using a Class 390, and this meant a 57/3 was attached at Crewe for the 106-mile journey to the end of the line in Anglesey. This was to offer a Pendolino service to the Welsh port, so releasing Class 221s for other duties, but also to keep up crew competency on the Class 57. It also allowed a regular use of the Dellner couplers, so ensuring they were always fit for purpose. Virgin also used 57/3s on some booked empty Pendolino drags for the same reasons of keeping both the equipment and crews' competency in good order.

When the 57/3s were introduced, Virgin still had several sets of Mk 3 coaches that operated in push-pull fashion with Class 87s, 90s and the odd 86/2. Therefore, it was not unknown to see a 57/3s hauling Mk 3 stock in place of a Class 87 or 90 if there was a shortage of electric locos, bringing them to Euston or Glasgow Central.

Sometimes they would do the same but with a dead AC electric loco still on the train.

The Class 57/3s were initially allocated to Willesden, although this later changed to Manchester Longsight from October 2005.

No. 57315 *The Mole* approaches Heyford with 1Z57, the 0955 Kensington Olympia–Chester private charter on 14 September 2007. Sister loco 57316 *FAB 1* is on the rear. The coaching stock is the 'Queen of Scots' rake, which includes various vintage coaches, the most notable of which is the 1891-built observation car, seen here coupled directly behind the loco. All the vehicles in this image are now owned by WCR. *Martin Loader*

GWR 57604 *Pendennis Castle* was on display at the Old Oak Common open day on 4 September 2017. *Jack Boskett*

The Class 57/6s are now allocated to Penzance and used in the main on Penzance–Paddington sleeper trains. In between duties the locos lay over at Old Oak Common or Penzance, and 57605 rests in the shed at Old Oak on 4 September 2017. *Jack Boskett*

DRS 57004 and 47832 ease in to Workington Station with a Maryport–Workington shuttle service along the Cambrian coast on 25 March 2010. In December 2009, serious flooding washed away the main road bridge to the north of Workington, so a free Workington to Maryport shuttle was provided by DRS, which ran all day between the two points for locals. One loco was always an ETS machine but the other end could be a freight loco and several 57/0s were used for the service, which ran until May 2010. *Jack Boskett*

Now painted in Arriva Trains livery, but returning to its original work, 57314 hauls 390021 *Virgin Dream* in to Crewe on 26 April 2012 on an empty stock move. *Rob France*

Great Western takes four

In 2003 First Great Western, happy with its extended trial running of 57601, ordered four Class 57s for its Paddington–Penzance 'sleeper' operations.

These were to be numbered 57602–605 and were similar in design and appearance to trial loco 57601. They were converted from ex-Freightliner locos and were, in order: 47337, 47349, 47209, 47206 *The Morris Dancer*. They entered traffic between November 2003 and September 2004. Of these, 47349 retained its skirting – the other three didn't – while 47209/337 both had MW equipment to remove at conversion.

These were released before 57313–316, which entered traffic in October to December 2004. So, Virgin's 57316 proved to be the thirty-third and final Class 57 conversion.

The 57/6s were outshopped in FGW green with a gold band close to the solebar and gold First logos at No. 1 end. The numbers were in green on the gold band and also on the cab fronts in green. Small yellow warning panels featured.

The FGW Class 57/6s were allocated to Laira to start with, then moved to Old Oak Common and then Swansea Landore – the latter might have seemed a strange decision considering the locos never went to Swansea at all in their day-to-day work, but the reality was their depot allocation was irrelevant. They were maintained at Old Oak Common – the FGW HST depot and not the ex-EWS depot.

All FGW 57/6s were soon named and, keeping with Western tradition, all were named after castles on the FGW route in Devon and Cornwall. Unlike the 57/3s, all had official ceremonies and the first to have its plates unveiled was 57605 *Totnes Castle*, named at the town's station on 21 September 2004.

A week later, on 28 September, 57602 was named *Restormel Castle* at Par station. Next was 57604, which was named *Pendennis Castle* at Truro station on 5 October, and finally 57603 was named *Tintagel Castle* at Penzance station on 19 October. As well as having their nameplates unveiled, they also had their numbers on cast plaques fitted behind the cab doors at No. 2 end.

In 2008, the four FGW locos were repainted into First Group blue, this work being undertaken by Hunslet Barclay at Kilmarnock. In June 2010, to commemorate 175 years since the formation of the Great Western Railway, 57604 was repainted at Brush into GWR green and had new cast number and nameplates – the latter in GWR upper case style. It was officially unveiled at an event at the Didcot Railway Centre on 20 June. Its snowploughs were painted black at the same time.

In 2015, First Great Western rebranded itself as Great Western Railway. Nos 57603/603/605 were repainted into the company's dark green livery, a throwback to the old GWR, the same year and these carried GWR cast emblems. No. 57604 retained its lighter – original lined GWR – green livery.

WCR duo 57316/601 pass Eldroth near Clapham in North Yorkshire on 2 October 2016 with an empty stock move. The Class 57s have been an exceptional buy for WCR allowing it to not only grow its business but have improved reliability on its most prestigious workings like the Royal Scotsman and more recently the Northern Belle. *Rob France*

Class 57/6 workings

The vast bulk of workings by 57/6s were exactly as intended – 'sleeper' trains between Paddington and Penzance, but they occasionally strayed on to other duties. For example, on 28 February 2006, 57604 hauled the 1040 Shoeburyness–Newport taking twelve ex-Southern Region Mk 1 EMU cars for scrapping.

On 8 May 2008, 57602 – now in First Group blue livery – was running light from the Barclay plant at Kilmarnock to the Western Region when it was intercepted at Oxenholme and sent north to assist a twelve-car Class 325 mail EMU train on 1M44, the 1532 Shieldmuir–Warrington. The 57 hauled the units through to their destination.

The FGW Class 57s have seen some other occasional passenger work away from their booked sleeper turns.

The summer timetables of 2008–10 saw FGW run a Saturdays-only loco-hauled train from Bristol TM to Weymouth and back, and this was booked for a DB Schenker Class 67. However, on 4 September 2010, 57604 was rostered for 2O72, the 0909 Bristol Temple Meads to Weymouth, and the 1655 return. This was the last time that duty was loco-hauled, but it has since been operated by HSTs. To get 57604 to Bristol TM for the turn, it was attached to the rear of the 2350 Paddington–Penzance and taken off at Exeter before running light to Bristol TM.

An equally unusual working was on 1 February 2010, when 57602 and 57605 top-and-tailed the 0901 Oxford–Paddington commuter train in place of an unavailable HST. The stock used was the fill rake off the 'sleeper' complete with the sleeping cars, which were locked out of use.

On 14 October 2011 57604 was used to haul 1A91, the 1400 Penzance–Paddington from Plymouth to Exeter, after 43063/191 were in trouble. The 57 provided extra power for the ailing HST to tackle the notorious hills between the two cities. Another HST drag – with a difference – was on 3 August 2013 when 57603 hauled power car 43150 on its own as 0Z77, the 1530 Westbury–Laira, after the power car had been dumped at Westbury after failing.

Spare 57s at Penzance during the day were used in the spring of 2014 for driver training in readiness for a forthcoming additional summer Saturday passenger turn. A loco and a couple of coaches were used to train Penzance drivers on loco handling on the main line as they generally only worked the ECS from the station to Long Rock Depot.

Running nearly an hour late, Virgin Thunderbird 57303 *Alan Tracy* is well off course as it climbs out of Patchway Tunnel, near Bristol with the Pathfinder Tours' 1Z64, 0618 Worcester Foregate Street–Penzance 'Virgin Territorial' railtour on 16 September 2006. *Martin Loader*

Then from that summer, the loco and three day coaches off the Down 'Night Riviera' were used on summer Saturdays to work an additional duty to Exeter and back to Penzance. The turn was the 1125 Par–Exeter and 1750 Exeter–Penzance, though in the summers of 2016 to 2018 this outward run ran just from Plymouth at 1335. This turn ended in 2018.

While four locos generally were fine for covering the sleeper turns, if any loco was on long-term maintenance, or suffered a serious failure, then cover would be needed and this usually came in the form of a DRS Class 57/3 hired in.

On 6 August 2014, 57603 failed on 1C99, the 2350 Paddington–Penzance, near Exeter and 57310 *Pride of Cumbria* was needed to assist. This DRS loco then led its FGW sister on the ECS to Penzance ready for that night's Up working back to Paddington.

However, 57310 then failed at Plymouth and had to visit Laira depot for repairs. The result was that the 2200

Penzance–Paddington was worked by an HST to Plymouth, where 57310/603 took over, top-and-tail with the Mk 3 coaches, but they failed near Bristol TM and needed 66413/518 to drag the train into Temple Meads station. It was duly cancelled!

The boot was on the other foot on 26 January 2015 when 66176 failed between Par and Lostwithiel on a china clay train. No. 57603 was sent from Long Rock to assist and take the train of CDAs to St Blazey yard before returning to its booked sleeper turns.

On 29 May 2016, 57605 was used to assist CrossCountry Trains' 1T55 1625 Plymouth–Newquay after 43366/378 were in trouble.

On 1 March 2018, the 2103 Paddington to Plymouth was affected by bad weather and arrived at its destination nearly six hours later. No. 57604 was then used to drag the HST to Penzance on 2 March – in the snow.

No 57306 *Her Majesty's Railway Inspectorate 175* passes Chalford as it climbs Sapperton Bank on 13 May 2016 with 1Z10, the 0634 Sheffield–Bristol Temple Meads Northern Belle luxury charter. These trains are now operated by West Coast Railways, although Class 57s are still the usual, and certainly preferred, traction. *Martin Loader*

No. 57306 runs along the down relief line at Circourt Bridge, Denchworth, on 1 October 2015 with 1Z31, the 1155 Paddington–Cardiff Central rugby special. Classmate 57310 is on the rear. This was one of three special trains run in connection with the Rugby World Cup Wales versus Fiji game at the Millennium Stadium. In the background, GBRf's 66748 slowly runs along the other relief line with 6M40, the 1156 Westbury–Stud Farm ballast empties. *Martin Loader*

Class 57 modifications

Early on in the career of the 57/3s, a clear design deficiency was immediately recognised; the job for which they were intended, rescuing a stricken Class 390, was not at all easy. At the time of their introduction, Virgin West Coast still had plenty of Class 87/90-hauled Mk 3 sets in use and a 57 could easily rescue one of these.

But the new Class 390s, which entered traffic in 2002, had a Dellner coupler hidden behind a moveable – and fragile – front panel. When a 57 was needed to couple to these, it was a convoluted, drawn out – and often unsuccessful – operation.

The solution was to fit retractable Dellner couplers to 57301 as a trial in 2003. This was quite a big job and needed a large section of the front being cut away and an indented recess fitted to accommodate the new equipment. This was not a cheap retro modification as it needed to be undertaken on 57301–312, while 57313–316 had the equipment fitted at conversions, but it was necessary.

The couplers would be folded away in the vertical position when needed but via the press of a button in the cab, the Dellner would extend and sweep down 90 degrees and be horizontal and at the same height as the Dellner coupler on both a Class 390 or a Class 220/221 Voyager DEMU. This meant a 57/3 could recover any stricken train much more easily and quicker – and indeed safer than when using a conventional Class 57.

The only other modification of note was that the four FGW locos have snowplough brackets added – although 47206, which became 57605, already had them fitted as a 47/0. This meant the locos started to sport three-piece miniature snowploughs, though they soon settled down to just sporting the outer side ploughs.

West Coast's first 57

The first Class 57 to be sold on was Porterbrook's prototype ETH loco 57601, which moved to West Coast Railways in April 2003, although it initially remained on hire to FGW. It finally moved to its new owner's home at Carnforth on 23 December 2003.

It was immediately taken into the paintshop at Carnforth and emerged in February painted in the first version of WCR's maroon livery, which featured a black stripe midway down the body between the two cabs. It had white 57601 numbers on all four cabsides and also on its front just above the bufferbeam.

It was the second Type 4 loco to join the WCR fleet after ex-VXC 47854 was acquired from Porterbrook in June 2003. The first working for 57601 with its new owner was on 29 February 2004 on a Bolton to Cardiff football special for Bolton Wanderers fans.

It soon settled down to becoming a reliable and popular addition to the WCR fleet and the fitters at Carnforth speak very highly of it. The loco has now clocked up more than fifteen years' work for WCR, and eighteen years in all since conversion. It was nicknamed Sheila – and even carried this 'name' in small font on the cabside for a period.

In October 2012 it was repainted in the company's standard darker maroon livery but in 2018 it was repainted again into Pullman umber and cream to match the coaches used in the Northern Belle train that WCR acquired from Belmond in 2017. It was also finally named for the first time in this guise, inheriting the Windsor Castle nameplates from withdrawn 47786. In September 2019, 57313 was the second WCR 57 to be painted in Pullman colours.

No. 57601 has been all over the country, often becoming the first of the class to visit some destinations. As well as charters, the loco has been used on saloon moves, hauling the Queen of Scots Pullman, which is now owned by WCR and used for special events only. It has also been used on infrastructure machine moves and the occasional freight train.

In plain, unbranded Arriva turquoise, 57313 passes non-stop through Hereford station with 1W91, the 1615 Cardiff Central–Holyhead Welsh Assembly-sponsored Arriva Trains Wales service on 2 June 2009. This loco-hauled train operates just once in each direction per day. It changed to a DB Cargo Class 67 turn in 2012. *Martin Loader*

Class 57/0s redeployed

After the sale of 57601 to WCR, the next 57s to find new owners would be the dozen original no-heat Class 57/0s. They had rapidly become non-standard in the Freightliner fleet following multiple orders to create a healthy Class 66s fleet – totalling 131 locos at one stage. It was clear once the 66s became the traction of choice for the company that the role for the 57s would be limited.

And as the 57/0s became non-standard, naturally they became costlier to operate and could create some issues with driver knowledge. They would also be due major expenditure as soon as works overhauls loomed.

The 57/0s were still owned by Porterbrook, so when their leases with Freightliner ended, they were simply returned to their owner, although that handover had to be with each loco in full working order. During 2007 most of the 57/0s were returned to Porterbrook and their owner sought new users for them.

Initially, 57007–012 were duly leased to DRS from May 2007 joined by 57002/003 in July 2008, while 57004 was bought outright by DRS in April 2008. All were repainted into DRS's 'Compass' livery, lost their original names and were fitted with multiple working to allow them to run with both other 57s and other locos in the DRS fleet.

The DRS Class 57/0s have seen use on nuclear, engineering and infrastructure, intermodal and charter trains. They have even seen passenger use on service trains when top-and-tailing with ETH locos.

No. 57008 was renamed by DRS *Telford International Railfreight Park June – 2009* to commemorate the reopening of a railhead at Donington.

Any of the DRS locos that retained indented headcode panels had them plated over, with the exception of 57009, which was withdrawn before this modification was implemented. The change also saw new white LED marker lights fitted.

On hire to Amec Spie, 57311 *Parker* passes Docker with 6J37, the 1327 Carlisle Yard–Chirk loaded timber train on 12 September 2007. *Bill Atkinson*

Still sporting Northern Belle livery, DRS's 57312 *Solway Princess* is one of two 57/3s on long-term lease to Rail Operations Group – along with 57303 – and used mostly for moving multiple units. On 11 April 2019, it hauls ex-Great Northern 313050 away for scrap as 5Q54, the 1018 Hornsey–Kingsbury Sidings, past Copleys Brook, Melton Mowbray.
Bill Atkinson

Advenza and WCR 57/0s

DRS's decision to take nine Class 57/0s left three available for Porterbrook to either dispose of or lease again.

In January 2008, 57005/006 were sold to small spot hire Open Access freight operator Gloucester-based Cotswold Rail, which operated under its Advenza Freight Operating Company banner.

The first working was by now-nameless 57005, still in Freightliner livery – even with branding – on 21 January on a Long Marston to Bescot move of tank wagons. No. 57005 was still green in early February but by March both had been repainted into the company's blue livery, which was not too dissimilar to BR blue. Nos 47237/375 also joined this operation in the same colour scheme.

They were used initially on scrap metal trains between Stockton and Cardiff Tidal, but they also worked other freight trains and rolling stock moves – including FGW Class 43 Power Cars – between works and depots. They also appeared on some short-term freight flows. Interestingly, for such a small, and new, company. Advenza's decision to ditch its 47s and 57s so soon in favour of Class 66 – in early 2009 – ultimately helped cause its downfall as it could not afford the leasing costs.

Following Advenza's demise in late 2009, the locos spent a period stored at Gloucester while the company's assets were disposed of. The two 57/0s were originally bought by Harry Needle Railroad Company in September 2009 and eventually, HNRC, which never used the locos, sold them to WCR in April 2011.

At the same time, WCR also did a deal to take 57001 directly from Porterbrook. In their final months with Freightliner, some locos had already endured periods in store while they were stopped waiting parts, but most returned to traffic. However, in December 2006, 57001 failed with a major engine defect and was duly withdrawn from traffic. It was taken to Marcroft Engineering at Stoke in July 2007 but then moved to the LNWR site at Crewe a month later, where it had its nameplates removed in early in 2008.

All 57s had to be handed back to Porterbrook in operational condition, so 57001 was returned to Brush at Loughborough in December 2008, but it was August 2010 before it was returned to serviceable condition. It was tested in October by Freightliner, working off its Leeds Midland Road Depot before being sold – not leased – to West Coast Railways in early 2011.

Once moved to Carnforth it was eventually repainted into WCR's brown livery and returned to use that year. However, in August 2012 it had been stopped again and would be laid up until October 2014. It worked intermittently for its new owners until being stopped in February 2016 again and then taken to Nemesis Rail's site at Burton in June 2018 for a repair, emerging in December 2018.

No. 57006 returned to use, repainted in WCR's maroon livery, and despite having no train supply it and 57001 could be used on charters as WCR mostly operated with top-and-tail locos for insurance and to avoid running round.

The 57/0s were also ideal for the Royal Scotsman luxury train, which had its own on-board train supply so heating from the locomotive was not needed. This was also perfect work for any WCR loco restricted to 75mph due to poor wheelsets as that was the maximum speed of this train.

No. 57006 returned to traffic in June 2012, but its returned was relatively brief as by October 2013, however, 57006 was stopped with poor wheelsets and has not worked since. In early 2019 there was a suggestion it could return to traffic.

The other loco acquired by WCR, 57005, was not so lucky and has remained at Carnforth since it arrived on 4 January 2012. Its return to traffic is highly unlikely and it has been a spares donor to the company's 57 fleet ever since.

There was a rumour that 57001/006 – and presumably 57005 as well – may have been sold by WCR to DRS in the summer of 2014, but such a deal never happened.

57/3s move on

VWC's need for Class 57/3s diminished following its decision to rescue failed Class 390s with another 390, and so the demand for the Virgin Thunderbirds was cut dramatically.

Before getting rid of its 57s, Virgin sub-leased some locos to other operators. Amec Spie hired three from January 2007 to work timber trains from Carlisle to Chirk. This work passed to Colas in March 2009 and while it initially continued to use the 57/3s, it later swapped its traction provider to DRS, who supplied a 57/0. In fact, 57002 actually had Colas logos applied to its bodysides.

Four locos, 57313–316, were also sub-hired to Arriva Trains Wales in 2009 for working Holyhead–Cardiff trains. They were repainted into Arriva colours, although only 57314/315 had branding vinyls applied, 57313/316 remaining in all-over base turquoise colours. They lost their names in the process.

This work only lasted until March 2012 when the haulage contract was changed to DB Schenker, which provided a Class 67 and a DVT. This left these locos spare and they were sold to WCR in November 2012, although the sale did not include the inclusion of the Dellner couplers as these were removed beforehand.

They were all repainted into WCR maroon and joined by 57001/006/601, which meant the Carnforth-based operator

– whose customer portfolio grew rapidly in the early 2000s – had seven operational Class 57s, five of them with ETH.

The other twelve Class 57/3 were split equally between DRS and Network Rail. DRS bought 57302/304/307–309/311 from Porterbrook but they were all dedicated to their same duties – standby rescue locos for Virgin.

The other six locos, 57301/303/305/306/310/312, were moved to Network Rail in November 2011 and duly repainted in the company's all-over yellow livery at Eastleigh, with 57310 the last of the sextet to be repainted. They were intended to be used for snow-clearing duties and other rescue missions, especially on the Southern Region.

They were to work in pairs top-and-tailing the new Snow and Ice Treatment Trains (SITT). The formation was a ZZA snowplough wagon, the 57, then four YXA wagons, the second 57 and then another ZZA wagon. During its time with NR, 57312 was renamed *Peter Henderson*.

The trains were operated by GB Railfreight and based at Tonbridge. However, their use with the national infrastructure owner was brief as in July 2014 they all moved to DRS as well, a deal that caused a level of consternation among GBRf management. They left the SR and left the SITTs to be covered by other locos, usually Class 73s. These six 57/3s remain owned by Porterbrook and merely leased by DRS.

All sixteen ex-Virgin Class 57/3s lost their Thunderbird names apart from 57307, for which dispensation was granted for it to keep its *Lady Penelope* nameplates.

Once with DRS, the ex-NR 57/3s were used for charters – including the Northern Belle, for which 57305/312 were painted in brown and cream Belle livery in 2014 as they replaced 47790/832, which had been the previous dedicated locos for this train. When this train was sold to WCR in late 2017, 57305/312 joined their classmates in general use.

As mentioned, DRS also hired 57/3s to boost the FGW fleet and some workings on the 'sleeper' trains were even made by the locos before they lost their yellow NR livery. Even in 2019, DRS Class 57/3s are still used by FGW from time to time.

So by 2015 of the sixteen ex-Virgin 57/3s, the first dozen were with DRS, with 57301/303/306/310 now sporting the new DRS Compass livery and 57307 having been adorned with 'Cable thieves we're watching you' branding. Nos 57305/312 were in Northern Belle. Nos 57313–315 had been repainted in WCR maroon in 2014 and 57316 followed in 2015.

DRS has renamed the locos, some more than once with 57301 named *Goliath*, 57302 *Chad Varah*, 57303 *Pride of Carlisle*, 57304 *Pride of Cheshire*, 57305 *Northern Princess*, 57306 *Her Majesty's Railway Inspectorate 175*, 57308 *Country of Staffordshire* then renamed *Jamie Ferguson*, 57309 *Pride of Crewe*, 57310 *Pride of Cumbria*, 57311 *Thunderbird* and 57312 *Solway Princess*. By 2019, WCR had not named any of its 57/3s.

In 2017–18, DRS 57302/310/311 were stored out of traffic, while in 2018 ex-Northern Belle pair 57305/315 were sub-hired to fellow FOC Rail Operations Group for use on multiple unit moves, moving into the GROG pool. They retained their Belle names and livery albeit with the branding painted out.

These hires left 57304/307–309 in the XHVT pool for the few remaining Thunderbird duties on the WCML and 57301/306 for general use – with 57306 often on hire to FGW.

The future

By 2019, of the original dozen 57/0s, WCR owned three – two of which, 57001/006, were in and out of the operational fleet and one, 57005, was withdrawn.

Of the nine DRS 57/0s, six locos, 57004/008–012, were in store at Longtown having been stood down in December 2015. The locos remain in store with the view of being able to be returned to traffic for season work such as every autumn when they can help cover the Railhead Treatment Train season as it puts an extra strain on the operator's resources.

That left just 57002/003/007 in the active fleet at the start of the year with DRS. No. 57002 was now named *Rail Express* with the nameplates from 47853, and 57007 was named *John Scott* using the nameplates from 47810.

Of the ETH Class 57/3 fleet, just three were withdrawn, 57302/310/311, while five were with WCR,

four with FGW, three were with ROG and six were retained by DRS.

In 2011, DRS had a plan to fit its nine Class 57/0s with Electric Train Supply as the company won more passenger work, but this plan was shelved. FGW had mooted the possibility of re-engineering its locos with MTU engines – to match its HST fleet – but again, this seems to have been little more than a 'thinking out loud' possibility rather than anything concrete.

However, as the Class 57s were only ever intended as a stopgap, and indeed they have spent most of their careers being just that, the time has come for most of them to be disposed of or redeployed.

The FGW locos and WCR locos seem safe for the moment. The WCML Thunderbird contract also seems unlikely to end any time soon, so employing four machines, but that leaves most of the 57/0s and some of the 57/3s as underutilised.

You cannot imagine WCR would turn down the opportunity to buy any 57/3s should they become available, and even GBRf would probably give serious consideration to any 57s that came on the market.

They were built to do a job, and while the bodysnatchers – as they were known – might not be everyone's cup of tea, you cannot deny they have been a useful tool over the last two decades.

Virgin Thunderbird 57307 *Lady Penelope* pauses at Sheffield while unusually working in place of a Class 221 Voyager on Virgin CrossCountry's 1M17, the 1717 Newcastle–Birmingham New Street, on 26 January 2007. *Ian Nightingale*

9

The MTU Class 43s
Rebuilding of a Classic

The High Speed Train, or InterCity 125, was a marketing revelation for British Rail when it was introduced in 1976. An HST had a formidable combined power output of 4,500hp from a locomotive at each end, allowing it to have excellent acceleration and a top speed of 125mph.

The locos were originally fitted with Paxman Valenta 12RP200L engines developing 2,250hp. Working in multiple in pairs – with one loco either end of seven or eight Mk 3 coaches – the HSTs cut journey times on every route they worked. Some 197 locos were built between 1975 and 1982, numbered 43002–198 – two prototype units built in 1972 being 43000/001.

They were introduced first on the Western Region, then the East Coast Main Line before later taking on the majority of workings on the Midland Main Line and most trains on the CrossCountry network, initially on the North East–South West Route before then later working to Manchester, Liverpool, Edinburgh, Glasgow Central, Poole and Weymouth. Only Brighton and Ramsgate on the CrossCountry network did not succumb to regular HST operation.

By the early 2000s, the HST power car fleet was beginning to show its age, especially as regards its Valenta engines. These were noisy, inefficient and dated, and if the trains were to remain in traffic, re-engineering the power cars was seen as a priority, plus a cost-effective way to reduce noise, emissions and fuel usage.

First Great Western 43005 passes Avoncliff on 18 April 2015 with the diverted 1C18, 1430 Paddington–Bristol Temple Meads. The River Avon is in the foreground, and the aqueduct carrying the Kennet & Avon Canal over the railway can just be seen in the background. *Martin Loader*

That solution came about in 2004 with the fitting of two locos, 43004/009, with testbed MTU engines, but before looking at this conversion, it is worth briefly recalling some of the re-engineering trials undertaken by British Rail on the HST power car fleet.

Over the years, 195 of the Class 43 power cars have had new engines fitted. Only accident write-offs 43011/019 were withdrawn still with their original Valenta engines. Interestingly, the first HST power car of all to be written off, 43173, had only just been re-engined from a Valenta to a VP185 before its fatal collision in 1997.

BR trials

Not all Class 43s retained their original engines at the turn of the millennium, and indeed there were only four years when the entire fleet was in traffic with the same, original, engines as from 1986, a start was made by BR to look into alternative power units.

It is beyond the remit of this book to look into too much detail of the re-engineering done before privatisation, but a brief recap is worthy of inclusion. The first power car to be re-engined was 43167 when it was fitted with a 12-cylinder Mirrlees MB190 engine at Derby Works in late 1986, entering traffic in January 1987.

Mirrlees MB190 units were then fitted to 43168-170 in 1987 to allow a lengthy evaluation on the InterCity routes from Paddington. The units were to prove ultimately unsuccessful and while the company also failed to win any orders for its engines to be fitted into rebuilt Class 37s (after an initial trial of two locos), it did win an order to provide engines to 100 Class 60s in the late 1980s. BR's InterCity sector had undertaken these engine tests aimed at finding better engine alternatives to the Valenta unit, but the Mirrlees engine never fulfilled their promise.

The first conversion to a VP185 engine was 43170 in 1994, when it lost its Mirrlees engine. The following year 43167/169 followed suit, losing their Mirrlees engines for VP185s, while around the same time, the Valenta engines were taken out of InterCity Midland Main Line's 43047/075 and switched for VP185s. Then in 1996, 43168 also swapped its Mirrlees engine for a VP185, leaving six VP185s in traffic – four on the WR and two on the MML.

In January 1996 43167 was moved from the Western fleet to Neville Hill to allow the VP185 to be evaluated on the East Coast Main Line, but it was an odd man out – and no other power car joined it. It ran with a VP185 in it into privatisation in 1996 when Sea Containers won the InterCity East Coast Franchise and created the new GNER operation.

Two of Network Rail's trio of MTU power cars, 43013 *Mark Carne CBE* and 43062 *John Armitt,* power the 1146 Hull– Heaton New Measurement Train run past Crabley Creek, near Brough, on 3 November 2018. *Anthony Hicks*

It inherited 43167 but when its engine was due overhaul it was duly converted back from a VP185 to a Valenta in 2001 to allow the fleet to be uniform with the rest of the GNER fleet. Despite its performance proving to be fine, it was non-standard and GNER wanted all of its Class 43s to be the same.

Privatisation

Great Western Trains was the Train Operating Company that had started running the InterCity Great Western (ICGW) franchise from 1996. The following year, GWT had Angel Trains' 43173/177/179/191 all converted to VP185 engines – with 43173 only working a matter of weeks before it crashed in 1997 and then scrapped. No. 43165 was converted to a VP185 in 2002 using the recovered engine out of 43173.

BR's InterCity Midland Main Line business sector, in conjunction with leasing company Porterbrook MML, had four VP185 conversions authorised initially: 43047/075 in 1996 with 43059/074 following in 1997–98 after the problems of the first two had been identified and rectified.

There was then a hiatus in conversions to VP185s until Midland Main Line decided to make it the engine of choice for its HST fleet, so progressively between 2002 and 2009 its remaining power cars were swapped to these new powerplants.

This decision was taken to assist with turnaround of overhauled engines, as there were not enough good Valenta engines available. Hence Porterbrook and MML agreed that half the fleet would be made VP185 and half retained as Valentas, allowing better utilisation of a small fleet (thirty required daily from thirty-six). The later conversions were driven by the availability of the engines from Angel cars following the MTU conversions

The conversions were 43048/049/052/055/072 in 2002, 43043–045/050/060/061/073/076/082 in 2003, 43046/054/058/066/081/083 in 2008 and finally 43064/089 in 2009.

By the time the last conversions to VP185s were taking place, there was a new option for the HST fleet – the MTU 16V4000 R41R.

No. 43198 *Driver Stan Martin 25 June 1950 – 6 November 2004* brings up the rear of GWR's 1Z23, the 0737 Paddington–Carmarthen 'Flying Banana' railtour, at Moreton-in-Marsh on 1 June 2019. No. 43002 *Sir Kenneth Grange* was leading the train and this was the last HST to visit Paddington for GWR. *Martin Loader*

With the chimney and cooling towers of Eggborough Power Station providing the dramatic backdrop, 43310 speeds past Heck Ings on 7 April 2015 with Virgin East Coast Trains' 1E05, the 0730 Edinburgh–King's Cross. The power car's livery is a temporary fix pending the roll-out of the company's new red colour scheme and is just a vinyl addition to the former East Coast livery. *Martin Loader*

The birth of the MTU HST

First Great Western, the new franchisee after GWT, in conjunction with Angel Trains and Brush Traction, rebuilt 43004/009 with the new V16-cylinder MTU engines in 2004–05 and they proved better on fuel, produced lower emissions and were far quieter than the noisy Valenta engines they replaced.

While the engine has a capability of producing 2,678hp, for use in an HST they are rated at 2,250hp, the same as a Valenta HST, mainly because the higher rating would have distorted the train performance and placed undue demands on the other traction equipment still fitted on the locos.

The MTU engine had already proved itself in Germany in the Class 218 diesel hydraulics, so it was tried and tested technology. The MTU engines have skip-firing, so after a period of idling only eight cylinders are working. This reduces fuel usage and emission when the units are stationary but idling. Both Valentas and VP engines were later also fitted with single-bank firing, providing the same effect.

FGW set about rebuilding its entire fleet. Those owned by Angel were 43002–010/012/015–018/020–037/040-042,
43124–152/163–165/168–172/174–177/179/181–183/185–192, while those owned by Porterbrook were 43053/056/063/069/071/078/079/086–088/091, 43156/159–162/180/193/195–197 and a dozen locos that First Group acquired from Porterbrook in 2004–05 after they were returned off lease by Virgin CrossCountry in 2003; namely 43092–094/097/098/122/153–155/158/194/198.

The two locos were fitted with a new Voith cooler group, which had also been fitted to thirty-five other original power cars at the time, replacing the Serck or Marston cooler groups. The cooler group has less 'work' to do as the MTU engines emit less heat.

The engine has common rail fuel injection, which makes power take up smoother and easier. If the engine gets too hot, it will automatically become derated so as to produce less power and cool it down, so preventing damage to the engine.

The locos also have the ability to be preheated so they don't start up the engine cold; this reduces emission and wear on the components. They have a superior tractive effort compared with their predecessors. In their early days of use, of course, a Valenta power car would 'hold them back'!

Grand Central was the last operator to have its Valenta HSTs upgraded to MTU engines. Nos 43484 and 43480 pass Metheringham with 1N24, the 1648 King's Cross–Sunderland, diverted via the Joint Line due to planned engineering on 22 October 2011. *Bill Atkinson*

On 21 May 2005 43009 entered traffic and undertook a number of test runs from its home depot, Bristol St Philip's Marsh, and then entered traffic on 14 June. On 23 June, 43004 entered passenger traffic. Their early days in traffic saw them supported by travelling fitters from Brush.

Externally, the only thing to set them apart from Valenta power cars in the FGW fleet were their revised light clusters, which were a smoother and cleaner design.

They initially worked only with Valenta-engined Class 43s for a while until they were put together to measure their performance as a wholly MTU-powered HST.

The MTU project started in earnest in 2006 with the twelve First Group-owned locos, which had been stored for years, being the first to be revived.

Nos 43093/097/098/198 were the first to be added to the programme in January, followed by 43092/094 in February.

GNER joins

In early 2006, GNER signed up to join the MTU party and have its HST fleet fitted with the new engines. The first two locos for GNER were 43090/100, which like the First

Group locos, were ex-Virgin CrossCountry locos, albeit owned by Porterbrook, and had also been stored for some considerable time.

Understandably, the level of work to resurrect those locos that had been stored for long periods was much greater, especially with corrosion repairs to be addressed.

On 13 April, FGW's 43175 moved to Loughborough for rebuilding, and this was the first of the active western fleet of locos that was stopped in traffic and taken for rebuilding. It arrived two weeks before 43154/155/158 – also long-time stored, ex-VXC locos – were added to the programme.

No. 43175, which had arrived with a Valenta engine, emerged on 7 July, initially sporting Angel branding for publicity pictures. Its rebuild had taken less than three months and once the project was in full swing, locos could reappear in under two months after their conversions. Locos were rewired and overhauled at the same time, so the production line at Brush was proving to be highly efficient.

Nos 43078/165/197 arrived in late June, with 43165 being a VP185 loco in the FGW fleet. First Group's 43153 was added to the programme in June, leaving just two of

In 2018–19, fifty-four Class 43s retired by Great Western Railway were transferred to ScotRail to work with four-car trailer sets on many inter-city lines from Glasgow and Edinburgh to Inverness and Aberdeen. No. 43140, with 43148 on rear, nears Greenloaning with 1A57, the 0940 Glasgow Queen Street–Aberdeen, on 13 March 2019. *Robin Ralston*

the First power cars, 43122/194, to be added to the programme. This happened in October, but not until other locos had been withdrawn from the FGW operational fleet for their moves to Loughborough.

The locos were usually moved in pairs, hauled by a Class 47 from the now defunct Spot Hire company Cotswold Rail, which then delivered the overhauled locos back to FGW depots.

It was December 2006 when the first two GNER locos emerged as they had been in a very sorry state of disrepair and hence needed a lot of work to get them back to running condition.

All the GNER Class 43s were renumbered when fitted with MTU engines, with 200 being added to their numbers, so 43090 became 43290, 43100 became 43300 and so on.

The first GNER power car to be taken out of traffic for rebuild was 43120 in October 2006 and it emerged – as 43320 – in January 2007. No. 43114 moved to Brush in November and appeared in February as 43314.

CrossCountry goes for MTU

In late 2007, Arriva-owned CrossCountry Trains (XCT) leased a small fleet of power cars, 43007/104/166/178/184 from Angel and 43085/101/103/121/157 from Porterbrook, as part of a franchise commitment to provide extra trains and supplement its Class 220/221 Voyager DEMU fleets.

Four were ex-VXC locos, 43101/103/104/121, while 43007/085/166/178/184 were from the Midland Main Line fleet and 43157 was ex-VXC but had spent a spell with MML on the Project Rio services from St Pancras to Manchester in 2004.

Project Rio trains were operated by MML using spare HSTs to provide direct trains and extra capacity between the two cities while the WCML was being upgraded.

In July 2007, these ten locos joined the MTU production line, and if some of the First Group locos were in poor shape, some of these were even worse. No. 43101 was in an especially bad state and needed a lot of work. In fact it was more than a year before these locos returned to traffic. XCT also adopted the renumbering scheme at re-engineering and so 43301/303 were the first to appear, in July 2008.

A First Great Western HST departs Moreton-in-Marsh on the Cotswold Line with a Paddington train on 6 May 2011. This scene has dramatically changed following route upgrading, while HSTs are now just a memory on the line. *Jack Boskett*

Old Oak Common maintained HSTs from 1976 until late 2018, but even though the locos were rebuilt with new engines a decade ago, they have still been superseded by newer rolling stock. *Jack Boskett*

Virgin Train East Coast 43295, with 43300 *Craigentinny* on the rear, passes Lamberton, near Berwick-upon-Tweed, working 1S21, the 1430 King's Cross–Edinburgh, on 5 May 2018. This train runs all its 393 miles under the wires but is still worked by a diesel. *Robin Ralston*

Initially, the last two FGW power cars to enter the programme were – coincidentally or otherwise, 43002/003 – which arrived at Loughborough on 4 January 2008 and emerged with their new engines on 6 March.

This left the Brush converting the last power cars used on the East Coast Main Line – now under the operations of National Express since August 2007 after GNER went bust. The last two NXEC power cars – 43051/110 – entered Brush on December 10 2008 followed two days later by 43053/056 which, although having been on lease to GNER and then NatEx, were to emerge as FGW locos after their rebuilding.

No. 43053 emerged on 7 April, sporting the number 43253, which while a correct number to signify its advanced electronics and Wheelslip Protection System, GWR changed its mind as it was thought it might cause driver issues by highlighting the differences so the loco was soon changed back to its original number. It was followed by 43056 on 25 April, which also had its original number.

However, the MTU production line wasn't over just yet as in 2009, the three power cars now in use with Network Rail – Porterbrook's 43013/014/062 – were added to the programme. Like the FGW locos, they emerged with their original numbers.

Their arrival left just six power cars in use with Valenta engines – the six locos owned and used by Open Access operator Grand Central;

43065/067/068/080/084/123. In March 2010 GC sold the Power Cars to Angel Trains and then leased them back after they had been fitted with MTU engines. The last two locos, 43084/123, entered Brush on 6 January 2011 and emerged a couple of months later.

When the Grand Central's power cars were converted to MTU engines, they had 400 added to their number, so 43067 became 43467. However, 43123 did not become 43523, but became the more sensible 43423. However, the re-engined locos are not classed as 43/2 or 43/4s.

The final two MTU conversions were 43072/074. These two Porterbrook locos, which had VP185 engines, were taken on by East Coast in May 2011 and in the autumn of 2011 43072 was sent to Brush for rebuilding; arriving on 18 September and emerging as 43272 on 28 November. That same date saw 43074 take its place in the Brush workshops, finally emerging as 43274 on 29 February 2012 – the last MTU HST conversion of the lot. A total of 170 locos were rebuilt with the new engines in less than six years.

No. 43131, with 43188 on the rear, heads along a deserted Dawlish sea wall on a fine and sunny 13 August 2018 with 1A12, the 0748 Paignton–Paddington. No. 43131 is now working with ScotRail while 43188, which has already been painted in GWR green, is still in use on the Western Region. *Robin Ralston*

HSTs have been an everyday sight at King's Cross since 1978, but their days are now coming to an end and by the end of 2019 it is highly likely they will no longer be working on the ECML. No. 43314 arrives at the terminus on 27 July 2016 with the 0755 from Inverness. *Jack Boskett*

HSTs ousted Class 50s from many top-link passenger jobs on the Western Region in the late 1970s, but to see both working on the main line in the twenty-first century is still remarkable. On 13 February 2015 CrossCountry Trains' 43366 heads for the South-west while 50007 *Hercules* waits in Ashchurch loop with two hopper wagons bound for Gloucester Yard. The 50 then ran light to Yeovil to pick up classmate 50050 *Fearless*. Jack Boskett

Why the MTU?

Before deciding on the MTU engine for its fleet of HST power cars, FGW looked at engine options from Cummins and Caterpillar as well as MTU, while also not ruling out fleet-wide fitting of VP185 engines.

The Cummins units were too big, so would need major internal re-engineering of the layout of the locos, and also the American company said it wouldn't be willing to support the engines in the UK market, thus making the proposal pointless.

The Caterpillar was too long and heavy for practical use in an HST, while more VP185s were ruled out as they were deemed to be more of the same and simply not reliable enough, and so would not solve the overall problem.

However, the MTU engine fitted the bill perfectly. It was the right size, offered up to 30 per cent lower fuel consumption, although that figure has been disputed and may be less, had superior emission standards and was quieter. MTU would also support the project and after every 3½ to 4½ years it would replace the engine with another. The removed engine would be returned to

Germany, overhauled and resupplied to a loco at a later date, all based on accumulated hours.

As regards who would rebuild the locos, Brush was the only company in the frame to do the re-engineering. Due to vibrations between the engine and the loco, a flexiplate was built in to absorb these. Brush could also undertake the complete rewiring of the locos that was needed.

The two trial locos chosen were 43004/009 as they had initially been taken off lease by FGW in May 2004 and sent to Devonport for a full rewire in 2004, although this rewiring was then modified for the MTU conversions. The locos moved to Brush on 14 September 2004.

The cooler groups were also replaced with a new Voith design, similar to the Brush groups, although the GNER locos continued to use a Brush cooler group.

Voith cooler groups were a development of the previous Serck equipment whereas the Brush design was a completely new product developed from a clean sheet of paper to address all the failings of both the Serck and Marston Groups. They actually arrived into being a few months later than the Voith Groups.

Above: CrossCountry Trains has just ten power cars running with seven trailers, despite its four- and five-car Class 220/221s often being overcrowded. No. 43384, with 43207 on rear, passes Powderham on 1V50, the 0606 Edinburgh–Plymouth, on 17 November 2017. *Robin Ralston*

Opposite: A striking view of a Virgin Trains East Coast HST heading south on the Forth Bridge taken from the top of the north cantilever. The train is 1E11, the 0752 Aberdeen–King's Cross, on 3 June 2016. *Rob France*

Below: The HSTs have shown great versatility and being diesel powered meant they could continue working when OLE was isolated or diversions were needed – either planned or unexpected. On 18 November 2017, 43316 brings up the rear of the 1130 King's Cross–Edinburgh led by 43319 as it heads away from Spalding. *Pip Dunn*

Once the first conversions had been completed and the staff at Brush were familiar with the project, it only took nine weeks to turn an original Class 43 into an MTU loco. The removed Valenta engines were returned to their ROSCOs for disposal, with some saved by HST preservation groups for possible retrofitting in the future.

The MTU conversion was for an initial ten-year life extension of the HSTs, but it was known they would be able to last longer if required, and that has proved to be the case. In fact, 2019 has finally seen some HSTs being taken off lease with no immediate user in mind, and that was after fifty-four power cars were taken by ScotRail.

The re-engineering was a no-brainer and since entering traffic the MTU HSTs have proved very reliable, certainly when compared with the Valenta locomotives. The fact ScotRail has identified short-form HSTs of four coaches as a viable traction option for its long-distance services between Edinburgh and Glasgow to Inverness and Aberdeen speaks volumes for both the HSTs in general and the MTU engine.

Operations

The MTU locos did pretty much everything that their Valenta stablemates had done before them. The FGW locos worked out of Paddington to Paignton, Plymouth, Penzance, Newquay, Bristol TM, Cardiff, Swansea, Fishguard, Pembroke Dock, Hereford, Oxford, Cheltenham and Weston-super-Mare.

FGW was very keen on diverted trains when lines were closed for engineering work, and occasionally HSTs would work out of Waterloo to the West Country and also via Banbury and the Chilterns lines.

The ECML power cars worked from King's Cross to Edinburgh, Aberdeen, Inverness, Hull, Harrogate, Skipton and Lincoln. They also occasionally strayed – especially on diversions – and would run via Spalding and Lincoln when diverted between Peterborough and Newark/Doncaster. They also worked from Newcastle to Edinburgh via Carlisle and also from Peterborough to Hitchin via Cambridge.

An iconic train on an iconic structure, 43290 heads south over the Royal Border Bridge at Berwick-upon-Tweed as it brings up the rear of 1E11, the 0752 Aberdeen–King's Cross, led by 43296, on 19 November 2016. *Rob France*

The first production series HST Power 43002 was returned to its original livery in 2016 and named *Sir Kenneth Grange*. It approaches Radley on 5 May 2016 with 1P39, the 1101 Oxford–Paddington GWR train. *Martin Loader*

No. 43145 speeds past Ascott-under-Wychwood signalbox on 25 July 2012 with 1P21, the 0535 Hereford–Paddington. Until 2011 this train would have been weaving across to join the line directly in front of the 'box, as it was single track from here all the way to Wolvercote Junction. The single track now commences near Charlbury station. *Martin Loader*

Outshopped in a striking and poignant commemorative livery to honour Harry Patch, who was the last survivor of the First World War trenches, 43172 passes Challow on 6 April 2017 with 1L34, the 0728 Swansea–Paddington. *Martin Loader*

The XCT locos worked between Edinburgh and the West Country via York, running mostly to Plymouth but also in the summer to Newquay and Penzance. Some trains also worked through to Glasgow Central and they occasionally worked to Aberdeen. There were very occasional uses by XCT sets on Birmingham NS to Manchester Piccadilly trains.

The GC units worked from Sunderland to King's Cross but only until the end of 2017 when the locos were moved to East Midlands Trains. This brought regular MTU operation for the TOC, which had hitherto been reliant on VP185 units.

Cross-hiring was not unknown, especially between the East Coast and XCT fleets, mainly because both fleets – as well as the three NR machines – were all allocated to Craigentinny depot in Edinburgh.

Virgin Trains East Coast – which took over the ECML franchise in March 2015 after NatEx had given up in November 2009 and the ECML was under the control of Directly Operated Railways, a DfT operation – often hired

the occasional power car, and very occasionally a full XCT rake, and likewise the odd VTEC power car worked for XCT.

In late October and early November 2011 a shortage of HSTs on the ECML fleet saw a full FGW rake, powered by 43041/163 hired by East Coast for a few days, while in 2019, a shortage of Class 180 units saw Hull Trains hire a full FGW rake, with 43010/020/023/027/165/190 all being used. In between, on 18 October 2018, 43163 – again – was in ECML use when the ScotRail power car was hired by LNER.

In 2019, HST operations started for ScotRail with its 'seven cities' operation linking Glasgow and Edinburgh with Dundee, Aberdeen, Inverness, Perth and Stirling. This saw HSTs working from both Glasgow QS and Edinburgh to Inverness and Aberdeen, and also from Aberdeen to Inverness.

Hazy early morning light at Little Heck on 22 February 2019 as 43206 speeds southwards leading LNER's 1E03, the 0526 Stirling–King's Cross. *Martin Loader*

CrossCountry Trains' 43303 heads past Tredington with 9V59, the 0900 Glasgow–Plymouth on 10 October 2008, with 43285 on the rear. *Martin Loader*

No. 43318, with 43299 on the rear, nears Houndwood, between Dunbar and Berwick-upon-Tweed, working 1S20, the 1400 King's Cross–Aberdeen on 7 July 2018. *Robin Ralston*

Liveries

When they were outshopped 43004/009 were in the same First Group blue with a pink stripe that started thin below the light clusters and went around the side under the door before fattening out, sweeping up and then running along the cant rail roof height and fading out. Gold and pink stripes were run along the bodyside for halfway before giving way to a gold First branding with 'flying F logo'. This then gave way to the First Group blue with wavy lines, which was seen on both the pioneer locos.

However, when 43175 emerged after its initial photo shoot with Angel branding (which had also been seen on 43009 on its release from Brush, but was removed before the locos entered traffic) it was in all-over First Group blue.

First Group all-over blue was then seen on 43002–005/009/010/012/015–018/020–037/040–042/053/056/063/069–071/078/079/086–088/091–094/097/098, 43122/124–156/158–165/168–172/174–177/179–183/185–198.

First Group saw the potential of using the power cars as travelling billboards and several locos spent periods in advertising wraps or commemorative artwork. Hewlett Packard advertising was bestowed on 43148/186 in 2013, while 43163 sported Singapore Airlines advertising for just five months from January 2014 and was then rebranded the same year with Visit Plymouth advertising.

Promoting the operator's own improvements to the railway were 43144/146, which had different versions of its 'Building a Greater West' advertising livery in 2015.

Finally, Bristol 2015 Advertising livery was seen on 43012/126/148/192.

To commemorate key events, 43186 carried special Diamond Jubilee graphics in 2012, while 43027 sported Queen 90th birthday decals from 2016. The artwork on 43172, applied via a wrap in 2015 as a commemoration of the First World War was very impressive and the loco was also named *Harry Patch The last survivor of the trenches* at the same time.

In 2016, 43002 was wrapped in retro BR blue, grey and yellow, its original livery complete with InterCity125 branding. It was named *Sir Kenneth Grange* after the designer of the iconic loco. Hot on the heels was 43185 *Great Western* appearing in retro InterCity Swallow colours in the same year.

In 2016 FGW rebranded as Great Western Railway and adopted a dark green livery, and although it was now in the process of gearing up for the introduction of Hitachi Class 800/801 InterCity Express Trains (IETs), it still had a requirement for HSTs on some operations in the West Country.

Accordingly, GWR green was applied to those power cars it was planning to retain, with 43004/005/016/040–042/092/093/098, 43153/154/170/186–189/194/198 all treated by mid-2019. This livery should be applied to 43094/097/122/155/158 in the near future. Welsh dragons graphics were later applied to 43187/188, while 43093 had Old Oak Common graphics added in 2018 to commemorate the closure of the depot that had been the home for HSTs from 1976.

GNER had adopted its blue livery in 1996 but not all its MTU power cars carried this livery with their new engines, although it was seen on 43208/238/290/296, 43300/306/309/313–316/318/320/367. Of these, 43290/300 ran for a short period with adverts promoting cheap fares between Leeds and London. When GNER morphed into National Express, a white stripe replaced the red stripe and was seen on 43208/238/296, 43306/309/313–315/316/318/320/367.

All the ECML allocation of HST power cars soon changed to National Express livery, with 43039/108 both actually repainted before their re-engineering and running traffic as such for a few weeks. The livery was then seen on 43206/208/238/239/251/257/277/295/290/296/299, 43300/302/305–320/367. This then changed to having East Coast branding instead of National Express and was seen on all these locos apart from 43300. However, a new light grey livery was adopted by East Coast and bestowed on the now-expanded ECML fleet, which also included 43272/274. Of these, 43300 *Craigentinny* had special branding applied to commemorate the depot's 100 years.

GWR held an open day at Bristol St Phillips Marsh on 2 May 2016 depot in aid of the Springboard Charity. The event celebrated forty years' service for the HST Power Cars with examples from all TOCs on show – namely FGW 43172 *Harry Patch*, Grand Central 43423 *Valenta 1972–2010*, Network Rail 43013, LNER 43300 *Craigentinny*, EMT 43048 *TCB Miller MBE* and GWR 43187 and on display. The GC locos have since moved to EMT. *Jack Boskett*

When Stagecoach took over the ECML franchise in 2015, trading under the name Virgin Trains East Coast – Virgin having a 10 per cent stake in the operation, pretty much to allow Stagecoach to use the Virgin name – it inherited HSTs in both old NatEx and East Coast liveries and set about slapping Virgin logos on them as quickly as possible.

The ECML power cars then lost their East Coast livery for VTEC's new red scheme and eventually all thirty-two of the power cars carried this with the exception of 43238, which appeared in a very grey-based livery to commemorate forty years of the National Railway Museum in York in 2015.

When Stagecoach was expelled from the franchise by the government, it came back into state ownership – for a third time – and LNER branding replaced the Virgin logo, but there was no new livery. It was hardly worth it given the fleet would soon be replaced by new Azuma IETs.

No. 43274 sported Spirit of Sunderland branding, 43300 had another version of Craigentinny branding, while 43295 dedicated 'Perth is the place' with special branding.

CrossCountry Trains adopted a fairly uninspiring silver and sludge brown livery for its entire train fleet and so was seen on 43207/285/301/303/304/321/357/366/378/384, while Network Rail all-over yellow was the treatment given to 43013/014/062. As an aside, 43067/089/154/196 all carried NR yellow for very short periods, but not while with their MTU engines.

Grand Central changed its black livery slightly when its power cars were re-engineered and so 43423/465/467/468/480/484 all featured an orange solebar stripe.

When they moved to East Midlands Trains, these six locos gained a revised version of the TOC's livery – slightly changed from that sported by its VP185 locos.

ScotRail started to paint its locos in 'Seven Cities' blue and light grey with graphics, and this had been bestowed on 43003/012/015/021/026/028/030-037, 43124-152/163/164/168/169/169/175-177/179/181-183 by late-2019. Other locos ran for ScotRail in unbranded First Group blue while 43132 ran with 'A New Era' branding, and the names of the seven cities on its side, for a period. All should be repainted into the seven cities liveries in the fullness of time.

Just a few miles into its 568-mile journey, 43308 *Highland Chieftain* crosses Culloden Viaduct with Virgin Trains East Coast's 0755 Inverness–King's Cross. *Jack Boskett*

CrossCountry Trains' 43366 and 43304 head a Leeds–Exeter train through Tibberton, Worcestershire, on 2 April 2012.
Jack Boskett

Most of the FGW HSTs that arrived at Brush with their nameplates had them removed, but a handful did retain these such as 43003/027/030/033/037/040/139/175/179/185/189. Others have been named since.

Of the GNER fleet, 43300 was renamed *Craigentinny* when it was overhauled. This had briefly been its name as 43100 in BR days, although the names were removed in December 1987 only to be refitted in June 1991 and then removed again in March 1998.

The future

When FGW rebuilt its HSTs it was with an anticipated life extension of ten years but with the knowledge they would be good for many more years beyond that if required. And the latter has proved to be the case.

Of the 197 power cars built, three were condemned before MTU came on the scene and twenty-four were retained with VP185s engines by East Midlands Trains. That left 170 of the fleet that were rebuilt.

FGW had 119 power cars and planned to retain twenty-four – twelve it owned and twelve leased from Angel Trains – and after redeploying fifty-four to ScotRail that meant it retained forty-one locos from both Angel and Porterbrook for which there were no immediate future users.

In 2017, FGW started to introduce IETs and this allowed HSTs to be redeployed. ScotRail agreed to take fifty-four power cars and a number of trailer vehicles to start running short-form four-car HSTs on routes north of Glasgow and Edinburgh. Those transferred to ScotRail were 43003/012/015/021/026/028/030–037, 43124–152/163/164/168/169/175–177/179/181–183.

The last day of long-distance HST operation on the GWR routes was 18 May 2019, when four sets were in use. Nos 43185 *Great Western* and 43009 started the day off working the 0645 Bristol–Swansea, then the 0929 Swansea–Paddington, 1330 Paddington–Bristol TM and 1600 Bristol–Paddington.

No. 43093 *Old Oak Common HST Depot* and 43188 were the last HSTs to leave Cornwall for London when they worked the 0650 Penzance–Paddington before continuing with the 1300 Paddington–Bristol and 1530 Bristol–Paddington.

On the third set were 43002 *Sir Kenneth Grange* and 43198 – now renamed sporting one name formerly carried by 43033, *Driver Brian Cooper 15 June 1947–5 October 1999*, and one nameplate formerly carried by 43139, *Driver Stan Martin 25 June 1950–6 November 2004*. These were two drivers tragically killed while driving HSTs for Great Western. They – the first and last production series

For several years from 2009 until 2015, the InterCity East Coast franchise was run by the state-owned Directly Operated Railways under the banner East Cost Trains. Showing off the TOC's far from inspiring grey livery, 43367 *Deltic 50* and 43312 pass Melkridge, near Haltwhistle, with the diverted 1F50 1500 Newcastle–Edinburgh on 12 October 2014. *Rob France*

power cars – set off on the 0657 Plymouth–Paddington and then worked the 1045 Paddington–Swansea and 1429 Swansea–Paddington; the last HST to work from London to South Wales for GWR.

Finally, 43172 *Harry Patch* and 43162 Exeter Panel Signal Box worked empty from Laira to Exeter St David's to work the 0729 to Paddington, followed by the 1122 Paddington–Great Malvern and 1435 back to London.

The workings allowed all four HSTs to line up at Paddington in the evening. The first to arrive was 43093/188 on platform 1, followed by 43172/162 on platform 2, then 43002/198 on platform 4 and finally 43185/009 on platform 3. There was then about forty minutes when all four were 'at the blocks' and gaining admiring glances from enthusiasts, rail managers and the general public alike.

The curtain was brought down in a twenty-seven-minute period. First 43188/093 set off on the 1803 Paddington–Plymouth, followed by 43162/172 on the 1815 to Cheltenham, then 43009/185 on the 1822 to Hereford and finally, the last ever HST left Brunel's terminus on an InterCity passenger train as 43198/002

departed on the 1830 Paddington–Taunton, extended to Exeter St David's before running empty to Plymouth Laira and so ending the long-distance HST workings by GWR.

On 1 June, a farewell charter using a GWR set ran with 43002/198, and this visited key routes worked by the trains over the decades. It started at Bristol TM and ran to Paddington. It then continued via Oxford, Hereford and Abergavenny and then on to Carmarthen via Cardiff. The return was then to Paddington via Gloucester before a planned non-stop run to Plymouth.

From there on, HSTs were only used on the Western on four-car sets on Cardiff–Taunton and Devon/Cornwall local trains, although CrossCountry sets continued to work to Devon and Cornwall from the north.

The FGW power cars due to be off lease by mid-2019 were 43002/009/010/017/018/020/022/023/025/027/029/053/056/063/069–071/078/079/086–088/091, 43156/159–162/165/171/172/174/180/185/190–193/195-197, although some had their leases extended to cover the new short-set diagrams.

Of these, 43195 had severe collision damage to its cab and had been robbed for spares, meaning its future looked

Nos 43024, 43160 and a classmate line up inside Old Oak Common HST depot on 4 September 2017. Scenes like this are never to be repeated as all inter-city turns on the GWR are now worked by Class 800 IETs. *Jack Boskett*

very bleak indeed. It had last worked on 31 December 2017 but while working 1C96, the 2003 Paddington–Plymouth, it collided with a tree on Hemerdon bank, which caused the career-ending damage. Although locos are meant to be returned to their ROSCOs in working condition, it seems that Porterbrook understands that repairing 43195 would not be worthwhile and by mid-June 2019 it was a stripped shell of a locomotive.

No. 43002 meanwhile had been claimed by the National Railway Museum for display at York. It was fully repainted by staff at Laira prior to being sent to the STEAM museum at Swindon for a brief display in June before moving to store in Ely pending its move to York for display which finally happened in October 2019, after a brief visit to the NRM's Locomotion site at Shildon.

By mid-June 2019, Angel's 43017/018/024/025, 43165/174/185/190 were in store at Ely and Porterbrook's 43053/056/069/070/087, 43159/193/197 were in store at Long Marston, with crash-damaged 43195 still dumped at Laira. There was some discussion about redundant HST sets going on short-term lease to other operators, such as CrossCountry Trains.

Add in the thirty-two that were due to come off lease from LNER in the second half of 2019 and that leaves just three locos with NR, six MTU and twenty-five VP185s with EMT and ten with XCT.

LNER was due to start returning its HSTs in late 2019. New Azuma sets started in traffic on 18 May and a start is expected to be made in storing HSTs as and when new Class 800s come into traffic. It was LNER's aspiration to have its HSTs all retired by the end of 2019 meaning power cars 43061/075, 43206/208/238/239/251/257/272/274/277/290/295/296/299, 43300/302/305–320/367 would all be returned to the ROSCOs for possible redeployment or disposal. Locomotive Services is expected to take two ex-LNER sets with at least four power cars in 2020.

Other sets are likely to get new users, with spot hire and charter operators possible outlets for these ultimately very versatile trains but it is unlikely there will be enough users for all the HST power cars that come off lease in 2019–20.

Further cascades are possible – many routes are crying out for additional or longer trains to provide capacity and, despite their age, it would be folly to send HSTs for scrap when they could be used for so many other useful operations. The question is, with the Department for Transport agree?

10
The Class 73/9s
MTU is the Future for GBRf

The Class 73 Electro-diesels were always deemed to be one of the most versatile locos ever. They were basically a third-rail 750V DC electric loco with a small 600hp English Electric four-cylinder diesel engine allowing them to operate in yards, on non-electrified branch lines or on the main line at times of the power being isolated.

A mixed traffic loco, mostly used on freight and infrastructure work, six prototypes were built in 1962 by BR at Eastleigh, which led to an order for forty-three delivered in 1965–66, built by English Electric at Newton-le-Willows.

Apart from a couple of early withdrawals, by the time of sectorisation of BR in the mid-1980s, forty-seven remained in traffic. Many passed into the privatised era; fourteen with Gatwick Express, twenty-five with EWS, five with Merseyrail, two with Eurostar and one with South West Trains.

Sasha, Alison & Janice! Two contrasting forms of transport are pictured at Crofton on 14 July 2018, as GB Railfreight's 73961 *Alison* and 73963 *Janice* pass the narrowboat *Sasha* on the Kennet & Avon Canal, as they head west with the UK Railtours' 1Z40, 0730 Stevenage–Weymouth 'Sunny South Express' railtour. *Martin Loader*

Many of the locos were progressively withdrawn by most of their new users, especially EWS, which completely overhauled its loco fleet with new 66s and 67s replacing nearly all the ex-BR locos it had inherited. Gatwick Express replaced its 73/2s with Class 460s in 2000–05.

GB takes spare 73s

An interesting development in 2001 was the decision by GB Railways to have 'first refusal' on the Porterbrook Class 73/2s as they were withdrawn by Gatwick Express. Over the years, GB took 73201/203–209/212/213 and they were placed in store before a decision was taken to overhaul some locos for GB Railfreight. Nos 73204–206/209 were the first to be revived, followed by 73201/207/208/212/213. One loco, 73203, was scrapped after it had donated parts.

The GBRf 73s were still essentially a Southern Region loco, operating off their third rail in the main. Their diesel engines were still used occasionally, although as they were quite old they were struggling to even produce the 600hp that was their nominal output.

However, it was clear that the 73s could not carry on for too much longer without being overhauled, but even overhauling them as standard 73s would do little to address their issues. The locos had not had full overhauls since the 1990s and GBRf was faced with the decision on what to do with them to make them cost-effective assets in the future. Having signed contracts with some customers based on the supply of Class 73s, it was inevitable that something needed to be done.

GBRf also wanted a go anywhere Type 3 rather than an 'old-style' ED where the diesel was there almost as a contingency 'get out of jail free' option. It wanted a loco that could run long distances, hauling sizeable loads. It wanted, in effect, an alternative to a Class 37.

The GBRf MTU Class 73/9s are now a go anywhere Type 3 and have brought the sight of Class 73s to routes that rarely, and often never, had welcomed the loco type before. Nos 73963 *Janice* and 73962 *Dick Mabbutt* work 5O73, the 1230 Derby RTC–Tonbridge West Yard, past Barrow-on-Soar, just south of Loughborough, on 1 July 2015. *Bill Atkinson*

On 10 April 2019, the new CAF Mk 5 sleeping cars were showed off to Scottish stakeholders and a circular run around the Scottish Lowlands saw 73969 and 73971 top-and-tailing the eight-coach train, which took in a trip over the iconic Forth Bridge. *Jamie McEwan*

The rebuilding of 73209 as 73961 – then expected to be numbered 73901 – is close to completion at Brush Loughborough Work on 14 January 2014. On the left is 73206, which is partway through its complete body overhaul. *Jack Boskett*

On 20 February 2019, 73968 came to the aid of 6E45, the 0807 Fort William–North Blyth, after 66746 failed at Spean Bridge and worked it through to Fort William. This was the very first instance of a 73/9 working a freight train on the West Highland Line. *Gary Lennon*

That said, acquiring Class 37s was not an option for GBRf, as they were old, had reliability issues and were poor on emissions. However, the advancements in diesel technology meant it was now possible to completely rebuilt Class 73s and replace their tired EE engines with new, state-of-the-art MTU engines which would produce 1,600hp while allowing the locos to keep their useful third rail capability.

An agreement to rebuild

In June 2011 the concept of re-engineering some Class 73s was first mooted and GBRf started discussions with various parties over a rebuilding programme. It soon became apparent that the best option was to use Brush Traction at Loughborough and fitting an MTU 8-cylinder engine. MTU was the only option, and the GBRf fleet director had experience with both the engines and Brush, having worked with both parties on the HST re-engineering programme while working for First Group. The costs of the MTU conversion was also acceptable to GBRf.

GBRf worked with Brush on the design specification, and the company was realistically the only sensible option for building the locos. This was in part because it already had experience with MTU re-engineering, having rebuilt 170 HST power cars with MTU engines. Brush could also supply the alternator and the electronic traction control, diagnostics and CAPOS (capacitor start system).

In January 2013 GBRf signed a deal for the first five locos to be rebuilt. These would be for Network Rail contracts, hauling infrastructure monitoring and infrastructure support trains. In 2014 another six conversions were ordered for the Caledonian Sleeper haulage contract that GBRf had won that year.

The locos were initially going to be numbered 73901–905, but due to these numbers being taken on the Rolling Stock Library, and the 7395x number series having been taken by Network Rail for its Loram Class 73 conversions (see Chapter 11) GBRf opted instead for the 7396x number series. The five NR locos would be 73961–965 and the 'sleeper' examples would follow on and be 73966–971, albeit very different.

The 'sleeper' contract required four locos a day, plus a spare – one each to haul portions of the Highlander sleeper from Edinburgh to Fort William and Aberdeen and a pair to haul the Inverness portion, although this could run with a single loco if required. A spare loco would be available allowing for that sixth loco to be on maintenance or cover.

When Class 73/9s were first introduced on the West Highland lines, there was an issue that prevented them taking full power so for their early days a pair were used on the Fort William leg of Caledonian Sleeper. Nos 73968/966 pause at Rannoch on 27 July 2016 with the 1950 Fort William–Edinburgh portion. *Pip Dunn*

73970 and 73968 work 1S25, the 2028 Euston-Inverness, past Dunachton, between Kingussie and Aviemore on 17 April 2017. In late 2019 this train was operated using CAF Mk 5 'sleeper' coaches, which necessitated 73966-971 to have Dellner couplers fitted. *Anthony Hicks*

The first, 73961 for NR, used 73209 as its donor loco, and it moved to Loughborough from Eastleigh, via Peterborough, in August 2011. No. 73962 was built from 73204 and it moved to Brush in late 2012.

The level of work on rebuilding the locos was immense. The new locos retain the same bodyshell, bogies, traction motors and shoe gear as a standard Class 73 but internally it is a different story. On arrival each loco was totally stripped internally and underwent a full programme of bodywork repairs to address the corrosion that had been a major issue in the locos, which date from the 1960s.

The new locos – and they were effectively new locos – also needed to be fitted with GSMR (Global System for Mobile Communications Railway). However, they were not fitted with European Railway Traffic Management System (ERTMS) equipment, however the space has been left inside the locos to make the fitting of this both practical and easy at a later date when, or if, this equipment is necessary.

There are a few differences between the five Network Rail locos and the six 'sleeper' locos. From 73966 onwards the locos have MZT brakes, which are digitally controlled, whereas the first five have the original Davies & Metcalfe brake system.

There are also fewer jumper cables on the 'sleeper' locos as they will not be needed to work in push-pull mode on test trains. They also, understandably, have snowploughs fitted but a single-piece plough and not the old three-piece set-up favoured by BR.

A complex job

The rebuilds were not easy, and as some of the spares were not available it was necessary to manufacture new bespoke items, such as windscreen wipers, desk instruments and lights.

The new locos were fitted with Bmac light clusters and an AAR multiple working receptacle mounted centrally on the cab front. The first five retained their waist level duplicate brake pipes, and because the twenty-seven-way multiple working jumper would have rested over the lights this has been stretched so its jumper holder is more centrally placed.

When the line north of Crianlarich is closed, either for planned engineering or unexpected incidents such as landslides, it is common practice to divert the Fort William 'sleeper' to Oban. A booked diversion was on 25 March 2017 and 73967 leads 1Y11, the 0450 Edinburgh–Oban, through Glen Cruitten on the final few miles of its journey. *Anthony Hicks*

No. 73963 *Janice* approaches Dunstall Bridge, Moreton-in-Marsh, on 21 June 2018 with 1Z74, the 1454 Long Marston–Paddington GBRf special, returning from the *RAIL* Live event. No. 73962 *Dick Mabbutt* is bringing up the rear. *Martin Loader*

Due to the constraints on the Class 73 layout, the loco's existing 310-gallon fuel tank were retained but the greater fuel efficiency of the MTU engine means GBRf was not unduly worried about the range and need for refuelling. The MTU engines are 3½ tonnes lighter than the EE units and are wider but lower in height. Because of this weight differential, ballast weights were added to keep the weight correct and retain the loco's route availability classification of 6. The tractive effort and braking capabilities are the same as a standard ED.

The MTU 8V4000R43L engine is married to a brush-less, three-phase synchronous alternator, as opposed to a main generator as used on an EE Class 73. The traction motors and their blowers were retained from a standard 73. The air management system was changed and the exhaust is a V-style.

The Train Protection and Warning System (TPWS) and On Train Monitoring and Recording (OTMR) equipment is behind No. 1 end cab. A Webasto pre-heater was fitted as this was a necessary requirement for the MTU engine, which must be at 25°C before it can be started. The cooler group was also improved – overheating was a major issue

for Class 73s when running on diesel power for any length of time – and an improved header tank was also fitted.

The electrical control was from MTU and all the DC control systems were removed, making the locos now totally AC in their wiring. The 73/9s also have the CAPOS capacitor system fitted, which allows the engine to be turned over without needing to use the batteries so there is no draining of the battery. The capacitors then recharge when the loco is on the move and retain their charge for quite a long period. This was the first time this system was used in the UK, but it had previously been commonplace in Europe.

The rebuilt locos can work in multiple with standard Class 73/1 and 73/2s as well as with each other, but because they have the AAR multiple working system added as well it means they can also work with Class 59s, 66s and 67s as well as DVTs and Class 489 GLVs. The latter has proved useful for the occasions they have been used on ice-breaking duties.

In theory it would be possible to run a Class 73/2+73/9+66 combination in multiple! That said, the ability to work in multi with a 66 has proved very useful for GBRf.

One feature of the Class 73s when they were designed for the Southern Region was their dual controls in the cab, meaning they could be driven from either the left or right-hand side of the cab. This feature was retained at conversion, although the driver's control desks were heavily modified with a modern dash.

The centre 'window' on a Class 73 was previously filled by SR two-character roller blinds but these were removed and blanked off on the first five locos as it was deemed to be too expensive to fit a glass window and the area in between the two remaining front windows was then used to house equipment. However, a centre window was fitted on the Scottish machines – along with an extra wiper. The windows in the cab doors were retained but they no longer open and the windows in the bulkheads behind the driver's seats were also removed.

The locos are still capable of running at 90mph on diesel or electric modes and ETS is retained, although the index was reduced from 66 to 38. However, ETS is available on both modes – it was only possible on electric running on a standard Class 73.

The wheels on 73961 were initially retained with tyres but those fitted on 73962 onwards were monobloc style, and 73961 has since changed to these wheels as well.

Breaking cover

In late 2014, 73961 – still retaining its *Alison* nameplates – broke cover and was taken to the nearby Great Central Railway for a series of running tests. On 18 October it worked a number of passenger trains between Loughborough and Leicester North, but being air-braked only had to run with 45041 *Royal Tank Regiment* inside as a brake translator.

Nos 73969 and 73966 arrive at Arrochar & Tarbet on 31 August 2016 with 1Y11, the 0450 Edinburgh–Fort William Caledonian Sleeper. *Martin Loader*

No. 73962, rebuilt from 73204, emerged in August 2014 – initially in a plain blue but it was returned to traffic in GBRf colours – after being named *Dick Mabbutt*. Next out was 73963, rebuilt from 73206, in March 2015, then 73964 in April after using 73205 as is body donor. The last was 73965, rebuilt from 73208 in May. The five NR locos were all painted in GBRf livery, which meant 73205/208 lost their BR-era liveries of InterCity main line and BR blue respectively.

The locos selected to be 73966–971 were, in order: 73005, 73006, 73117, 73105, 73103 and 73207. This left 73107/109/119/128/136/141/201/212/213 in the operational GBRf fleet as standard EDs.

The first five conversions all arrived at Brush with nameplates – they had all been named after female office staff and they retained their names if the staff still worked for the company. The exceptions were 73204 *Lisa*, which was renamed after conversion, while 73208 *Kirsten* emerged unnamed as 73965.

GBRf learned a lot from the first batch and did a few modifications for the second batch mid-build. Once the contract for six additional locos was agreed, it led to GBRf acquiring further original 73s from other sources, including other train operators and preservation groups.

In fact, from 2009 to 2019, the company acquired a further sixteen Class 73s. These were 73005/006 from preservation groups in May 2014, 73103/105/117 from Nemesis Rail in July 2015 and 73134 in April 2015, 73107/109/128 from Michael Owen in April 2014,

November 2013 and October 2014 respectively, 73119 from Bruce Knights in September 2011, 73136 from the Class 73/1 Preservation Group in May 2013, which had main-line registered the loco and used it for spot hire, 73141/212/213 from Network Rail in June 2009, and more recently 73110 from the EE Preservation Group in September 2017 and 73101/139 from Loram in July 2018. No. 73134 was heavily stripped for the conversion programme but not rebuilt and in mid-2019 it remained as a shell at Brush available to be revived if further orders of 73/9s are ever sanctioned.

Into traffic

As the new locos were delivered by Brush, GBRf embarked on a series of driver training. This was a two-day conversion course from a standard Class 73 and three days from other traction.

The five NR locos are allocated to St Leonards – in the GBNR pool – and sometimes visit the depot for maintenance, but they tend to be out-stationed at Tonbridge, which is also the core operating base for the GBRf's last remaining active original Class 73s. However, the locos were still maintained by Brush for an initial ten-year period, and sometimes return to Loughborough for major work. The locos all returned to Brush for modifications to make their power take up correct. The 'sleeper' locos were also fitted with Dellner couplers at Eastleigh to enable them to haul the new CAF Mk 5 sleeper coaches introduced in 2019.

On 12 September 2018, 73967 passes at Achnabobane, near Spean Bridge, on the final few miles of the 0450 Edinburgh-Fort William, a portion of the Caledonian Sleeper from Euston. *Glen Batten*

The first five MTU Class 73/9 conversions were for Network Rail test and infrastructure trains. No. 73961 *Alison* passes St Denys with 1Q53, the 1035 Eastleigh Arlington–Eastleigh Arlington test train, on 31 August 2016. *Mark Pike*

The six Scottish locos, all now in Caledonian Sleeper livery, are allocated to Edinburgh Craigentinny depot and are in the GBCS pool.

Brush did not woo any other customers to have their 73s rebuilt with MTU engines, which is not surprising given the cost, and considering the level of work they do there is little call for Southern or South West Trains to have their fleets of a single loco converted.

Interestingly, despite being designated by the Railway Heritage Committee for eventual preservation, should it be required, 73201 can still be upgraded as the loco will retain its specification as an electro-diesel locomotive. However, regardless of budgets, there will be no more than twenty-three conversions due to limits on how many MTU engines can be used in the UK as a result of limitations via derogation.

Operations

Once in traffic and with sufficient drivers trained, the two fleets of locos settled down to fairly bespoke work. The NR locos are used for test trains, often top-and-tailing and sometimes operating with a DBSO in push-pull mode.

While much of this test train work is on their traditional old SR stamping ground – Class 37s in the main work train across the rest of the network, the 73s have been used in the North-west, where they work test trains on Merseyrail lines, banned to the likes of 37s. Some of this latter work is now covered by the Loram 73/9s conversions.

Because all the test train vehicles are based at Derby for maintenance and calibration, the 73/9s frequently work empty test trains along the Midland Main Line to Derby, usually on Fridays or Saturdays and returning on Monday.

The locos are also used for infrastructure support trains, especially on lines where 73s are needed for gauge purposes, such as to Moorgate. For this, two locos, 73962/964, have be treated to a minor modification whereby a frame is mounted to both ends to allow a ladder to be clipped to the locos' front for emergency evacuation in the Moorgate tunnel should one be necessary.

The Caledonian Sleeper locos tend to have fairly self-contained duties as described on page 199.

Until mid-2019, they shared these duties with 66s and hired DB Cargo 67s, although the Fort William turn was usually a solid 73 turn, When the locos first entered traffic, there was an issue with them taking full power, so for a period pairs of 73s were used. However, the need to release the 73s to return to Brush to have modifications to allow them to take full power saw several of the trains – especially to Fort William – worked by a 73/9 in multiple with a Class 66/7. This operation had to be with the 66 on the front so the ED could provide train supply.

From the late summer of 2019, CAF Mk 5 coaches were introduced on the 'Highlander' sleeper, meaning the only locos that would work these trains had to be fitted with Dellner couplers, a modification undertaken on 73966–971 in 2018. This means 67s could no longer be hired nor GBRf's own Class 66s used unless they have a Class 73/9 in between them and the Mk 5 coaches.

On 20 February 2019, 73968 came to the aid of a failed freight train at Spean Bridge and worked it through to Fort William. The 73/9 was working 1Y11, the 0450 Edinburgh–Fort William 'sleeper', when it got as far as Tulloch before it initially was sent to rescue 66746, which had failed half a mile north of Tulloch, working 6E45, the

0807 Fort William–North Blyth. The 73 left its coaches behind at Tulloch station to drag the 66 and its train into Tulloch station to clear the main line. The 73 then was taken off 6E45 and returned to collect 1Y11 and continue to its destination, some eighty-five minutes late.

After the late arrival at Fort William, the ED then ran light engine back to Tulloch to collect 6E45 and take that to Fort William, arriving back around 1345. This was the very first instance of a 'sleeper' 73/9 working a freight train on the West Highland Line. No. 66737 *Lesia* was then sent to Fort William the following day on the rear of 1Y11 to work 6Z45, the 1207 Fort William–North Blyth with dead 66746 on the rear.

But while the 73/9s have undoubtedly been reliable, occasionally they have blotted their copybook and one of the most high-profile failures occurred on the night of 28/29 June 2019 in the most awkward place imaginable as 73971 failed between Corrour and Rannoch on the middle of Rannoch Moor at about 2100 on the Friday night.

Painted in undercoat, the new-look front end of the 73/9 locos is clear in this view of the first loco to be rebuilt. *Jack Boskett*

Eventually 73966 was sent from Polmadie to assist but the train had already been sat for nine hours by the time it reached the stricken train. Finally the train got on its way, but then 73966 was unable to tackle the climb from Arrochar to Glen Douglas with the added weight of the dead 73971. The train duly set back to Arrochar and was further delayed while 73971 was detached and dumped in the siding. Finally 73966 was able to continue at 0950, and arriving at Dalmuir at 1050, 11 hours later where the train was – understandably cancelled.

Charter work for the super EDs

Occasionally the 'sleeper' 73s have strayed on to other work, and most notable was on 9 June 2018 when a pair reached Kyle of Lochalsh on a charter. The train, promoted by the Scottish Railway Preservation Society, set off behind 73966/967 from Paisley and on arrival at Inverness 73968/969 was added to the rear for the trip to the west coast. After a break, 73968/969 then worked back from Kyle, with the original pair detached at Inverness, and then they returned the train to Paisley.

The locos have also been to Oban when the 'sleeper' was booked to run from the town because the West Highland Line north of Crianlarich was closed for routine engineering work. They have also worked to Fort William on a charter, on 6 October 2018 when 73966/968 worked a trip from Edinburgh via Carstairs, Motherwell and Glasgow Central Low Level. On 30 September 2017, 73970 and 66764 worked an Ayr–Inverness trip for the SRPS.

There has occasionally been charter work in England for the five NR Class 73/9s. On 16 July 2016, UK Railtours' 'Herd of Wildebeest' trip ran with 73962/963 working from Basingstoke to Exeter, although 73963 was dead until Salisbury. There the train reversed and 73107 *Tracy* and 73128 *OVS Bulleid* took over for the run to Paignton to then allow the MTU locos to return the train to Waterloo.

There was an interesting day out for 73961/964 on 9 September 2016 when they worked the second day of GBRf's charity fundraising tour 'GBRf 15'. The 73/9s worked from King's Cross to Whitemoor Yard, then later in the day from Peterborough to Norwich and finally from Great Yarmouth to Harwich International via Berney Arms and Ipswich.

The 8-cylinder MTU engine in the 73/9s is much smaller and lower in height than the English Electric unit it replaces, but delivers two and half times the power. *Jack Boskett*

The new look front end is seen to good effect as 73968/966 wait at Fort William on 27 July 2016 with the 1950 to Edinburgh. The locos use the same AAR multiple working as a Class 66 but they also retain their original Blue Star MW. The waist-level duplicate brake pipes were removed when 73966–971 were rebuilt. *Pip Dunn*

No. 73963 got an unexpected passenger job on 5 May 2018 when it filled in for a failed 73107 to partner 73141 *Charlotte* for a few stretches of a trip that was in the main worked by 20189/205. However, the 73s worked from Mountfield British Gypsum to Mountfield Sidings and later from Tonbridge to Dungeness.

On 14 July 2018 73961/963 worked UK Railtours' 'Sunny South Express' from Stevenage to Weymouth and back via Reading, Westbury, Castle Cary and Yeovil Pen Mill while the return was via Bournemouth, Eastleigh, Basingstoke and Reading.

As part of the second GBRf four-day charity train, 'GBRf 18', 73961/963 were used for the Bristol TM to Pengam leg, running via Avonmouth and then from Bridgend to Didcot via Gloucester and Swindon.

The locos sometimes help out on the Royal Scotsman luxury charter train. When it visits Mallaig the train must be top and tailed from Fort William, and if a second 66 is not available then a 73/9 could be used.

The 73/9s have also visited the occasional preserved railway, such as 73964 to the Bluebell Railway in April 2016, 73961 to Swanage in May 2017 and 73965 to the Severn Valley Railway in May 2017. Scottish 73966/967 also visited the Bo'ness and Kinneil Railway and worked trains in January 2016.

More locos

GBRf Managing Director John Smith has made no secret that he would like to undertake more Class 73/9s conversions but can only do so with a sound business case, which is presently not there. Nevertheless, the company tends to buy any Class 73s that come on the market, including some from preservation groups. The price to rebuild the locos is now quite high and it could become quite prohibitive.

Another six to ten conversions are plausible – the company cannot do any more than another dozen – and with this in mind GBRf has 73101/110/134/139 in store and 73107/109/119/128/136/141, 73201/212/213 in active use. If more conversions were done, they would be to the same specification as the six 'sleeper' locos, apart from not having Dellner couplers fitted.

They would also be fitted with a phase 3 diesel and would retain third-rail capability and have MZT brakes. They would most likely be numbered 73972 onwards if agreed, but a specific contract would be needed to facilitate any further conversions.

The locos nevertheless have proved themselves and are popular with crews. They are now achieving 44,000 miles between failures, with the 'sleeper' locos proving slightly more reliable than that.

11

The Class 73/9s
Assemble the Minions

In the late 1950s and early 1960s there was a myriad of loco builders all trying to woo British Railways with their new diesel loco offerings. History tells us some were successful and some not so, and the same can be said of two very different plans to rebuild Class 73s that came to fruition in the early 2010s.

While GBRf worked with Brush and MTU to deliver a new, go anywhere Type 3, Derby-based Rail Vehicle Engineering Limited (RVEL) was hard at work with a rebuild project of its own that it announced in June 2011.

In agreement with Network Rail it planned a new-build Class 73 electro-diesel loco, and in a similar fashion to the MTU project, out would go the elderly, weak and unreliable EE 600hp four-cylinder engine and in its place something new.

In the case of the RVEL project, that would be two Cummins QSK 19-litre 750hp engines, similar to that used in the Bombardier Class 220/221/222 DEMU types and the Alstom Class 180 DMUs.

Twin-engined locos have a lot going for them; mainly if an engine fails, they can usually carry on to a sensible place to stop, or at least clear the running lines by continuing on their remaining good engine. BR put this to good practice with its Class 42/43 Warship and Class 52 Western diesel hydraulic locos of the 1950s and '60s, and English Electric did the same with its ground-breaking Napier-powered Class 55 Deltic diesel locos that speeded up the ECML immeasurably in the early 1960s. Even the HST concept is similar, although that relies on two locomotives rather than a single twin-engined loco.

As well as that belt and braces, 'get out of jail free' insurance policy of two engines, drivers could, if they so desired, deliberately run on one engine if hauling a light load; for example there was little point using all 2,700hp of a Western on a Cornish local with four coaches!

Not all twin-engine locos were a success, however, and the Class 17 Clayton Type 1s, which used a pair of Paxman 6ZHXL 450hp engines, were widely regarded as an unmitigated failure. Part of the Clayton sales pitch was

that the locos could be used on one engine for shunting and light trip duties. The reality was single engine running was often commonplace on the main line because one of the engines had failed!

But with two engines, the RVEL concept had a lot going for it, and the company went public in 2012 with the news that it was rebuilding an initial two locos, with two more due to follow, for Network Rail Infrastructure Monitoring trains.

No. 73211 was selected as the first to be converted, with 73104 to be the second. Waiting in the wings were 73101/139 with the company optimistic it could secure more 73s – ironically from RVEL's former 'partner' Nemesis Rail – should it need to if the project proved to be a success.

The plan was that the locos would be in the 73/3 number series, but like so many announcements, these series were often revealed before anyone had spoken with the Rolling Stock Library to see if they were vacant. As it transpired, 73301/302 had already been used, so the locos were duly allocated the numbers 73951/952.

The conversion of the locos can best be described as convoluted and painful for RVEL, which entered into a partnership with American company Loram in 2014, after which it bought a majority stake in the firm. During the project Loram took full control of RVEL and the name slowly slipped away into the railway history books.

No. 73211 was totally stripped down and all its inner equipment – which dated from the 1960s – was removed. The engine room had to be totally reconfigured with plenty of reworking to accommodate both the engines and the upgraded third-rail system.

Despite initial hopes that the first loco would be ready by 2012, this deadline slipped into 2013, then slipped again and then very badly slipped even further. It caused the RVEL press spokesman to get a little heated with the media when he, naturally, was asked questions about the project's progression.

Network Rail's Loram-rebuilt locos 73952 and 73951 with their *Janis Kong* and *Malcolm Brinded* nameplates covered run light past Ashwell on 22 February 2016 as they run light to Whitemoor for naming. *Bill Atkinson*

Minions break cover

However, in October 2015, 73951 finally broke cover from the Derby workshops. It had been radically redesigned externally with a completely new side grille arrangement, while the front-end jumper cables and brake pipes were removed, leaving a flush front end with new light clusters. Their 'strange' look earned the locos the nickname 'Minions' after the characters from the *Despicable Me* films – as the 73/9s were all yellow and the light clusters looked like the goggles worn by the little 'aliens' from the films! The first conversion was moved to Eastleigh for further electrical tests and preparation for main-line testing.

On 16 December, 37219 collected the 73/9 from Eastleigh and returned it to Derby. The following month, 73952 was finished at Derby and the two locos were ready to start their main-line tests. Their first test was a light engine run on 26 January from Derby to Crewe and back, something they repeated twice the following day before undertaking a trip to Kettering on 28 January, again running light engine.

On 19 February they undertook another test to Crewe and back, both sporting covered nameplates, and on 22 February, the two Minions ran light to Whitemoor for an event that saw them named *Malcolm Brinded* and *Janis Kong* respectively. They returned to Derby on the 25th. On 3 March they undertook a partially 'loaded'

test run when they worked a Derby to Crewe trip with NR DVTs 82111/145 sandwiched in between the 73s. The return was via Stafford.

The locos did not do much other than test runs and driver training, but on 19–21 May they starred at the Severn Valley Railway's diesel gala, so giving people a first chance to travel behind the locos on a passenger train. Because the locos are air-braked only, many of their turns were piloting dual-braked locos on the railway's vacuum-braked stock but there was also a former Southern Region 4-TC set brought to the gala that was air braked.

This allowed the two EDs to work on their own and as a pair, and there was one trip booked for the new look locos. That was the 1244 Bewdley–Kidderminster and it was clear a lot of people had the same idea – this was a chance to travel behind the locos and see and hear how they performed. Sadly with only four coaches, the train was rammed – akin to the old days of commuting into London in the 1970s, and not a pleasant travel experience at all!

Just after leaving the station, and about a quarter of a mile into the 3½-mile journey, 73951 failed and the train was held for some time while fitters tried to fix the loco, but sadly to no avail. Eventually the train continued with 73952 pushing its dead classmate and it arrived some half an hour late. With NR managers in attendance, this was an embarrassing failure for the new locomotives. They returned to Derby on 24 May.

On 10 November 2012, 73211 (left) and 73104 (right) are being stripped back to their bare, empty shells in readiness for conversions to new Cummins-powered locos. At this time the locos were expected to be 73301/302 but this was later changed to 73951/952. *Jason Rogers*

DC electric locos were an everyday sight at Hadfield in the 1960s and '70s but that has not been the case since July 1981 when the Woodhead line closed and the Class 76s were withdrawn. Now it is the terminus of the suburban Manchester lines, but on the night of 12 June 2019, 73951 visited the town on a test train. *Jason Rogers*

It was 22 June before they appeared again, with a test run to Lichfield but all was not well and an aspiration by NR to have the locos working test trains later that month was shelved as 73952 failed to complete on a loaded Derby to Crewe test run – with 73138 and 37057/254 as dead weight and 73951 on the rear – on 29 June.

On 13 July, the two locos returned to the SVR for NR testing in a convoy led by 97304 and with the EDs either side of 31233 and 97301 bringing up the rear. The two 73s then returned on 3 August. It was 12 September when 73951 next appeared on the network, on a light engine test with 31233 to collect 37800, while on the 23rd it was south on test again with the 31 for insurance.

In early October they were sent to Bournemouth for more electrical tests and on the 11th 73951 undertook a test run to Weymouth to test the third-rail capability was still working, with 97301 as insurance. However, the two Minions were still not working trains as intended. So not only were they two years behind schedule in terms of rebuilding, they were now the best part of another year late in terms of actually hauling a train.

On 5 December, so a year after the first of the pair appeared in public complete, 73951 was released into traffic and sent to Tonbridge with original classmate 73138. The next day it worked to Tunbridge Wells with GBRf 73965 and 66718 *Sir Peter Hendy CBE*.

On 21 December 73952 was on test – with 73951 and 73138 – on a Derby–Crewe run but the locos still seemed reluctant to work any trains and by the end of December 73951 was being used solo for route learning in Nottinghamshire.

In January 2017 the two locos were still only being used on test runs and route learning, plus moving NR stock, but they were still not being used on the test trains for which they were intended. On 11 January 2017 they took a rail grinder to the High Marnham test track – a typical duty for the locos.

On 7 and 8 February the pair of Minions ran light from Derby to Plymouth and back as a mileage accumulation trip, and test runs continued into March and April. Then, on 23 June, the locos finally entered traffic, being used on a Doncaster–Derby test train.

Since then they have finally started to work many test trains and have finally built up a level of reliability, with each problem arising being ironed out by Loram engineers to make them more trustworthy. They are usually crewed by Colas drivers and can work on any route that a normal 73 can work over. There are certain routes where they are preferred, especially the third-rail lines of the Merseyrail network, plus every sixteen weeks they make a trip around the Harrogate circle line. They have also been used in the North-west and have visited places such as Glossop and Hadfield, the Manchester area and Chester as well as Ilkley and Knaresborough in Yorkshire.

The locos have some operational limitations – namely they can only work in multiple with each other and not with anything else. However, although the locos are now finally performing satisfactorily, no more conversions will be undertaken, and indeed Loram sold its spare locos 73101/139 – which would have been converted if NR has continued with the project – to GBRf.

Class 73s are nothing new at Shakespeare Cliffe, near Dover, but this was a first visit by the Minions as 73951/952 pass on 22 May 2019 with a driver training run. After a very shaky start, the issues on these locos have been ironed out and they are now working satisfactorily. *Jason Rogers*

Network Rail's 73951 *Malcolm Brinded* and 73952 *Janis Kong* work 3Q60, the 1303 Derby–Derby test train, past Crigglestone in West Yorkshire on 7 April 2019. No more conversions of these locos with Cummins engines are expected. *Anthony Hicks*

On 11 June 2019, 73952 waits at Liverpool Lime Street with a test train working. These trains run under Q headcodes and cover the length and breadth of the Network Rail infrastructure monitoring the condition of the track. *Jason Rogers*

The level of work undertaken on the locos is amazing, and indeed NR refers to them as Ultra 73s. Only the basic bodyshell and the bogies are the same as everything inside has been completed changed. They also have no train supply fitted any longer.

If the project hadn't fallen so behind schedule, and so over budget, and the locos had been into traffic much sooner after conversion, then it could have been a wholly different story. As it transpired, the MTU Class 73 rebuild was head and shoulders the better of the two projects.

On one of their first outings, 73952 and 73951 pass Woking with 0Z73, the 1000 Derby RTC–Woking Up Yard light engine run, on 15 June 2017. *Mark Pike*

12

The Class 93

The Tri-Mode Future of the Electro-Diesel

As this book went to the printers, a plan by Rail Operations Group to order ten Class 93s from Stadler was in the final stages of being rubberstamped.

The Class 93 is basically an updated and enhanced Class 88 – in fact it could conceivably be a Class 88/1 – but rather than just being a plain electro-diesel, the Class 93s are a tri-mode loco and will run, in the main, off 25kV AC overhead lines but have a small diesel engine supported by battery power as well not just for last mile operations but also to work over non-electrified lines for some distances if required.

The locos will share the same body as a Class 88 with any necessary changes to the bodyside grilles. They are expected to cost about £4.5 million each and will be financed by ROSCO Beacon Rail. They are to be built by Stadler in the same Valencia factory that built the Class 68s and 88s for DRS – also financed in the main by Beacon.

The 93s will have batteries to support the diesel and the combined diesel/battery will have an output of 1,745hp, so equivalent to a Class 37 Type 3, which makes them ideal for healing trains of a decent weight for a long time.

The range the locos will have away from the OLE is not yet clear, as it obviously depends on the trailing load and the route, however, they will have a 1,500-litre fuel tank for the diesel engine. That said, ROG says the locos will never be too far away from the OLE, so a huge range on diesel is not seen as a major requirement.

The ROG fleet comprises ex-BR Class 37s and 47s, as well as long-term hired Class 57/3s from DRS. It has also hired other locos from other companies to meet short-term and ad hoc traffic requirements.

The plan for the 93s is to supplement this fleet, which specialises in moving rolling stock, especially coaches and multiple units to and from overhaul or store, and also delivering brand new units, either that have arrived in the UK from builders abroad or been built in the UK.

The 93s' arrival could spell the end for the 47s in the ROG fleet but the 37s will be retained as they have tightlock couplers fitted for moving some multiple units. The 93s, however, will have a Dellner coupler than can be used at varying heights.

Despite the high initial cost of each loco, ROG believes they will offset that by having running costs of about a quarter of that to run a Class 66.

An official artist's impression of the ROG Class 93 design, which shares the same bodyshell as the Class 68/88s. Ten locos are expected to be ordered, although the hope is for more. *ROG*

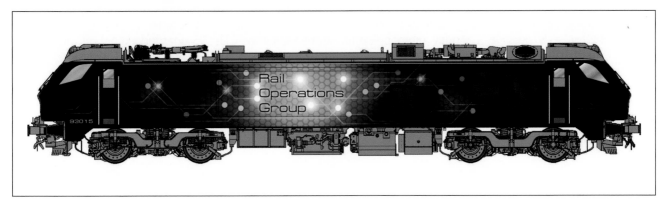

ROG also has aspirations to start a logistics type of operation similar to the old Rail Express Systems, which would handle less than trainload freight in vans.

Speaking to *Rail* magazine in late 2018, Chief Executive Officer Karl Watts said: 'We have gone for the Class 93 as it is the Class 68/88 UKLIGHT platform. We needed that platform and the approvals that go with it. That is still two years from the order placed to the locomotive entering traffic in revenue-earning service. If we hadn't got that, it would be four years.'

In the same interview, Mr Watts said he had looked at the Eurodual locomotive offered by Stadler, but this did not fit the UK loading gauge. However, the Swiss manufacturer offered a solution involving an updated diesel alternator set plus Lithium Titanate Oxide (LTO).

As of mid-September 2019, Beacon Rail and Stadler were still finalising a few legal issues prior to the contact being signed. The final specifications for the testing and approval of the new locomotives were also being agreed.

As the locos are 95 per cent the same as a Class 88, there is no need to go through such an intense approval process as a wholly brand new loco design and this should speed their entry into traffic somewhat. However, as the locos are designed for 110mph there will be some differences in their dynamics when running at their top speed, plus their kinematic envelope will be marginally different when compared with an 88.

They will have a Mk 2 high-speed pantograph to allow for the increased speed – a Class 88 is only passed for 100mph. There will also be a different electrical (electro-magnetic compatibility) footprint for the locos because of their batteries.

The plan is for 93001/002 to be the test bed locos to be used to gain the certification and then it is hoped that 93003–010 will be ready to be put straight into work as soon as they arrive off the boat from Spain, in the same way the Class 66s were unloaded at Newport and put straight into use. It is planned to be just fifty-five days from the delivery of 93001/002 to them entering traffic.

From the moment the contract is signed, it is expected to be twenty-one months before 93001/002 are constructed and ready or testing, and ROG is looking at summer 2021 for their entry into traffic. The locos will be maintained by Arlington Fleet services at Eastleigh.

The current specification will see the diesel engine used being the Caterpillar C32 – so slightly bigger and more powerful than the C27 used in the Class 88 – and this can deliver 1,205hp on its own, while the batteries add another 540hp. It is possible a slightly more powerful engine could be incorporated by the time the construction of the locos actually starts but this is still to be finalised.

The Class 88s had the smaller 940hp engine but by the time the drawings for the 93s were ready there was scope for the more powerful engine, and by the time construction of the 93s starts there is every chance that power could have been upped once again and the locos could be further enhanced to get even more power out of the same dimensions and weights.

Also, battery technology is improving by the day and so equally there is most likelihood there will be more power achievable from the same size and weights of batteries. The more 'installed' power there is in the bodyshell, the better it will be for ROG.

The locos will weigh the same as a Class 88 – 87 tonnes – as any heavier would make them increase to a Route Availability classification of 8, whereas ROG requires RA7.

To accommodate the extra weight of the batteries while maintaining the weight the locos will sacrifice the rheostatic brake resistors, which is not seen as a big issue. The locos will still use regenerative power to brake.

They will not appear in ROG's blue livery as seen on some of its Class 47s, but instead a new futuristic livery designed by AST Rail of Penrith will be applied using vinyls. The initial lease will be for ten years.

ROG says the locos as a 'classic mixed traffic loco', and describes them as 'the 47 for the future'. The deal allows for further 93 orders if required.

They will have an ETS index of 95 – the same as an 88 – and will be perfect for passenger operation as well as express freight. They won't be used for Trainload work, although that is not something in the ROG portfolio. They could be used for intermodal traffic and there is also scope to use them with refurbished Mk 3s and an HST power car as a high-speed freight mover.

This proposal would need some modifications to allow the MTU-engined HST to work with the 93, but it is – in laymen's terms – just a case of a new wiring, cabling and software combination.

The Class 93s will represent a useful loco deign for the UK's railway and assuming they are as successful as the 68s and 88s from the Stadler stable, then there is every chance the production won't end at 93010.

ROG first talked publicly about it Class 93 proposal as late as 2018 and was still on board with the project in the summer of 2019. However, since then the project has gone very quiet and no orders have yet to be placed. It remains to be seen if the Class 93 does indeed get off the ground.

13

The Class 69

A Cost-Effective Rebuild?

Of all the rebuilding programmes in recent times the decision by GB Railfreight to sign up to turn elderly and unreliable Class 56s into new Class 69 locos with General Motors engines is one of the most interesting. The change of 56s to 69s is very similar to the change of 47s to 57s.

GBRf Managing Director John Smith had long joked that GBRf would have Class 56s in its fleet 'over his dead body, having been 'scarred for life' by their appalling reliability when he was a BR manager. GBRf grew beyond his wildest dreams in the mid-2010s, and the clamour for new traction saw it acquire Class 66s from mainland Europe, followed by Class 66s from DB Cargo, Class 47s and 60s from Colas Rail Freight, Class 73s from anyone who had them for sale and Class 92s from SNCF and Europorte.

But it was still not enough and having bought twenty-eight new Class 66s from Progress Rail, the last 66s off the production line and the last to meet emission regulations, followed by ten more 66s from DBC, GBRf had to look elsewhere for new locos.

In 2018 it acquired eighteen Class 56s mostly from UK Rail Leasing, namely 56007/009/018/031/032/037/038/060/065/069/077/081/098, 56104/106/128, 56311/312 – the last two previously being 56057 and 56003 respectively. Some of these locos had recently been acquired by UKRL from DC Rail, while 56128, also an ex-DC Rail machine, had been sold to CF Booth for disposal but not physically broken up.

Of the locos, just 56081/098, 56104, and 56311/312 had seen any main-line use with the spot hire company or DC Rail, the others having not run for more than a decade or even longer. Some locos were in a very poor state indeed, especially 56009/037/077/128, while 56106 already had a cab removed to be sold to Hungarian operator Floyd to repair crash-damaged 56115. Accordingly, this loco was the first to be dismissed from the conversion plan and will be used solely as a spare parts donor.

There are no issues with converting a Class 56 from any batch of locos built – and GBRf has acquired examples of Romanian (56007/009/018/312), Doncaster (56031/ 032/ 037/038/060/065/069/077/081/098, 56104/106/311) and Crewe machines (56128).

Most of the locos were stored at UKRL's Leicester Depot, apart from those that were in active use. No. 56009 was dumped at the Battlefield Line in Leicestershire, while 56128 was at the CF Booth scrapyard in Rotherham.

The conversion work was due to be undertaken by EMD at its Longport site near Stoke-on-Trent, and GBRf set about moving the locos there. No. 56009 was the first to arrive, moving by road in June 2018, at the same time a press release was issued by GBRf. It announced: 'GB Railfreight is again expanding its fleet of locomotives as a result of continued growth in the services that it runs. GBRf is pleased to confirm that it has purchased 16 Class 56 locomotives from UK Rail Leasing (UKRL), along with a number of spares and materials.'

This was actually incorrect as it was seventeen locos, and then 56128 was a later purchase.

It added: 'In the first instance, some of these locomotives will be moved from Leicester to be stored at various locations pending a decision on their future re-engineering, while others may be returned to service if required. At this time GBRf is not able to confirm any projected re-engineering as this is still subject to final contract.'

John Smith said: 'This is an important deal for us as it provides much needed capacity for our expanding business. At a time when rail freight is facing an uncertain future, GBRf is able to say it is growing and confident that the industry will overcome current challenges. With ambitious housing and infrastructure targets, growing consumer demand, and the need to reduce carbon emissions, rail freight must be ready to play a central role.'

On 6 July 2018. 66769 hauled 56031/032/037/311 followed by 56069 being taken on its own by 66781 on 13 July. Nos 56018/081/098/104/312 initially moved to store in Castle Donington, although 56081/098/312 were later revived for heavy shunting at Peak Forest.

The GBRf Class 69s are being rebuilt using redundant Class 56s. One of the locos seen in its earlier guise is 56312, which hauls East Midlands Trains' 222101 as the 5Z56 Derby–Crofton, past Denaby on 6 July 2013. This loco started life as 56003 and was built in Romania in 1976. It was renumbered 56312 in June 2008 when sold to DC Rail, which painted it in these colours before repainting it in a garish purple livery. *Anthony Hicks*

On 10 September, 56128 arrived by road from Rotherham and then 56007/018/038 arrived from Leicester on 20 December – 56018 having been collected from Castle Donington. That left 56060/065/077 and 56104/106 at Leicester in to early 2019.

In early 2019 a provisional contract was signed for the rebuilding of ten locos with the option to increase that order to sixteen, and this was finalised in mid-March. It was then that it announced the locos would receive a new class number – Class 69 – and not be staying in the 56xxx number series.

The rebuild plan

The Class 56s date from 1976, with the first thirty locos built by subcontractor Electroputere in Romania. They were shipped to the UK in 1976–77 and suffered from numerous faults due to poor build quality. The next eighty-five locos, 56031–115, were built by BREL at Doncaster, and 56116–135 were constructed by BREL at Crewe.

The locos featured a Ruston Paxman 16RK3CT engine, derived from the English Electric 16CSVT engine fitted to the Class 50s, rated at 3,250hp.

This engine was not the best in its heavy freight application. Withdrawal of the 56s started in the early 1990s not long after the last loco, 56135, rolled off the production line in 1984.

The Class 69 rebuild sees the inside of the loco, between the cabs, completely stripped out and the old Ruston engines disposed of along with the existing coolant groups.

In its place, a new 3a compliant EMD 710A engine, as fitted to the 66752–779 batch of Class 66s, will be fitted. It will also have and new compressors, blower motors and electronic cubicles.

The underframe, bogies, traction motors and brake system will remain the same as a Class 56 but will be fully overhauled. The brake frames will be overhauled and retained.

The cabs will be markedly changed and the fronts will have new, compliant, restyled lights fitted, while the multiple working cables will be removed and changed to the AAR system to allow a Class 69 to work in multiple with a Class 59, 66, 67 or 73/9.

New 'Cyclops'-style middle headlights will also be fitted on the cab roofs, while the horn grilles will be retained but

The first Class 69 will be built using the bodyshell of 56311. This picture on 3 April 2019 shows the stripped out shell of the ex-DC Rail loco being shunted by 08220 at Longport, where it will be fitted with a GM engine and returned to traffic as 69001 in a unique livery. *Cliff Beeton*

changed – there are two different types of horn grilles on Class 56s. Yellow warning panels will be retained and new Class 66-style buffers and drawgear will also be fitted.

Inside, the cabs will also be totally remodelled to be more like a Class 66 in design, with a pedestal set up for the power handle. New gauges, cab instruments lights, switches and seats will be fitted.

The roofs will be completely changed, with a new exhaust fitted in a flat cutaway section of the roof. More grilles and windows will be added to the bodysides. GBRf expects the first Class 69 to be delivered in June 2020 and the last of the order should be in traffic twelve months later.

No. 69001 will be outshopped in a special livery and will be named but the remainder of the fleet should be unveiled in standard GBRf livery and all sixteen locos should look the same despite the differences in cab designs of some of the donor locos.

Where the 69s will work

The haulage capability of a Class 69 compared with a 56 will be the same and the track dynamics are unaffected. They will weigh the same as a Class 56 – approximately 126 tonnes.

The locos will have an advantage over a Class 56 as they will be more reliable and have individual traction motor control, thus allowing them to haul their trains more efficiently and with no wheelslip. There will be wheelslip probes on every axle, which will be computer controlled. They will be fitted with sanding equipment.

The Class 69s are intended to be general purpose locos for use across the entire GBRf work portfolio. They will work intermodal trains and bulk trainloads, although they won't be used on the heaviest trainload flows, which will remain operated by 59003, the ten Class 60s and Class 66s.

There is scope for GBRf to order more Class 69s on top of the ten planned, and GBRf has also said it will be happy to allow other Class 56 operators such as Colas or DC Rail to tag on the build process if they wish to do so with their locos.

The locos are anticipated to have a twenty-five-year life between overhauls and are deemed to be a new loco with a lifespan in excess of forty years. A new Class 69 is considerably cheaper than acquiring a new Class 66. Once converted, all 69s will be owned by Progress Rail Leasing.

14

The Future for Locos in the UK

What the future holds for new locomotives being ordered for the UK's railways is incredibly hard to predict and it is highly likely that legislation aiming to reduce carbon emissions – probably on a global scale – will be a driving factor in dictating what, if any, new locos are ordered any time in the near future.

Any TOC or FOC looking to order any new locos in the current climate has few choices. The Class 66 production run is over, leaving the Stadler Class 68 and the General Electric Class 70 as the only realistic diesel options. GE Transportation is now owned by Wabtec, but to date has not been rebranded.

On the electric loco front, the Class 88 or 93 versions of the Stadler design are good bets and would also be available as a straight electric or probably a dual-voltage option if there was enough demand for a third-rail-equipped version.

Other locos for the UK market will depend purely on orders. Because of our restrictive loading gauge, few manufacturers in Europe or further afield will entertain the costly design and build process of a prototype purely on the *hope* of winning a contract.

The Bombardier TRAXX and Siemens Vectron platforms – both of which are doing well in mainland Europe – could both conceivably be redesigned for the UK, but such a redesign is not easy to do and only worthwhile if the manufacturers either perceive there to be a real chance of orders or if a franchise bid or a freight operator actually comes knocking on their doors with a cast-iron order.

The other factor is what demand is there for new locos? The Class 66s and 68s certainly have a long life ahead of them. Even though the oldest 66s are now over 20 years old, yet they are probably still not even halfway through their potential working lives. They are bulletproof! The new 68s again should be looking at achieving at least a forty year life.

GB Railfreight is always on the lookout for new locos – as demonstrated by its Class 69 project – and freely admits it will take on any 66 it can acquire if cost-effective to do so. It has former Freightliner, DRS an DB Cargo locos already in its fleet, as well as locos sourced from Europe, and more 66s will inevitably follow.

Stadler presently has the UK market sewn up and has its UK designs. It has also sold a version of the Class 88 to South Africa. It is also now offering the six-axle version of its Euro 4000 diesel and bi-mode Eurodual designs, with the latter effectively an electro-diesel with the same diesel power as a Class 68 and a 7MW electric loco. There is also a straight electric version, which can deliver a massive 9MW output. All of these are probably too powerful for the UK market, assuming the equipment could fit in a 68 body. It's hard to see too many alternatives for these locos in the next ten years or even more. There is even a suggestion Stadler might be able to offer a light, RA5, version of the 'Class 68' platform.

Alstom, which is a European-based company and a mass builder of new locos, does not actually serve the European market very much. Most of its build is for Asia, with the Prima designs popular in Kazakhstan and India.

China has some builders of new locos and while a handful have been sold into Europe, such as Macedonia, and a couple of hybrid locos have been built for the German market for infrastructure trains, the UK market is, again, not on the radar.

General Electric, which has had limited success with its Class 70s and the other PowerHaul designs in Turkey, has also sold large numbers of locos to Ukraine and Kazakhstan. The Class 70 has the advantage that it has a design that is UK-friendly in terms of measurements, but its reliability problems have been a cause for concern.

Some of these locos were sold to Turkish operators – with a massively different body design compared with the Class 70 – but the plan to deliver six locos to an operator in Germany has been beset with difficulties and the project was running at least five years behind schedule. The demonstration loco was displayed at Innotrans in 2012 but was still awaiting approval to run in Germany as this book went to press in 2019. Some of these locos, have, however, been sold to South Korea and are apparently running satisfactorily.

Bombardier did look at the UK market and a UK-gauge version of the TRAXX design was a serious proposition for the ECML before the InterCity Express Programme train was chosen. Obviously nothing was built, but the concept was seriously worked up and could be again.

Siemens has a popular Vectron platform, and that includes the VectronDual, which is an electro-diesel that runs off 15kV AC and has a decent size diesel – the 3,200hp MTU engine – capable of main-line running.

The Vectron comes in all sorts of options for electric and can also be acquired as a straight diesel. However, nine of the latter were built but none were sold as such to operators. These demonstrator locos have been leased to various operators in Germany but due to the low take-up, barring any large orders, it is unlikely any of these would roll of the production line any time soon.

Emissions

The biggest driving factor for new locos will be exhaust emissions and these will only get more and more restrictive. Euro Stage 4 is now being built. Noise emissions are also becoming an issue and, again, they will only get more stringent in years to come.

In fact, new diesels may be a thing of the past, and the fuel could go the same way as steam – eventually 'barred'. However, so long as there are grandfather rights it's unlikely there will be so much deviation away from diesel in the next decade or two for freight operations.

For passenger options it's a different story as this is a market where battery power can be more effective for certain applications. In fairness, loco haulage for passenger trains remains a dying breed in the UK, especially with new units. There's the odd exception to the rule, such as the Mk 5 coaches from CAF with Class 68 power from Stadler recently introduced by TransPennine Express on its Liverpool to Scarborough, but huge contracts for new rolling stock on several intercity franchises have been awarded to multiple unit manufacturers.

Battery and hydrogen power remains unlikely for locos hauling freight trains in the currently climate as the technology is currently not suitable for this market.

The Vectron design has proved popular in mainland Europe, but sadly is too big for the UK's restrictive loading gauge. However, if there were enough interest and some firm orders, a scaled down version could possibly be offered by Siemens. Regiojet ELL 193.206 leaves Olomouc on 10 April 2017. *Keith Fender*

A third-rail 750V DC Stadler 'Class 88' (a Class 78 perhaps?) is always plausible, but there is not really any need for such a loco, certainly not as a straight electric-only machine.

Unless there is any introduction of emission standards that call for a ban on existing locos, and such a ban would receive such a fierce backlash from existing operators it would effectively force freight on to the already congested UK's roads – it's hard to see the 66s not still running into the second half of this century

The future for lower emissions is electrification but while there is still some ongoing in the UK, especially in Scotland, after the Paddington–Cardiff wiring is completed there are not expected to be too many long-distance electrification projects, other than the proposed trans-Pennine and the extension of the current Midland Main Line project.

This leaves freight operators reliant on diesel. The Class 88/93 concept has much merit for long-distance freight flows where running under the wires is still possible and the diesel or battery propulsion mode for the last few miles into yards, on to branches and on other short sections of unwired main line is acceptable.

Re-engineering

For the UK loco market, re-engineering existing locos is always an option and it has many advantages, least of all cost. It allows modern technology to be incorporated in an older bodyshell, thus saving on construction costs, but also makes certification much easier than for a brand new loco design.

The Class 57 concept has proved that fact, and although Brush never gained the orders that were talked about – as the 57s were usurped by the 66s – nevertheless, the 57 offered a cost-effective alternative for new locos for the likes of Virgin and FGW especially.

Likewise, the MTU Class 43 project was a major success, allowing the HST fleet to gain another twenty years plus of life.

The locos that gave rise to the Class 88; the first of the Eurodual locos under construction at Stadler's Valencia plant. *Keith Fender*

The same could be said about the MTU Class 73/9s project, albeit this particular rebuild has proved to be a bit more costly that first envisaged. The Cummins/Loram Class 73 project, however, reminds us that rebuilding an old loco does not always work as well as operators would have liked.

Plans to convert Class 37s with Caterpillar engines has died a quiet death, and given the poor bodyshells on Class 37s are both dated and prone to rust this does make the idea unlikely to see the light of day.

This book was published before the first Class 69 took to the rails – where old Class 56s are rebuilt with the innards of a Class 66. Time will tell if this was a sensible option.

It's unlikely there will be many major new loco orders before 2030. It is possible, in fact even likely, more Class 68s could be ordered – DRS is rumoured to want another ten locos at least, but these might be of a different, lighter, specification while the Class 88 and 93 projects also have a lot of potential for further orders.

There is unlikely to ever be the same kind of seismic shift in traction that there was from steam to diesel, where the whole of the UK fleet was effectively replaced in little more than a decade.

The future demand for locos in the UK will be dependent the main factors: traction propulsion choice, suppliers willing to enter the market with a product that meets the UK's loading gauge making and a demand for loco haulage. The problem is, all three factors are so, so hard to predict.

One thing is for sure: there will always be some ideas, trials and suggestions to keep the story of new locomotives an ongoing story!

Appendices

Fleet list 1: Class 43 HST Power cars with MTU engines

HST MTU conversions

Loco	Rebuilt from	Owner	Operator	Current Livery	Name
43002		National Railway Museum		BR Blue/grey	*Sir Kenneth Grange*
43003		Angel	ScotRail	ScotRail Seven Cities	
43004		Angel	Great Western Railway	Great Western Railway green	
43005		Angel	Great Western Railway	Great Western Railway green	
43009		Angel	Great Western Railway	First Great Western blue	
43010		Angel		First Great Western blue	
43012		Angel	ScotRail	ScotRail Seven Cities	
43013		Porterbrook	Network Rail	Network Rail yellow	*Mark Carne CBE*
43014		Porterbrook	Network Rail	Network Rail yellow	*The Railway Observer*
43015		Angel	ScotRail	ScotRail Seven Cities	
43016		Angel	Great Western Railway	Great Western Railway green	
43017		Angel		First Great Western blue	
43018		Angel		First Great Western blue	
43020		Angel		First Great Western blue	*mtu Power Passion Partnership*
43021		Angel	ScotRail	ScotRail Seven Cities	
43022		Angel		First Great Western blue	
43023		Angel	Hull Trains*	First Great Western blue	*SQN LDR HAROLD STARR ONE OF THE FEW*
43024		Angel		First Great Western blue	
43025		Angel		First Great Western blue	
43026		Angel	ScotRail	ScotRail Seven Cities	
43027		Angel	Hull Trains*		
43028		Angel	ScotRail	ScotRail Seven Cities	
43029		Angel		First Great Western blue	
43030		Angel	ScotRail	ScotRail Seven Cities	
43031		Angel	ScotRail	ScotRail Seven Cities	
43032		Angel	ScotRail	ScotRail Seven Cities	
43033		Angel	ScotRail	ScotRail Seven Cities	
43034		Angel	ScotRail	ScotRail Seven Cities	
43035		Angel	ScotRail	ScotRail Seven Cities	
43036		Angel	ScotRail	ScotRail Seven Cities	
43037		Angel	ScotRail	ScotRail Seven Cities	
43040		Angel	Great Western Railway	Great Western Railway green	*Bristol St Philip's Marsh*
43041		Angel	Great Western Railway	Great Western Railway green	*Meningitis Trust Support for Life*

Loco	Rebuilt from	Owner	Operator	Current Livery	Name
43042		Angel	Great Western Railway	Great Western Railway green	
43053		Porterbrook		First Great Western blue	
43056		Porterbrook		First Great Western blue	
43062		Network Rail		Network Rail yellow	*John Armitt*
43063		Porterbrook		First Great Western blue	
43069		Porterbrook		First Great Western blue	
43070		Porterbrook		First Great Western blue	
43071		Porterbrook		First Great Western blue	
43078		Porterbrook		First Great Western blue	
43079		Porterbrook		First Great Western blue	
43086		Porterbrook		First Great Western blue	
43087		Porterbrook		First Great Western blue	
43088		Porterbrook		First Great Western blue	
43091		Porterbrook		First Great Western blue	
43092		First Group	FGW	Great Western Railway green	
43093		First Group	FGW	Great Western Railway green	*Old Oak Common HST Depot 1976–2018*
43094		First Group	FGW	Great Western Railway green	
43097		First Group	FGW	Great Western Railway green	*Environment Agency*
43098		First Group	FGW	Great Western Railway green	
43122		First Group	FGW	Great Western Railway green	
43124		Angel	ScotRail	ScotRail Seven Cities	
43125		Angel	ScotRail	ScotRail Seven Cities	
43126		Angel	ScotRail	ScotRail Seven Cities	
43127		Angel	ScotRail	ScotRail Seven Cities	
43128		Angel	ScotRail	ScotRail Seven Cities	
43129		Angel	ScotRail	ScotRail Seven Cities	
43130		Angel	ScotRail	ScotRail Seven Cities	
43131		Angel	ScotRail	ScotRail Seven Cities	
43132		Angel	ScotRail	ScotRail Seven Cities	
43133		Angel	ScotRail	ScotRail Seven Cities	
43134		Angel	ScotRail	ScotRail Seven Cities	
43135		Angel	ScotRail	ScotRail Seven Cities	
43136		Angel	ScotRail	ScotRail Seven Cities	
43137		Angel	ScotRail	ScotRail Seven Cities	
43138		Angel	ScotRail	ScotRail Seven Cities	
43139		Angel	ScotRail	ScotRail Seven Cities	
43140		Angel	ScotRail	ScotRail Seven Cities	
43141		Angel	ScotRail	ScotRail Seven Cities	
43142		Angel	ScotRail	ScotRail Seven Cities	
43143		Angel	ScotRail	ScotRail Seven Cities	
43144		Angel	ScotRail	ScotRail Seven Cities	
43145		Angel	ScotRail	ScotRail Seven Cities	
43146		Angel	ScotRail	ScotRail Seven Cities	
43147		Angel	ScotRail	ScotRail Seven Cities	
43148		Angel	ScotRail	ScotRail Seven Cities	
43149		Angel	ScotRail	ScotRail Seven Cities	
43150		Angel	ScotRail	ScotRail Seven Cities	
43151		Angel	ScotRail	ScotRail Seven Cities	
43152		Angel	ScotRail	ScotRail Seven Cities	
43153		First Group	Great Western Railway	Great Western Railway green	
43154		First Group	Great Western Railway	First Great Western blue	
43155		First Group	Great Western Railway	Great Western Railway green	
43156		Porterbrook	Great Western Railway	First Great Western blue	*Dartington International Summer School*
43158		First Group	Great Western Railway	First Great Western blue	
43159		Porterbrook		First Great Western blue	
43160		Porterbrook		First Great Western blue	
43161		Porterbrook		First Great Western blue	
43162		Porterbrook		First Great Western blue	

Loco	Rebuilt from	Owner	Operator	Current Livery	Name
43163		Angel	ScotRail	ScotRail Seven Cities	
43164		Angel	ScotRail	ScotRail Seven Cities	
43165		Angel		First Great Western blue	
43168		Angel	ScotRail	ScotRail Seven Cities	
43169		Angel	ScotRail	ScotRail Seven Cities	
43170		Angel	Great Western Railway	Great Western Railway green	
43171		Angel	Great Western Railway	First Great Western blue	
43172		Angel	Great Western Railway	We will remember them wrap	Harry Patch The last survivor of the trenches
43174		Angel		First Great Western blue	
43175		Angel	ScotRail	ScotRail Seven Cities	
43176		Angel	ScotRail	ScotRail Seven Cities	
43177		Angel	ScotRail	ScotRail Seven Cities	
43179		Angel	ScotRail	ScotRail Seven Cities	
43180		Porterbrook		First Great Western blue	
43181		Angel		ScotRail Seven Cities	
43182		Angel	ScotRail	ScotRail Seven Cities	
43183		Angel	ScotRail	ScotRail Seven Cities	
43185		Angel		InterCity	
43186		Angel	Great Western Railway	Great Western Railway green	
43187		Angel	Great Western Railway	Great Western Railway green	
43188		Angel	Great Western Railway	Great Western Railway green	
43189		Angel	Great Western Railway	Great Western Railway green	
43190		Angel		First Great Western blue	
43191		Angel		First Great Western blue	
43192		Angel	Great Western Railway	Great Western Railway green	
43193		Porterbrook		First Great Western blue	
43194		First Group	Great Western Railway	Great Western Railway green	Okehampton Castle
43195		Porterbrook		First Great Western blue	
43196		Porterbrook		First Great Western blue	
43197		Porterbrook		First Great Western blue	
43198		First Group	Great Western Railway	Great Western Railway green	Driver Brian Cooper 15 June 1947–5 October 1999/ Driver Stan Martin 25 June 1950–6 November 2004
43206	43006	Angel	LNER	LNER red/white	
43207	43007	Angel	XC	CrossCountry Trains brown/silver	
43208	43008	Angel	LNER	LNER red/white	Lincolnshire Echo
43238	43038	Angel	LNER	National Railway Museum wrap	National Railway Museum 40 Years 1975–2015
43239	43039	Angel	LNER	LNER red/white	
43251	43051	Porterbrook	LNER	LNER red/white	
43257	43057	Porterbrook	LNER	LNER red/white	Bounds Green
43272	43072	Porterbrook	LNER	LNER red/white	
43274	43074	Porterbrook	LNER	LNER red/white	Spirit of Sunderland
43277	43077	Porterbrook	LNER	LNER red/white	
43285	43085	Porterbrook	CrossCountry Trains	CrossCountry Trains brown/silver	
43290	43090	Porterbrook	LNER	LNER red/white	mtu Fascination of Power
43295	43095	Angel	LNER	LNER red/white	
43296	43096	Angel	LNER	LNER red/white	
43299	43099	Porterbrook	LNER	LNER red/white	
43300	43100	Porterbrook	LNER	LNER red/white	Craigentinny
43301	43101	Porterbrook	CrossCountry Trains	CrossCountry Trains brown/silver	
43302	43102	Porterbrook	LNER	LNER red/white	
43303	43103	Porterbrook	CrossCountry Trains	CrossCountry Trains brown/silver	
43304	43104	Angel	CrossCountry Trains	CrossCountry Trains brown/silver	
43305	43105	Angel	LNER	LNER red/white	
43306	43106	Angel	LNER	LNER red/white	
43307	43107	Angel	LNER	LNER red/white	
43308	43108	Angel	LNER	LNER red/white	HIGHLAND CHIEFTAIN

Loco	Rebuilt from	Owner	Operator	Current Livery	Name
43309	43109	Angel	LNER	LNER red/white	
43310	43110	Angel	LNER	LNER red/white	
43311	43111	Angel	LNER	LNER red/white	
43312	43112	Angel	LNER	LNER red/white	
43313	43113	Angel	LNER	LNER red/white	
43314	43114	Angel	LNER	LNER red/white	
43315	43115	Angel	LNER	LNER red/white	
43316	43116	Angel	LNER	LNER red/white	
43317	43117	Angel	LNER	LNER red/white	
43318	43118	Angel	LNER	LNER red/white	
43319	43119	Angel	LNER	LNER red/white	
43320	43120	Angel	LNER	LNER red/white	
43321	43121	Porterbrook	CrossCountry Trains	CrossCountry Trains brown/silver	
43357	43157	Porterbrook	CrossCountry Trains	CrossCountry Trains brown/silver	
43366	43166	Angel	CrossCountry Trains	CrossCountry Trains brown/silver	
43367	43167	Angel	LNER	LNER red/white	DELTIC 50 1955–2005
43378	43178	Angel	CrossCountry Trains	CrossCountry Trains brown/silver	
43384	43184	Angel	CrossCountry Trains	CrossCountry Trains brown/silver	
43423	43123	Angel	East Midland Railway	East Midlands Railway plain Blue	
43465	43065	Angel	East Midland Railway	East Midlands Railway plain Blue	
43467	43067	Angel	East Midland Railway	East Midlands Railway plain Blue	
43468	43068	Angel	East Midland Railway	East Midlands Railway plain Blue	British Transport Police Nottingham/ Nottinghamshire Fire and Rescue Service
43480	43080	Angel	East Midland Railway	East Midlands Railway plain Blue	West Hampstead PSB
43484	43084	Angel	East Midland Railway	East Midlands Railway plain Blue	

Note: 43011/019/173 were written off before the MTU project. 43043–050/052/054/055/058–061/064/066/073/075/076/081–083/089 were not MTU fitted but did have their Valenta engines replaced by VP185s.

Fleet list 2: Class 57s

Class 57/0 Original locos built for Freightliner without train heating

Loco	Rebuilt from	Owner	Operator	Livery	Name
57001	47356	West Coast Railways	West Coast Railways	West Coast Railways	
57002	47322	Direct Rail Services	Direct Rail Services	Revised Direct Rail Services Compass	RAIL Express
57003	47317	Direct Rail Services	Direct Rail Services	Revised Direct Rail Services Compass	
57004	47347	Direct Rail Services	Direct Rail Services	Direct Rail Services Compass	
57005	47350	West Coast Railways	West Coast Railways	Advenza Blue	
57006	47187	West Coast Railways	West Coast Railways	West Coast Railways	
57007	47332	Direct Rail Services	Direct Rail Services	Revised Direct Rail Services Compass	John Scott 12.5.45–22.5.12
57008	47060	Direct Rail Services	Direct Rail Services	Direct Rail Services Compass	
57009	47079	Direct Rail Services	Direct Rail Services	Direct Rail Services Compass	
57010	47231	Direct Rail Services	Direct Rail Services	Revised Direct Rail Services Compass	
57011	47329	Direct Rail Services	Direct Rail Services	Direct Rail Services Compass	
57012	47204	Direct Rail Services	Direct Rail Services	Direct Rail Services Compass	

Class 57/3 ETH locos originally ordered by Virgin Trains

Loco	Rebuilt from	Owner	Operator	Livery	Name
57301	47845	Porterbrook	Direct Rail Services	Revised Direct Rail Services Compass	Goliath
57302	47827	Direct Rail Services	Direct Rail Services	Direct Rail Services Compass	Chad Varah
57303	47705	Porterbrook	Direct Rail Services	Revised Direct Rail Services Compass	Pride of Carlisle
57304	47807	Direct Rail Services	Direct Rail Services	Revised Direct Rail Services Compass	Pride of Cheshire
57305	47822	Porterbrook	Rail Operations Group	Northern Belle	Northern Princess
57306	47814	Porterbrook	Direct Rail Services	Revised Direct Rail Services Compass	Her Majesty's Railway Inspectorate 175
57307	47225	Direct Rail Services	Direct Rail Services	Direct Rail Services 20 Years	LADY PENELOPE

Loco	Rebuilt from	Owner	Operator	Livery	Name
57308	47846	Direct Rail Services	Direct Rail Services	Revised Direct Rail Services Compass	*Jamie Ferguson*
57309	47806	Direct Rail Services	Direct Rail Services	Revised Direct Rail Services Compass	*Pride of Crewe*
57310	47831	Porterbrook	Direct Rail Services	Revised Direct Rail Services Compass	*Pride of Cumbria*
57311	47817	Direct Rail Services	Direct Rail Services	Direct Rail Services Compass	*Thunderbird*
57312	47330	Porterbrook	Rail Operations Group	Northern Belle	*Solway Princess*
57313	47371	West Coast Railways	West Coast Railways	West Coast Railways	
57314	47372	West Coast Railways	West Coast Railways	West Coast Railways	
57315	47234	West Coast Railways	West Coast Railways	West Coast Railways	
57316	47290	West Coast Railways	West Coast Railways	West Coast Railways	

Class 57/6 Locos ordered by First Great Western

Loco	Rebuilt from	Owner	Operator	Livery	Name
57601	47825	West Coast Railways	West Coast Railways	Northern Belle	*Windsor Castle*
57602	47337	Porterbrook	Great Western Railway	GWT green	*Restormel Castle*
57603	47349	Porterbrook	Great Western Railway	GWT green	*Tintagel Castle*
57604	47209	Porterbrook	Great Western Railway	Great Western Railway green	*PENDENNIS CASTLE*
57605	47206	Porterbrook	Great Western Railway	GWT green	*Totnes Castle*

Fleet list 3: Class 66

Class 66/0 Locos ordered by English Welsh & Scottish Railway (Now DB Cargo)
Some now with other operators

Loco	Later numbers	Owner	Operator	Livery	name
66001	-	DB Cargo	DB Cargo	DB Cargo	
66002	-		DB Cargo	English Welsh & Scottish Railway	
66003	-	DB Cargo	DB Cargo	English Welsh & Scottish Railway	
66004	-	DB Cargo	DB Cargo	English Welsh & Scottish Railway	
66005	-	DB Cargo	DB Cargo	Maritime blue	*Maritime Intermodal One*
66006	-	DB Cargo	DB Cargo	English Welsh & Scottish Railway	
66007	-	DB Cargo	DB Cargo	English Welsh & Scottish Railway	
66008*	66780	GB Railfreight			
66009	-	DB Cargo	DB Cargo	DB Cargo	
66010	92 70 0 066010-4	DB Cargo	Euro Cargo Rail	English Welsh & Scottish Railway	
66011	-	DB Cargo	DB Cargo	English Welsh & Scottish Railway	
66012	-	DB Cargo	DB Cargo	English Welsh & Scottish Railway	
66013	-	DB Cargo	DB Cargo	English Welsh & Scottish Railway	
66014	-	DB Cargo	DB Cargo	English Welsh & Scottish Railway	
66015	-	DB Cargo	DB Cargo	English Welsh & Scottish Railway	
66016*	66781	GB Railfreight			
66017	-	DB Cargo	DB Cargo	DB Cargo	
66018	-	DB Cargo	DB Cargo	DB Cargo	
66019	-	DB Cargo	DB Cargo	DB Cargo	
66020	-	DB Cargo	DB Cargo	DB Cargo	
66021	-	DB Cargo	DB Cargo	DB Cargo	
66022	92 70 0 066022-9	DB Cargo	Euro Cargo Rail	English Welsh & Scottish Railway	
66023	-	DB Cargo	DB Cargo	English Welsh & Scottish Railway	
66024	-	DB Cargo	DB Cargo	English Welsh & Scottish Railway	
66025	-	DB Cargo	DB Cargo	English Welsh & Scottish Railway	
66026	92 70 0 066026-0	DB Cargo	Euro Cargo Rail	English Welsh & Scottish Railway	
66027	-	DB Cargo	DB Cargo	DB Cargo	
66028	92 70 0 066028-6	DB Cargo	Euro Cargo Rail	English Welsh & Scottish Railway	
66029	92 70 0 066029-4	DB Cargo	Euro Cargo Rail	English Welsh & Scottish Railway	
66030	-	DB Cargo	DB Cargo	English Welsh & Scottish Railway	
66031	-	DB Cargo	Direct Rail Services	English Welsh & Scottish Railway	
66032	92 70 0 066032-8	DB Cargo	Euro Cargo Rail	English Welsh & Scottish Railway	
66033	92 70 0 066033-6	DB Cargo	Euro Cargo Rail	English Welsh & Scottish Railway	
66034	-	DB Cargo	DB Cargo	DB Cargo	

Loco	Rebuilt from	Owner	Operator	Livery	Name
66035	-	DB Cargo	DB Cargo	DB Cargo	*Resourceful*
66036	92 70 0 066036-9	DB Cargo	Euro Cargo Rail	English Welsh & Scottish Railway	
66037	-	DB Cargo	DB Cargo	English Welsh & Scottish Railway	
66038	92 70 0 066038-5	DB Cargo	Euro Cargo Rail	English Welsh & Scottish Railway	
66039	-	DB Cargo	DB Cargo	English Welsh & Scottish Railway	
66040	-	DB Cargo	DB Cargo	English Welsh & Scottish Railway	
66041	-	DB Cargo	DB Cargo	DB Cargo	
66042	92 70 0 066042-7	DB Cargo	Euro Cargo Rail	English Welsh & Scottish Railway	
66043	-	DB Cargo	DB Cargo	English Welsh & Scottish Railway	
66044	-	DB Cargo	DB Cargo	DB Cargo	
66045	92 70 0 066045-0	DB Cargo	Euro Cargo Rail	English Welsh & Scottish Railway	
66046*	66782	GB Railfreight			
66047	-	DB Cargo	DB Cargo	Maritime blue	*Maritime Intermodal Two*
66048	-	EMD		Plain black	
66049	92 70 0 066049-2	DB Cargo	Euro Cargo Rail	English Welsh & Scottish Railway	
66050	-	DB Cargo	DB Cargo	English Welsh & Scottish Railway	*EWS Energy*
66051	-	DB Cargo	DB Cargo	Maritime blue	*Maritime Intermodal Four*
66052	92 70 0 066052-6	DB Cargo	Euro Cargo Rail	English Welsh & Scottish Railway	
66053	-	DB Cargo	DB Cargo	English Welsh & Scottish Railway	
66054	-	DB Cargo	DB Cargo	English Welsh & Scottish Railway	
66055	-	DB Cargo	DB Cargo	DB Cargo	*Alain Thauvette*
66056	-	DB Cargo	DB Cargo	English Welsh & Scottish Railway	
66057	-	DB Cargo	DB Cargo	English Welsh & Scottish Railway	
66058*	66783				
66059	-	DB Cargo	DB Cargo	English Welsh & Scottish Railway	
66060	-	DB Cargo	DB Cargo	English Welsh & Scottish Railway	
66061	-	DB Cargo	DB Cargo	English Welsh & Scottish Railway	
66062	92 70 0 066062-5	DB Cargo	Euro Cargo Rail	English Welsh & Scottish Railway	
66063	-	DB Cargo	DB Cargo	English Welsh & Scottish Railway	
66064	92 70 0 066064-1	DB Cargo	Euro Cargo Rail	English Welsh & Scottish Railway	
66065	-	DB Cargo	DB Cargo	DB Cargo	
66066	-	DB Cargo	DB Cargo	DB Cargo	*Geoff Spencer*
66067	-	DB Cargo	DB Cargo	English Welsh & Scottish Railway	
66068	-	DB Cargo	DB Cargo	English Welsh & Scottish Railway	
66069	-	DB Cargo	DB Cargo	English Welsh & Scottish Railway	
66070	-	DB Cargo	DB Cargo	DB Cargo	
66071	92 70 0 066071-6	DB Cargo	Euro Cargo Rail	English Welsh & Scottish Railway	
66072	92 70 0 066072-4	DB Cargo	Euro Cargo Rail	English Welsh & Scottish Railway	
66073	92 70 0 066073-2	DB Cargo	Euro Cargo Rail	English Welsh & Scottish Railway	
66074	-	DB Cargo	DB Cargo	DB Cargo	
66075	-	DB Cargo	DB Cargo	English Welsh & Scottish Railway	
66076	-	DB Cargo	DB Cargo	English Welsh & Scottish Railway	
66077	-	DB Cargo	DB Cargo	DB Cargo	
66078	-	DB Cargo	DB Cargo	DB Cargo	
66079	-	DB Cargo	DB Cargo	English Welsh & Scottish Railway	*James Nightall G.C.*
66080	-	DB Cargo	DB Cargo	English Welsh & Scottish Railway	
66081*	66784				
66082	-	DB Cargo	DB Cargo	DB Cargo	
66083	-	DB Cargo	DB Cargo	English Welsh & Scottish Railway	
66084	-	DB Cargo	DB Cargo	English Welsh & Scottish Railway	
66085	-	DB Cargo	DB Cargo	DB Cargo	
66086	-	DB Cargo	DB Cargo	English Welsh & Scottish Railway	
66087	-	DB Cargo	DB Cargo	English Welsh & Scottish Railway	
66088	-	DB Cargo	DB Cargo	English Welsh & Scottish Railway	
66089	-	DB Cargo	DB Cargo	English Welsh & Scottish Railway	
66090	-	DB Cargo	DB Cargo	Maritime Blue	*Maritime Intermodal Six*
66091	-	DB Cargo	Direct Rail Services	English Welsh & Scottish Railway	
66092	-	DB Cargo	DB Cargo	English Welsh & Scottish Railway	
66093	-	DB Cargo	DB Cargo	English Welsh & Scottish Railway	
66094	-	DB Cargo	DB Cargo	DB Cargo	

Loco	Rebuilt from	Owner	Operator	Livery	Name
66095	-	DB Cargo	DB Cargo	English Welsh & Scottish Railway	
66096	-	DB Cargo	DB Cargo	English Welsh & Scottish Railway	
66097	-	DB Cargo	DB Cargo	DB Schenker	
66098	-	DB Cargo	DB Cargo	English Welsh & Scottish Railway	
66099	-	DB Cargo	DB Cargo	English Welsh & Scottish Railway	
66100	-	DB Cargo	DB Cargo	DB Cargo	*Armistice 100*
66101	-	DB Cargo	DB Cargo	DB Schenker	
66102	-	DB Cargo	DB Cargo	English Welsh & Scottish Railway	
66103	-	DB Cargo	DB Cargo	English Welsh & Scottish Railway	
66104	-	DB Cargo	DB Cargo	DB Cargo	
66105	-	DB Cargo	DB Cargo	DB Cargo	
66106	-	DB Cargo	DB Cargo	English Welsh & Scottish Railway	
66107	-	DB Cargo	DB Cargo	DB Cargo	
66108	-	DB Cargo	Direct Rail Services	English Welsh & Scottish Railway	
66109	-	DB Cargo	DB Cargo	PD Ports blue	*Teesport Express*
66110	-	DB Cargo	DB Cargo	English Welsh & Scottish Railway	
66111	-	DB Cargo	DB Cargo	English Welsh & Scottish Railway	
66112	-	DB Cargo	DB Cargo	English Welsh & Scottish Railway	
66113	-	DB Cargo	DB Cargo	DB Cargo	
66114	-	DB Cargo	DB Cargo	DB Schenker	
66115	-	DB Cargo	DB Cargo	DB Cargo	
66116	-	DB Cargo	DB Cargo	English Welsh & Scottish Railway	
66117	-	DB Cargo	DB Cargo	DB Cargo	
66118	-	DB Cargo	DB Cargo	DB Schenker	
66119	-	DB Cargo	DB Cargo	English Welsh & Scottish Railway	
66120	-	DB Cargo	DB Cargo	English Welsh & Scottish Railway	
66121	-	DB Cargo	DB Cargo	English Welsh & Scottish Railway	
66122	-	DB Cargo	Direct Rail Services	English Welsh & Scottish Railway	
66123	92 70 0 066123-5	DB Cargo	Euro Cargo Rail	English Welsh & Scottish Railway	
66124	-	DB Cargo	DB Cargo	DB Cargo	
66125	-	DB Cargo	DB Cargo	English Welsh & Scottish Railway	
66126	-	DB Cargo	Direct Rail Services	English Welsh & Scottish Railway	
66127	-	DB Cargo	DB Cargo	English Welsh & Scottish Railway	
66128	-	DB Cargo	DB Cargo	DB Cargo	
66129	-	DB Cargo	DB Cargo	English Welsh & Scottish Railway	
66130	-	DB Cargo	DB Cargo	DB Cargo	
66131	-	DB Cargo	DB Cargo	DB Cargo	
66132*	66785				
66133	-	DB Cargo	DB Cargo	English Welsh & Scottish Railway	
66134	-	DB Cargo	DB Cargo	DB Cargo	
66135	-	DB Cargo	DB Cargo	DB Cargo	
66136	-	DB Cargo	DB Cargo	DB Cargo	
66137	-	DB Cargo	DB Cargo	DB Cargo	
66138	-	DB Cargo	DB Cargo	English Welsh & Scottish Railway	
66139	-	DB Cargo	DB Cargo	English Welsh & Scottish Railway	
66140	-	DB Cargo	DB Cargo	English Welsh & Scottish Railway	
66141*	66786				
66142	-	DB Cargo	DB Cargo	Maritime blue	*Maritime Intermodal Three*
66143	-	DB Cargo	DB Cargo	English Welsh & Scottish Railway	
66144	-	DB Cargo	DB Cargo	English Welsh & Scottish Railway	
66145	-	DB Cargo	DB Cargo	English Welsh & Scottish Railway	
66146	92 70 0 066146-6	DB Cargo	DB Polska	English Welsh & Scottish Railway	
66147	-	DB Cargo	DB Cargo	English Welsh & Scottish Railway	
66148	-	DB Cargo	DB Cargo	English Welsh & Scottish Railway	
66149	-	DB Cargo	DB Cargo	DB Cargo	
66150	-	DB Cargo	DB Cargo	DB Cargo	
66151	-	DB Cargo	DB Cargo	English Welsh & Scottish Railway	
66152	-	DB Cargo	DB Cargo	DB Schenker	*Derek Holmes Railway Operator*
66153	92 70 0 066153-2	DB Cargo	DB Polska	English Welsh & Scottish Railway	

Loco	Rebuilt from	Owner	Operator	Livery	Name
66154	-	DB Cargo	DB Cargo	English Welsh & Scottish Railway	
66155	-	DB Cargo	DB Cargo	English Welsh & Scottish Railway	
66156	-	DB Cargo	DB Cargo	English Welsh & Scottish Railway	
66157	92 70 0 066157-3	DB Cargo	DB Polska	English Welsh & Scottish Railway	
66158	-	DB Cargo	DB Cargo	English Welsh & Scottish Railway	
66159	92 70 0 066159-9	DB Cargo	DB Polska	English Welsh & Scottish Railway	
66160	-	DB Cargo	DB Cargo	English Welsh & Scottish Railway	
66161	-	DB Cargo	DB Cargo	English Welsh & Scottish Railway	
66162	-	DB Cargo	DB Cargo	Maritime Blue	Maritime Intermodal Five
66163	92 70 0 066163-1	DB Cargo	DB Polska	DB European	
66164	-	DB Cargo	DB Cargo	English Welsh & Scottish Railway	
66165	-	DB Cargo	DB Cargo	DB Cargo	
66166	92 70 0 066166-4	DB Cargo	DB Polska	English Welsh & Scottish Railway	
66167	-	DB Cargo	DB Cargo	DB Cargo	
66168	-	DB Cargo	DB Cargo	English Welsh & Scottish Railway	
66169	-	DB Cargo	DB Cargo	English Welsh & Scottish Railway	
66170	-	DB Cargo	DB Cargo	English Welsh & Scottish Railway	
66171	-	DB Cargo	DB Cargo	English Welsh & Scottish Railway	
66172	-	DB Cargo	DB Cargo	English Welsh & Scottish Railway	PAUL MELLANY
66173	92 70 0 066173-0	DB Cargo	DB Polska	English Welsh & Scottish Railway	
66174	-	DB Cargo	DB Cargo	English Welsh & Scottish Railway	
66175	-	DB Cargo	DB Cargo	DB Cargo	
66176	-	DB Cargo	DB Cargo	English Welsh & Scottish Railway	
66177	-	DB Cargo	DB Cargo	English Welsh & Scottish Railway	
66178	92 70 0 066178-9	DB Cargo	DB Polska	DB European	
66179	92 70 0 066179-7	DB Cargo	Euro Cargo Rail	English Welsh & Scottish Railway	
66180	92 70 0 066180-5	DB Cargo	DB Polska	English Welsh & Scottish Railway	
66181	-	DB Cargo	DB Cargo	English Welsh & Scottish Railway	
66182	-	DB Cargo	DB Cargo	DB Cargo	
66183	-	DB Cargo	DB Cargo	English Welsh & Scottish Railway	
66184*	66787				
66185	-	DB Cargo	DB Cargo	DB Cargo	DP WORLD London Gateway
66186	-	DB Cargo	DB Cargo	English Welsh & Scottish Railway	
66187	-	DB Cargo	DB Cargo	English Welsh & Scottish Railway	
66188	-	DB Cargo	DB Cargo	English Welsh & Scottish Railway	
66189	92 70 0 066189-6	DB Cargo	DB Polska	DB European	
66190	92 70 0 066190-4	DB Cargo	Euro Cargo Rail	English Welsh & Scottish Railway	
66191	92 70 0 066191-2	DB Cargo	Euro Cargo Rail	English Welsh & Scottish Railway	
66192	-	DB Cargo	DB Cargo	DB Cargo	
66193	92 70 0 066193-8	DB Cargo	Euro Cargo Rail	English Welsh & Scottish Railway	
66194	-	DB Cargo	Euro Cargo Rail	English Welsh & Scottish Railway	
66195	92 70 0 066195-3	DB Cargo	Euro Cargo Rail	English Welsh & Scottish Railway	
66196	92 70 0 066196-1	DB Cargo	DB Polska	English Welsh & Scottish Railway	
66197	-	DB Cargo	DB Cargo	English Welsh & Scottish Railway	
66198	-	DB Cargo	DB Cargo	English Welsh & Scottish Railway	
66199	-	DB Cargo	DB Cargo	English Welsh & Scottish Railway	
66200	-	DB Cargo	DB Cargo	English Welsh & Scottish Railway	
66201	92 70 0 066201-9	DB Cargo	Euro Cargo Rail	English Welsh & Scottish Railway	
66202	92 70 0 066202-7	DB Cargo	Euro Cargo Rail	English Welsh & Scottish Railway	
66203	92 70 0 066203-5	DB Cargo	Euro Cargo Rail	English Welsh & Scottish Railway	
66204	92 70 0 066204-3	DB Cargo	Euro Cargo Rail	English Welsh & Scottish Railway	
66205	92 70 0 066205-1	DB Cargo	Euro Cargo Rail	English Welsh & Scottish Railway	
66206	-	DB Cargo	DB Cargo	DB Cargo	
66207	-	DB Cargo	DB Cargo	English Welsh & Scottish Railway	
66208	92 70 0 066208-4	DB Cargo	Euro Cargo Rail	English Welsh & Scottish Railway	
66209	92 70 0 066209-2	DB Cargo	Euro Cargo Rail	English Welsh & Scottish Railway	
66210	92 70 0 066210-0	DB Cargo	Euro Cargo Rail	English Welsh & Scottish Railway	
66211	92 70 0 066211-8	DB Cargo	Euro Cargo Rail	English Welsh & Scottish Railway	
66212	92 70 0 066212-6	DB Cargo	Euro Cargo Rail	English Welsh & Scottish Railway	

Loco	Rebuilt from	Owner	Operator	Livery	Name
66213	92 70 0 066213-4	DB Cargo	Euro Cargo Rail	English Welsh & Scottish Railway	
66214	92 70 0 066214-2	DB Cargo	Euro Cargo Rail	English Welsh & Scottish Railway	
66215	92 70 0 066215-9	DB Cargo	Euro Cargo Rail	English Welsh & Scottish Railway	
66216	92 70 0 066216-7	DB Cargo	Euro Cargo Rail	English Welsh & Scottish Railway	
66217	92 70 0 066217-5	DB Cargo	Euro Cargo Rail	English Welsh & Scottish Railway	
66218	92 70 0 066218-3	DB Cargo	Euro Cargo Rail	English Welsh & Scottish Railway	
66219	92 70 0 066219-1	DB Cargo	Euro Cargo Rail	English Welsh & Scottish Railway	
66220	92 70 0 066220-9	DB Cargo	DB Polska	DB European	
66221	-	DB Cargo	Euro Cargo Rail	English Welsh & Scottish Railway	
66222	92 70 0 066222-5	DB Cargo	Euro Cargo Rail	English Welsh & Scottish Railway	
66223	92 70 0 066223-3	DB Cargo	Euro Cargo Rail	English Welsh & Scottish Railway	
66224	92 70 0 066224-1	DB Cargo	Euro Cargo Rail	English Welsh & Scottish Railway	
66225	92 70 0 066225-8	DB Cargo	Euro Cargo Rail	English Welsh & Scottish Railway	
66226	92 70 0 066226-6	DB Cargo	Euro Cargo Rail	English Welsh & Scottish Railway	
66227	92 70 0 066227-4	DB Cargo	DB Polska	DB European	
66228	92 70 0 066228-2	DB Cargo	Euro Cargo Rail	English Welsh & Scottish Railway	
66229	92 70 0 066229-0	DB Cargo	Euro Cargo Rail	English Welsh & Scottish Railway	
66230	-	DB Cargo	DB Cargo	DB Cargo	
66231	92 70 0 066231-6	DB Cargo	Euro Cargo Rail	English Welsh & Scottish Railway	
66232	92 70 0 066232-4	DB Cargo	Euro Cargo Rail	English Welsh & Scottish Railway	
66233	92 70 0 066233-2	DB Cargo	Euro Cargo Rail	English Welsh & Scottish Railway	
66234	92 70 0 066234-0	DB Cargo	Euro Cargo Rail	English Welsh & Scottish Railway	
66235	92 70 0 066235-7	DB Cargo	Euro Cargo Rail	English Welsh & Scottish Railway	
66236	92 70 0 066236-5	DB Cargo	Euro Cargo Rail	English Welsh & Scottish Railway	
66237	92 70 0 066237-3	DB Cargo	DB Polska	English Welsh & Scottish Railway	
66238*	66788				
66239	92 70 0 066239-9	DB Cargo	Euro Cargo Rail	English Welsh & Scottish Railway	
66240	92 70 0 066240-7	DB Cargo	Euro Cargo Rail	English Welsh & Scottish Railway	
66241	92 70 0 066241-5	DB Cargo	Euro Cargo Rail	English Welsh & Scottish Railway	
66242	92 70 0 066242-3	DB Cargo	Euro Cargo Rail	English Welsh & Scottish Railway	
66243	92 70 0 066243-1	DB Cargo	Euro Cargo Rail	English Welsh & Scottish Railway	
66244	92 70 0 066244-9	DB Cargo	Euro Cargo Rail	English Welsh & Scottish Railway	
66245	92 70 0 066245-6	DB Cargo	Euro Cargo Rail	English Welsh & Scottish Railway	
66246	92 70 0 066246-4	DB Cargo	Euro Cargo Rail	English Welsh & Scottish Railway	
66247	92 70 0 066247-2	DB Cargo	Euro Cargo Rail	English Welsh & Scottish Railway	
66248	92 70 0 066248-9	DB Cargo	DB Polska	DB European	
66249	92 70 0 066249-8	DB Cargo	Euro Cargo Rail	English Welsh & Scottish Railway	
66250*	66789				

* 66008/016/046/058/081/132/141/184/238/250 now operated by GB Railfreight as 66780–789.

Class 66/3 Locos ordered by Fastline Freight (Now with Direct Rail Services)

Loco	Later numbers	Owner	Operator	Livery	Name
66301	-	Beacon Rail	Direct Rail Services	Direct Rail Services plain blue	*Kingmoor TMD*
66302	-	Beacon Rail	Direct Rail Services	Direct Rail Services plain blue	*Endeavour*
66303	-	Beacon Rail	Direct Rail Services	Direct Rail Services plain blue	
66304	-	Beacon Rail	Direct Rail Services	Direct Rail Services plain blue	
66305	-	Beacon Rail	Direct Rail Services	Direct Rail Services plain blue	

Notes: Ordered and operated by Fastline Freight 6/08–7/10

Class 66/4 Locos ordered by Direct Rail Services (now with other operators)

Loco	Later numbers	Owner	Previous operators	Livery	Name
66401*	66733				
66402*	66734				
66403*	66735				
66404*	66736				
66405*	66737				
66406*	66841, 66742				

Loco	Later numbers	Owner	Previous operators	Livery	Name
66407*	66842, 66743				
66408*	66843, 66744				
66409*	66844, 66745				
66410*	66845, 66746				
66411	66013	Macquarie Group	Freightliner Poland	Freightliner Powerhaul Poland	
66412	66015	Macquarie Group	Freightliner Poland	Freightliner Powerhaul Poland	
66413	-	Macquarie Group	Freightliner	Genesee & Wyoming lighter orange	*Lest We Forget*
66414	-	Macquarie Group	Freightliner	Freightliner Powerhaul	
66415	-	Macquarie Group	Freightliner	Genesee & Wyoming darker orange	
66416	-	Macquarie Group	Freightliner	Freightliner Powerhaul	
66417	66014	Macquarie Group	Freightliner Poland	Freightliner Powerhaul Poland	
66418	-	Macquarie Group	Freightliner	Freightliner Powerhaul	*PATRIOT – IN MEMORY OF FALLEN RAILWAY EMPLOYEES*
66419	-	Macquarie Group	Freightliner	Genesee & Wyoming darker orange	
66420	-	Macquarie Group	Freightliner	Freightliner Powerhaul	

* 66401–410 now operated by GB Railfreight as 66733–745 (66734 is scrapped).

Class 66/4 Locos ordered by Direct Rail Services

Loco	Later numbers	Owner	Operator	Livery	Name
66421	-	Macquarie Group	Direct Rail Services	Direct Rail Services plain blue	*Gresty Bridge TMD*
66422	-	Macquarie Group	Direct Rail Services	Direct Rail Services plain blue	
66423	-	Macquarie Group	Direct Rail Services	Direct Rail Services plain blue	
66424	-	Macquarie Group	Direct Rail Services	Direct Rail Services plain blue	
66425	-	Macquarie Group	Direct Rail Services	Direct Rail Services plain blue	
66426	-	Macquarie Group	Direct Rail Services	Direct Rail Services plain blue	
66427	-	Macquarie Group	Direct Rail Services	Direct Rail Services plain blue	
66428	-	Macquarie Group	Direct Rail Services	Direct Rail Services plain blue	*Carlisle Eden Mind*
66429	-	Macquarie Group	Direct Rail Services	Direct Rail Services plain blue	
66430	-	Macquarie Group	Direct Rail Services	Direct Rail Services plain blue	
66431	-	Macquarie Group	Direct Rail Services	Direct Rail Services plain blue	
66432	-	Macquarie Group	Direct Rail Services	Direct Rail Services plain blue	
66433	-	Macquarie Group	Direct Rail Services	Direct Rail Services plain blue	
66434	-	Macquarie Group	Direct Rail Services	Direct Rail Services plain blue	

Class 66/5 Locos ordered by Freightliner (some now with Freightliner Poland, Colas Railfreight or GB Railfreight)

Loco	Later numbers	Owner	Operator	Livery	Name
66501	-	Porterbrook	Freightliner	Freightliner	*Japan 2001*
66502	-	Porterbrook	Freightliner	Freightliner	*Basford Hall Centenary 2001*
66503	-	Porterbrook	Freightliner	Freightliner	*The RAILWAY MAGAZINE*
66504	-	Porterbrook	Freightliner	Freightliner Powerhaul	
66505	-	Porterbrook	Freightliner	Freightliner	
66506	-	Eversholt	Freightliner	Freightliner	*Crewe Regeneration*
66507	-	Eversholt	Freightliner	Freightliner	
66508	-	Eversholt	Freightliner	Freightliner	
66509	-	Eversholt	Freightliner	Freightliner	
66510	-	Eversholt	Freightliner	Freightliner	
66511	-	Eversholt	Freightliner	Freightliner	
66512	-	Eversholt	Freightliner	Freightliner	
66513	-	Eversholt	Freightliner	Freightliner	
66514	-	Eversholt	Freightliner	Freightliner	
66515	-	Eversholt	Freightliner	Freightliner	
66516	-	Eversholt	Freightliner	Freightliner	
66517	-	Eversholt	Freightliner	Freightliner	

Loco	Later numbers	Owner	Operator	Livery	Name
66518	-	Eversholt	Freightliner	Freightliner	
66519	-	Eversholt	Freightliner	Freightliner	
66520	-	Eversholt	Freightliner	Freightliner	
66521	-				
66522	-	Eversholt	Freightliner	Freightliner	
66523	-	Eversholt	Freightliner	Freightliner	
66524	-	Eversholt	Freightliner	Freightliner	
66525	-	Eversholt	Freightliner	Freightliner	
66526	-	Eversholt	Freightliner	Freightliner	*Driver Steve Dunn (George)*
66527	66016	Eversholt	Freightliner Poland	Freightliner	
66528	-	Porterbrook	Freightliner	Freightliner Powerhaul	*Madge Elliot MBE Borders Railway Opening 2015*
66529	-	Porterbrook	Freightliner	Freightliner	
66530	66017	Porterbrook	Freightliner Poland	Freightliner	
66531	-	Porterbrook	Freightliner	Freightliner	
66532	-	Porterbrook	Freightliner	Freightliner	*P&O Nedlloyd Atlas*
66533	-	Porterbrook	Freightliner	Freightliner	*Hanjin Express/ Senator Express*
66534	-	Porterbrook	Freightliner	Freightliner	*OOCL Express*
66535	66018	Porterbrook	Freightliner Poland	Freightliner	
66536	-	Porterbrook	Freightliner	Freightliner	
66537	-	Porterbrook	Freightliner	Freightliner	
66538	-	Eversholt	Freightliner	Freightliner	
66539	-	Eversholt	Freightliner	Freightliner	
66540	-	Eversholt	Freightliner	Freightliner	*Ruby*
66541	-	Eversholt	Freightliner	Freightliner	
66542	-	Eversholt	Freightliner	Freightliner	
66543	-	Eversholt	Freightliner	Freightliner	
66544	-	Eversholt	Freightliner	Freightliner	
66545	-	Porterbrook	Freightliner	Freightliner	
66546	-	Porterbrook	Freightliner	Freightliner	
66547	-	Porterbrook	Freightliner	Freightliner	
66548	-	Porterbrook	Freightliner	Freightliner	
66549	-	Porterbrook	Freightliner	Freightliner	
66550	-	Porterbrook	Freightliner	Freightliner	
66551	-	Porterbrook	Freightliner	Freightliner	
66552	-	Porterbrook	Freightliner	Freightliner	*Maltby Raider*
66553	-	Porterbrook	Freightliner	Freightliner	
66554	-	Eversholt	Freightliner	Freightliner	
66555	-	Eversholt	Freightliner	Freightliner	
66556	-	Eversholt	Freightliner	Freightliner	
66557	-	Eversholt	Freightliner	Freightliner	
66558	-	Eversholt	Freightliner	Freightliner	
66559	-	Eversholt	Freightliner	Freightliner	
66560	-	Eversholt	Freightliner	Freightliner	
66561	-	Eversholt	Freightliner	Freightliner	
66562	-	Eversholt	Freightliner	Freightliner	
66563	-	Eversholt	Freightliner	Freightliner	
66564	-	Eversholt	Freightliner	Freightliner	
66565	-	Eversholt	Freightliner	Freightliner	
66566	-	Eversholt	Freightliner	Freightliner	
66567	-	Eversholt	Freightliner	Freightliner	
66568	-	Eversholt	Freightliner	Freightliner	
66569	-	Eversholt	Freightliner	Freightliner	
66570	-	Eversholt	Freightliner	Freightliner	
66571	-	Eversholt	Freightliner	Freightliner	
66572	-	Eversholt	Freightliner	Freightliner	
66573*	66846				
66574*	66847				
66575*	66848				

Loco	Later numbers	Owner	Operator	Livery	Name
66576*	66849				
66577*	66850				
66578*	66738				
66579*	66739				
66580*	66740				
66581*	66741				
66582	66009	Eversholt	Freightliner Poland	Freightliner	
66583	66010	Eversholt	Freightliner Poland	Freightliner	
66584	66011	Eversholt	Freightliner Poland	Freightliner	
66585	-	Macquarie Group	Freightliner	Freightliner	The Drax Flyer
66586	66008	Macquarie Group	Freightliner Poland	Freightliner	
66587	-	Macquarie Group	Freightliner	ONE Pink	AS ONE, WE CAN
66588	-	Macquarie Group	Freightliner	Freightliner	
66589	-	Macquarie Group	Freightliner	Freightliner	
66590	-	Macquarie Group	Freightliner	Freightliner	
66591	-	Macquarie Group	Freightliner	Freightliner	
66592	-	Macquarie Group	Freightliner	Freightliner	Johnson Stevens Agencies
66593	-	Macquarie Group	Freightliner	Freightliner	3MG MERSEY MULTIMODAL GATEWAY
66594	-	Macquarie Group	Freightliner	Freightliner	NYK Spirit of Kyoto
66595	-	Beacon Rail	Freightliner Poland	Freightliner	
66596	-	Beacon Rail	Freightliner	Freightliner	
66597	-	Beacon Rail	Freightliner	Freightliner	Viridor
66598	-	Beacon Rail	Freightliner	Freightliner	
66599	-	Beacon Rail	Freightliner	Freightliner	

* Locos have since moved to other operators and their new numbers are detailed. They also appear in their new operators' tables.

Class 66/6 Regeared locos ordered by Freightliner (some now with Freightliner Poland)

Loco	Later numbers	Owner	Operator	Livery	Name
66601		Porterbrook	Freightliner	Freightliner	The Hope Valley
66602	-	Porterbrook	Freightliner	Freightliner	
66603	-	Porterbrook	Freightliner	Freightliner	
66604	-	Porterbrook	Freightliner	Freightliner	
66605	-	Porterbrook	Freightliner	Freightliner	
66606	-	Porterbrook	Freightliner	Freightliner	
66607	-	Porterbrook	Freightliner	Freightliner	
66608	66603	Porterbrook	Freightliner Poland	Freightliner	
66609	66605	Porterbrook	Freightliner Poland	Freightliner	
66610	-	Porterbrook	Freightliner	Freightliner	
66611	66604	Porterbrook	Freightliner Poland	Freightliner	
66612	66606	Porterbrook	Freightliner Poland	Freightliner	
66613	-	Eversholt	Freightliner	Freightliner	
66614	-	Eversholt	Freightliner	Freightliner	1916 POPPY 2016
66615	-	Eversholt	Freightliner	Freightliner	
66616	-	Eversholt	Freightliner	Freightliner	
66617	-	Eversholt	Freightliner	Freightliner	
66618	-	Eversholt	Freightliner	Freightliner	Railways Illustrated Annual Photographic Awards Alan Barnes
66619	-	Eversholt	Freightliner	Freightliner	Derek W. Johnson MBE
66620	-	Eversholt	Freightliner	Freightliner	
66621	-	Eversholt	Freightliner	Freightliner	
66622	-	Eversholt	Freightliner	Freightliner	
66623	-	Macquarie Group	Freightliner	Genesee & Wyoming darker orange	
66624	66602	Macquarie Group	Freightliner Poland	Freightliner	
66625	66601	Macquarie Group	Freightliner Poland	Freightliner	

Class 66/7 Locos ordered or acquired by GB Railfreight

Loco	Previous numbers	Owner	Operator	Livery	Name
66701	-	Eversholt	GB Railfreight	GBRf version 1	
66702	-	Eversholt	GB Railfreight	GBRf version 2	Blue Lightning
66703	-	Eversholt	GB Railfreight	GBRf version 2	Doncaster PSB 1981–2002
66704	-	Eversholt	GB Railfreight	GBRf version 2	Colchester Power Signalbox
66705	-	Eversholt	GB Railfreight	GBRf version 2	Golden Jubilee
66706	-	Eversholt	GB Railfreight	GBRf version 2	Nene Valley
66707	-	Eversholt	GB Railfreight	GBRf version 2	Sir Sam Fay
66708	-	Eversholt	GB Railfreight	GBRf version 2	Jayne
66709	-	Eversholt	GB Railfreight	Medite Shipping company	Sorrento
66710	-	Eversholt	GB Railfreight	GBRf version 2	Phil Packer BRIT
66711	-	Eversholt	GB Railfreight	Aggregates industries	Sence
66712	-	Eversholt	GB Railfreight	GBRf version 2	Peterborough Power Signalbox
66713	-	Eversholt	GB Railfreight	GBRf version 2	Forest City
66714	-	Eversholt	GB Railfreight	GBRf version 2	Cromer Lifeboats
66715	-	Eversholt	GB Railfreight	GBRf version 2	VALOUR
66716	-	Eversholt	GB Railfreight	GBRf version 2	LOCOMOTIVE & CARRIAGE INSTITUTION CENTENARY 1911–2011
66717	-	Eversholt	GB Railfreight	GBRf version 2	Good Old Boy
66718	-	Eversholt	GB Railfreight	London Underground black	Sir Peter Hendy CBE
66719	-	Eversholt	GB Railfreight	GBRf version 2	METRO-LAND
66720	-	Eversholt	GB Railfreight	Artistic	
66721	-	Eversholt	GB Railfreight	London Underground white	Harry Beck
66722	-	Eversholt	GB Railfreight	GBRf version 2	Sir Edward Watkin
66723	-	Eversholt	GB Railfreight	GBRf with branding	Chinook
66724	-	Eversholt	GB Railfreight	GBRf version 2	Drax Power Station
66725	-	Eversholt	GB Railfreight	GBRf with branding	SUNDERLAND
66726	-	Eversholt	GB Railfreight	GBRf version 2	SHEFFIELD WEDNESDAY
66727	-	Eversholt	GB Railfreight	Maritime	Maritime One
66728	-	Eversholt	GB Railfreight	GBRf version 2	Institution of Railway Operators
66729	-	Eversholt	GB Railfreight	GBRf version 2	DERBY COUNTY
66730	-	Eversholt	GB Railfreight	GBRf version 2	Whitemoor
66731	-	Eversholt	GB Railfreight	GBRf version 2	InterhubGB
66732	-	Eversholt	GB Railfreight	GBRf version 2	GBRF The First Decade 1999–2009 John Smith MD
66733	66401	Porterbrook	GB Railfreight	GBRf version 2	Cambridge PSB
66734	66402				
66735	66403	Porterbrook	GB Railfreight	GBRf version 2	PETERBOROUGH UNITED
66736	66404	Porterbrook	GB Railfreight	GBRf version 2	WOLVERHAMPTON WANDERERS
66737	66405	Porterbrook	GB Railfreight	GBRf version 2	Lesia
66738	66578	Beacon Rail	GB Railfreight	GBRf version 2	HUDDERSFIELD TOWN
66739	66579	Beacon Rail	GB Railfreight	GBRf version 2	Bluebell Railway
66740	66580	Beacon Rail	GB Railfreight	GBRf version 2	Sarah
66741	66581	Beacon Rail	GB Railfreight	GBRf version 2	Swanage Railway
66742	66406, 66841	Beacon Rail	GB Railfreight	GBRf version 2	ABP Port of Immingham Centenary 1912–2012
66743	66407, 66842	Beacon Rail	GB Railfreight	Royal Scotsman	
66744	66408, 66843	Beacon Rail	GB Railfreight	GBRf version 2	Crossrail
66745	66409, 66844	Beacon Rail	GB Railfreight	GBRf version 2	Modern Railways The first 50 years
66746	66410, 66845	Beacon Rail	GB Railfreight	Royal Scotsman	
66747	20078968-007	GB Railfreight	GB Railfreight	Newell & Wright	Made in Sheffield
66748	20078968-004	GB Railfreight	GB Railfreight	GBRf version 2	West Burton 50
66749	20078968-006	GB Railfreight	GB Railfreight	GBRf version 2	
66750	20038513-01	Beacon Rail	GB Railfreight	GBRf version 2	Bristol Panel Signal Box

Loco	Previous numbers	Owner	Operator	Livery	Name
66751	20038513-04	Beacon Rail	GB Railfreight	GBRf version 2	*Inspirational Delivered Hitachi Rail Europe*
66752	-	GB Railfreight	GB Railfreight	GBRf version 2	*The Hoosier State*
66753	-	GB Railfreight	GB Railfreight	GBRf version 2	*EMD Roberts Road*
66754	-	GB Railfreight	GB Railfreight	GBRf version 2	*Northampton Saints*
66755	-	GB Railfreight	GB Railfreight	GBRf version 2	*Tony Berkeley OBE RFG Chairman 1997–2018*
66756	-	GB Railfreight	GB Railfreight	GBRf version 2	*Royal Corps of Signals*
66757	-	GB Railfreight	GB Railfreight	GBRf version 2	*West Somerset Railway*
66758	-	GB Railfreight	GB Railfreight	GBRf version 2	*The Pavior*
66759	-	GB Railfreight	GB Railfreight	GBRf version 2	*Chippy*
66760	-	GB Railfreight	GB Railfreight	GBRf version 2	*David Gordon Harris*
66761	-	GB Railfreight	GB Railfreight	GBRf version 2	*Wensleydale Railway Association 25 Years 1990–2015*
66762	-	GB Railfreight	GB Railfreight	GBRf version 2	
66763	-	GB Railfreight	GB Railfreight	GBRf version 2	*Severn Valley Railway*
66764	-	GB Railfreight	GB Railfreight ·	GBRf version 2	
66765	-	GB Railfreight	GB Railfreight	GBRf version 2	
66766	-	GB Railfreight	GB Railfreight	GBRf version 2	
66767	-	GB Railfreight	GB Railfreight	GBRf version 2	
66768	-	GB Railfreight	GB Railfreight	GBRf version 2	
66769	-	GB Railfreight	GB Railfreight	GBRf version 2	
66770	-	GB Railfreight	GB Railfreight	GBRf version 2	
66771	-	GB Railfreight	GB Railfreight	GBRf version 2	*Amanda*
66772	-	GB Railfreight	GB Railfreight	GBRf version 2	*Maria*
66773	-	GB Railfreight	GB Railfreight	GBRf Pride	*Pride in GB Railfreight*
66774	-	GB Railfreight	GB Railfreight	GBRf version 2	
66775	-	GB Railfreight	GB Railfreight	GBRf with branding	*HMS Argyll*
66776	-	GB Railfreight	GB Railfreight	GBRf version 2	*Joanne*
66777	-	GB Railfreight	GB Railfreight	GBRf version 2	*Annette*
66778	-	GB Railfreight	GB Railfreight	GBRf version 2	*Cambois Depot 25 Years*
66779	-	GB Railfreight	GB Railfreight	British Railways green	*EVENING STAR*
66780	66008	GB Railfreight	GB Railfreight	Cemex	*The Cemex Express*
66781	66016	GB Railfreight	GB Railfreight	GBRf version 2	
66782	66046	GB Railfreight	GB Railfreight	GBRf with branding	
66783	66058	GB Railfreight	GB Railfreight	Biffa red	*The Flying Dustman*
66784	66081	GB Railfreight	GB Railfreight	GBRf version 2	*Keighley & Worth Valley Railway 50th Anniversary 1968–2018*
66785	66132	GB Railfreight	GB Railfreight	GBRf version 2	
66786	66141	GB Railfreight	GB Railfreight	GBRf version 2	
66787	66184	GB Railfreight	GB Railfreight	GBRf version 2	
66788	66238	GB Railfreight	GB Railfreight	GBRf version 2	*LOCOMOTION 15*
66789	66250	GB Railfreight	GB Railfreight	British Rail 'Large Logo' blue	*British Rail 1948–1997*
66790	T66403	Beacon Rail	GB Railfreight	Rush Rail Blue	
66791	T66404	Beacon Rail	GB Railfreight	Rush Rail Blue	
66792	T66405	Beacon Rail	GB Railfreight	Rush Rail Black	

Note: 66734 is scrapped.

Class 66/8: Locos acquired by Colas Rail Freight

Loco	Previous numbers	Owner	Operator	Livery	All names carried
66846	66573	Beacon Rail	Colas Rail Freight	Colas Rail Freight	*Terry Baker*
66847	66574	Beacon Rail	Colas Rail Freight	Colas Rail Freight	
66848	66575	Beacon Rail	Colas Rail Freight	Colas Rail Freight	
66849	66576	Beacon Rail	Colas Rail Freight	Colas Rail Freight	*Wylam Dilly*
66850	66577	Beacon Rail	Colas Rail Freight	Colas Rail Freight	*David Maidment OBE*

Class 66/9 Low-emission locos ordered by Freightliner (some now with Freightliner Poland)

Loco	Previous numbers	Owner	Operator	Livery	All names carried
66951	-	Eversholt	Freightliner	Freightliner	
66952	-	Eversholt	Freightliner	Freightliner	
66953	-	Beacon Rail	Freightliner	Freightliner	
66954	-	Beacon Rail	Freightliner Poland	Freightliner	
66955	-	Beacon Rail	Freightliner	Freightliner	
66956	-	Beacon Rail	Freightliner	Freightliner	
66957	-	Beacon Rail	Freightliner	Freightliner	Stephenson Locomotive Society 1909–2009

Fleet list 4: Class 67

Class 67 Locos ordered by English Welsh & Scottish Railway (Now DB Cargo). Some now with Colas Rail Freight

Loco	Previous numbers	Owner	Operator	Livery	Name
67001	-	DB Cargo	DB Cargo	Arriva unbranded	
67002	-	DB Cargo	DB Cargo	Arriva unbranded	
67003	-	DB Cargo	DB Cargo	Arriva unbranded	
67004	-	DB Cargo	DB Cargo	DB Cargo	
67005	-	DB Cargo	DB Cargo	Royal Train version 3	Queen's Messenger
67006	-	DB Cargo	DB Cargo	Royal Train version 3	Royal Sovereign
67007	-	DB Cargo	DB Cargo	English Welsh & Scottish Railway	
67008	-	DB Cargo	DB Cargo	English Welsh & Scottish Railway	
67009	-	DB Cargo	DB Cargo	English Welsh & Scottish Railway	
67010	-	DB Cargo	DB Cargo	DB Cargo	
67011	-	DB Cargo	DB Cargo	English Welsh & Scottish Railway	
67012	-	DB Cargo	DB Cargo	Wrexham & Shropshire silver	
67013	-	DB Cargo	DB Cargo	DB Cargo	
67014	-	DB Cargo	DB Cargo	Wrexham & Shropshire silver	
67015	-	DB Cargo	DB Cargo	DB Cargo	
67016	-	DB Cargo	DB Cargo	English Welsh & Scottish Railway	
67017	-	DB Cargo	DB Cargo	English Welsh & Scottish Railway	
67018	-	DB Cargo	DB Cargo	DB Schenker	Keith Heller
67019	-	DB Cargo	DB Cargo	English Welsh & Scottish Railway	
67020	-	DB Cargo	DB Cargo	English Welsh & Scottish Railway	
67021	-	DB Cargo	DB Cargo	Pullman umber and cream	
67022	-	DB Cargo	DB Cargo	English Welsh & Scottish Railway	
67023	-	Beacon Rail	Colas Rail Freight	Colas Rail Freight	Stella
67024	-	DB Cargo	DB Cargo	Pullman umber and cream	
67025	-	DB Cargo	DB Cargo	English Welsh & Scottish Railway	Western Star
67026	-	DB Cargo	DB Cargo	Diamond Jubilee silver	Diamond Jubilee
67027	-	Beacon Rail	Colas Rail Freight	Colas Rail Freight	Charlotte
67028	-	DB Cargo	DB Cargo	DB Cargo	
67029	-	DB Cargo	DB Cargo	DB Managers' Trains silver	Royal Diamond
67030	-	DB Cargo	DB Cargo	English Welsh & Scottish Railway	

Fleet list 5: Class 68

Locos ordered by Direct Rail Services

Loco		Owner	Operator	Livery	Name
68001	-	Beacon Rail	Direct Rail Services	Revised Direct Rail Services Compass	Evolution
68002	-	Beacon Rail	Direct Rail Services	Revised Direct Rail Services Compass	Intrepid
68003	-	Beacon Rail	Direct Rail Services	Revised Direct Rail Services Compass	Astute
68004	-	Beacon Rail	Direct Rail Services	Revised Direct Rail Services Compass	Rapid
68005	-	Beacon Rail	Direct Rail Services	Revised Direct Rail Services Compass	Defiant
68006	-	Beacon Rail	ScotRail*	ScotRail Saltire	Daring
68007	-	Beacon Rail	ScotRail*	ScotRail Saltire	Valiant
68008	-	Beacon Rail	Chiltern Railways*	Revised Direct Rail Services Compass	Avenger
68009	-	Beacon Rail	Chiltern Railways*	Revised Direct Rail Services Compass	Titan
68010	-	Beacon Rail	Chiltern Railways*	Chiltern Railways silver	Oxford Flyer
68011	-	Beacon Rail	Chiltern Railways*	Chiltern Railways silver	
68012	-	Beacon Rail	Chiltern Railways*	Chiltern Railways silver	
68013	-	Beacon Rail	Chiltern Railways*	Chiltern Railways silver	
68014	-	Beacon Rail	Chiltern Railways*	Chiltern Railways silver	
68015	-	Beacon Rail	Chiltern Railways*	Chiltern Railways silver	
68016	-	Beacon Rail	Direct Rail Services	Revised Direct Rail Services Compass	Fearless
68017	-	Beacon Rail	Direct Rail Services	Revised Direct Rail Services Compass	Hornet
68018	-	Beacon Rail	Trans Pennine Express*	Revised Direct Rail Services Compass	Vigilant
68019	-	Beacon Rail	Trans Pennine Express*	Trans Pennine Express	Brutus
68020	-	Beacon Rail	Trans Pennine Express*	Trans Pennine Express	Reliance
68021	-	Beacon Rail	Trans Pennine Express*	Trans Pennine Express	Tireless
68022	-	Beacon Rail	Trans Pennine Express*	Trans Pennine Express	Resolution
68023	-	Beacon Rail	Trans Pennine Express*	Trans Pennine Express	Achilles
68024	-	Beacon Rail	Trans Pennine Express*	Trans Pennine Express	Centaur
68025	-	Beacon Rail	Trans Pennine Express*	Trans Pennine Express	Superb
68026	-	Beacon Rail	Trans Pennine Express*	Trans Pennine Express	Enterprise
68027	-	Beacon Rail	Trans Pennine Express*	Trans Pennine Express	Splendid
68028	-	Beacon Rail	Trans Pennine Express*	Trans Pennine Express	Lord President
68029	-	Beacon Rail	Trans Pennine Express*	Trans Pennine Express	Courageous
68030	-	Beacon Rail	Trans Pennine Express*	Trans Pennine Express	Black Douglas
68031	-	Beacon Rail	Trans Pennine Express*	Trans Pennine Express	Felix
68032	-	Beacon Rail	Trans Pennine Express*	Trans Pennine Express	Destroyer
68033	-	Direct Rail Services	Direct Rail Services	Revised Direct Rail Services Compass	
68034	-	Direct Rail Services	Direct Rail Services	Revised Direct Rail Services Compass	

* locos' principal user, but will be used by DRS for general duties when spare

Fleet list 6: Class 69

Locos ordered by GB Railfreight, rebuilt using Class 56 donor bodyshells

Loco	Previous numbers	Owner	Operator	Livery	Name
69001	56057, 56311	Beacon Rail	GB Railfreight		
69002		Beacon Rail	GB Railfreight		
69003		Beacon Rail	GB Railfreight		
69004		Beacon Rail	GB Railfreight		
69005		Beacon Rail	GB Railfreight		
69006		Beacon Rail	GB Railfreight		
69007		Beacon Rail	GB Railfreight		
69008		Beacon Rail	GB Railfreight		
69009		Beacon Rail	GB Railfreight		
69010		Beacon Rail	GB Railfreight		
69011		Beacon Rail	GB Railfreight		
69012		Beacon Rail	GB Railfreight		
69013		Beacon Rail	GB Railfreight		

Loco	Previous numbers	Owner	Operator	Livery	Name
69014		Beacon Rail	GB Railfreight		
69015		Beacon Rail	GB Railfreight		
69016		Beacon Rail	GB Railfreight		
69017		Beacon Rail	GB Railfreight		

Fleet list 7: Class 70

Class 70/0 Locos ordered by Freightliner

Loco	-	Owner	Operator	Livery	Name
70001	-	Macquarie Group	Freightliner	Freightliner Powerhaul	*PowerHaul*
70002	-	Macquarie Group	Freightliner	Freightliner Powerhaul	
70003	-	Macquarie Group	Freightliner	Freightliner Powerhaul	
70004	-	Macquarie Group	Freightliner	Freightliner Powerhaul	*The Coal Industry Society*
70005	-	Macquarie Group	Freightliner	Freightliner Powerhaul	
70006	-	Macquarie Group	Freightliner	Freightliner Powerhaul	
70007	-	Macquarie Group	Freightliner	Freightliner Powerhaul	
70008	-	Macquarie Group	Freightliner	Freightliner Powerhaul	
70009	-	Macquarie Group	Freightliner	Freightliner Powerhaul	
70010	-	Macquarie Group	Freightliner	Freightliner Powerhaul	
70011	-	Macquarie Group	Freightliner	Freightliner Powerhaul	
70012	-	General Electric		Freightliner Powerhaul	
70013	-	Macquarie Group	Freightliner	Freightliner Powerhaul	
70014	-	Macquarie Group	Freightliner	Freightliner Powerhaul	
70015	-	Macquarie Group	Freightliner	Freightliner Powerhaul	
70016	-	Macquarie Group	Freightliner	Freightliner Powerhaul	
70017	-	Macquarie Group	Freightliner	Freightliner Powerhaul	
70018	-	Macquarie Group	Freightliner	Freightliner Powerhaul	
70019	-	Macquarie Group	Freightliner	Freightliner Powerhaul	
70020	-	Macquarie Group	Freightliner	Freightliner Powerhaul	

Note: 70012 was damaged during unloading and returned to America. It is now used as a ted bed loco by General Electric.

Class 70/8 Locos ordered by Colas Rail Freight

Loco	Previous numbers	Owner	Operator	Livery	Name
70801	70099	Lombard Finance	Colas Rail Freight	Colas Rail Freight	
70802		Lombard Finance	Colas Rail Freight	Colas Rail Freight	
70803		Lombard Finance	Colas Rail Freight	Colas Rail Freight	
70804		Lombard Finance	Colas Rail Freight	Colas Rail Freight	
70805		Lombard Finance	Colas Rail Freight	Colas Rail Freight	
70806		Lombard Finance	Colas Rail Freight	Colas Rail Freight	
70807		Lombard Finance	Colas Rail Freight	Colas Rail Freight	
70808		Lombard Finance	Colas Rail Freight	Colas Rail Freight	
70809		Lombard Finance	Colas Rail Freight	Colas Rail Freight	
70810		Lombard Finance	Colas Rail Freight	Colas Rail Freight	
70811		Beacon Rail	Colas Rail Freight	Colas Rail Freight	
70812		Beacon Rail	Colas Rail Freight	Colas Rail Freight	
70813		Beacon Rail	Colas Rail Freight	Colas Rail Freight	
70814		Beacon Rail	Colas Rail Freight	Colas Rail Freight	
70815		Beacon Rail	Colas Rail Freight	Colas Rail Freight	
70816		Beacon Rail	Colas Rail Freight	Colas Rail Freight	
70817		Beacon Rail	Colas Rail Freight	Colas Rail Freight	

Fleet list 8: Class 73/9

Class 73/9 Loram rebuilt locos for Network Rail

Loco	Rebuilt from	Owner	Operator	liveries	Name
73951	73104	Network Rail	Network Rail	Network Rail yellow	*Malcolm Brinded*
73952	73211	Network Rail	Network Rail	Network Rail yellow	*Janis Kong*

Class 73/9 Brush rebuilt locos for GB Railfreight

Loco	Rebuilt from	Owner	Operator	liveries	Name
73961	73209	GB Railfreight	Network Rail	GB Railfreight	*Alison*
73962	73204	GB Railfreight	Network Rail	GB Railfreight	*Dick Mabbutt*
73963	73206	GB Railfreight	Network Rail	GB Railfreight	*Janice*
73964	73205	GB Railfreight	Network Rail	GB Railfreight	*Jeanette*
73965	73208	GB Railfreight	Network Rail	GB Railfreight	
73966	73005	GB Railfreight	Caledonian Sleeper	Caledonian Sleeper	
73967	73006	GB Railfreight	Caledonian Sleeper	Caledonian Sleeper	
73968	73117	GB Railfreight	Caledonian Sleeper	Caledonian Sleeper	
73969	73105	GB Railfreight	Caledonian Sleeper	Caledonian Sleeper	
73970	73103	GB Railfreight	Caledonian Sleeper	Caledonian Sleeper	
73971	73207	GB Railfreight	Caledonian Sleeper	Caledonian Sleeper	

Fleet list 9: Class 88

Locos ordered by Direct Rail Services

Loco	Previous numbers	Owner	Operator	liveries	Name
88001	-	Beacon Rail	Direct Rail Services	Revised Direct Rail Services Compass	*Revolution*
88002	-	Beacon Rail	Direct Rail Services	Revised Direct Rail Services Compass	*Prometheus*
88003	-	Beacon Rail	Direct Rail Services	Revised Direct Rail Services Compass	*Genesis*
88004	-	Beacon Rail	Direct Rail Services	Revised Direct Rail Services Compass	*Pandora*
88005	-	Beacon Rail	Direct Rail Services	Revised Direct Rail Services Compass	*Minerva*
88006	-	Beacon Rail	Direct Rail Services	Revised Direct Rail Services Compass	*Juno*
88007	-	Beacon Rail	Direct Rail Services	Revised Direct Rail Services Compass	*Electra*
88008	-	Beacon Rail	Direct Rail Services	Revised Direct Rail Services Compass	*Ariadne*
88009	-	Beacon Rail	Direct Rail Services	Revised Direct Rail Services Compass	*Diana*
88010	-	Beacon Rail	Direct Rail Services	Revised Direct Rail Services Compass	*Aurora*

Fleet list 10: Class 93

Locos to be ordered by Rail Operations Group

Loco	Previous numbers	Owner	Operator	liveries	Name
93001	-	Beacon Rail	Rail Operations Group	Rail Operations Group	
93002	-	Beacon Rail	Rail Operations Group	Rail Operations Group	
93003	-	Beacon Rail	Rail Operations Group	Rail Operations Group	
93004	-	Beacon Rail	Rail Operations Group	Rail Operations Group	
93005	-	Beacon Rail	Rail Operations Group	Rail Operations Group	
93006	-	Beacon Rail	Rail Operations Group	Rail Operations Group	
93007	-	Beacon Rail	Rail Operations Group	Rail Operations Group	
93008	-	Beacon Rail	Rail Operations Group	Rail Operations Group	
93009	-	Beacon Rail	Rail Operations Group	Rail Operations Group	
93010	-	Beacon Rail	Rail Operations Group	Rail Operations Group	

Note: These locos had not been ordered as this book went to print.

Specifications

Class 43 MTU

TOPS number range:	**various from 43002–198, 43207–384, 43423–484,**

Rebuilt by:	Brush Loughborough
Years introduced:	2004–11
Wheel arrangement:	Bo-Bo
Weight:	70 tons
Height:	12ft 10in (3.90m)
Length:	58ft 5in (17.80m)
Width:	8ft 11in (2.73m)
Wheelbase:	42ft 4in (12.90m)
Bogie wheelbase:	8ft 7in (2.60m)
Bogie pivot centres:	33ft 9in (10.28m)
Wheel diameter:	3ft 4in (1.02m)
Min curve negotiable:	4 chains (80.46m)
Replacement engines:	MTU16V4000 R41R
Engine output:	2,700hp (2,010kW)
Power at rail:	1,770hp (1,320kW)
Tractive effort:	17,980lb
Cont Tractive effort:	10,340lb
Maximum speed:	125mph (200km/h)
Route availability:	6
Bogie type:	BP16
Main alternator type:	Brush BA1001B
Auxiliary ETH alternator:	Brush BAH601B
Traction motor type:	43002–123/153–198 (Brush TMH68-46)
	43124–152 (GECG417AZ)
No of traction motors:	4
Gear ratio:	59:23
Fuel tank capacity:	1,030gal (4,680lit)
Luggage capacity	1.5 tons, increased to 2.5 tons

Class 57

TOPS number range:	**57001–012, 57301–316, 57601–605**

Rebuilt by:	Brush Traction
Originally built by:	Brush
Years introduced	1998–2005
Wheel arrangement:	Co-Co
Weight:	120.6 tons
Height:	12ft 10in (3.91m)
Length:	63ft 6in (19.38m)
Width:	9ft 2in (2.79m)
Wheelbase:	51ft 6in (15.69m)
Bogie wheelbase:	14ft 6in (4.41m)
Bogie pivot centres:	37ft (11.27m)
Wheel diameter:	3ft 9in (1.14m)
Min curve negotiable:	4 chains (80.46m)
Engine type:	General Motors 645-12E3
	General Motors 645-12F3B
Engine output:	2,500hp (1,860kW)
	2,750hp (2,051kW)
Power at rail:	2,025hp (1,507kW)
	2,200hp (1,640kW)
Tractive effort:	55,000lb
Maximum speed:	75mph (121km/h)
	95mph (153km/h)
Brake force:	80 tons

Route availability:	6
Main alternator type:	Brush BA1101A
Auxiliary alternator type:	Brush BAA602A
ETH alternator type:	Brush BAA
Traction motor type:	Brush TM68-46
No of traction motors:	6
Gear ratio:	66:17
Fuel tank capacity:	1,221gal, 5,551lit (57/0); 1,308gal, 5,887lit (57/3), 727gal, 3,273lit (57/6)

Class 66

TOPS number range:	**66001–66250, 66301–305, 66401–434, 66501–599, 66601–625, 66701–792, 66841–850, 66951–957**

Built by:	General Motors, London, Canada and Progress Rail, Muncie, Indiana USA
Construction model (GM):	JT-42-CWR
Years introduced:	from 1998
Wheel arrangement:	Co-Co
Weight:	126 tons
Height:	12ft 10in (3.91m)
Length:	70ft 1in (21.40m)
Width:	8ft 8in (2.65m)
Wheelbase:	56ft 9in (17.29m)
Bogie wheelbase:	13ft 7in (4.15m)
Bogie pivot centres:	43ft 6in (13.25m)
Wheel diameter:	3ft 6in (1.06m)
Min curve negotiable:	4 chains (80.46m)
Engine type:	GM 12N-710G3B-EC
Engine output:	3,300hp (2,462kW)
Power at rail:	3,000hp (2,238kW)
Maximum tractive effort:	92,000lb – 66/0; 105,080lb – 66/6
Continuous tractive effort:	58,390lb – 66/0; 66,630lb – 66/6
Maximum speed:	75mph (120km/h)
Brake force:	68 tons
Bogie type:	HTCR Radial
Route availability:	7
Traction alternator:	GM-EMD AR8
Companion alternator:	GM-EMD CA6
Traction motor type:	GM-EMD D43TR
No of traction motors:	6
Gear ratio:	81:20 66/0, 83:18 66/6
Fuel tank capacity:	1,145–1,440gal (5,150–6,550lit)

Class 67

TOPS number range:	**67001–030**

Built by:	Alstom/General Motors, Valencia, Spain
Construction model (GM):	JT-42-HWHS
Years introduced:	1999–2000
Wheel arrangement:	Bo-Bo
Weight:	90 tons
Height:	12ft 9in (3.93m)
Length:	64ft 7in (19.71m)
Width:	8ft 9in (2.71m)
Wheelbase:	47ft 3in (14.43m)
Bogie wheelbase:	9ft 2in (2.80m)
Bogie pivot centres:	38ft 1in (11.63m)
Wheel diameter:	3ft 2in (965mm)
Min curve negotiable:	3.8 chains (75m)
Engine type:	GM 12N-710G3B-EC

Engine output:	2,980hp (2,223kW)
Maximum tractive effort:	31,750lb
Continuous tractive effort:	20,200lb
Design speed:	125mph (200kph) restricted to 110mph (177kph)
Brake force	78 tons
Bogie type:	Alstom high speed
Route availability:	8
Traction alternator:	GM-EMD AR9A
Companion alternator:	GM-EMD CA6HEX
Traction motor type:	GM-EMD D43FM
No of traction motors:	4
Gear ratio:	59:28
Fuel tank capacity:	1,201gal (5,460lit)

Class 68

TOPS number range:	68001–034

Design Code:	68-0AA
Built by:	Vossloh/Stadler, Valencia
Years introduced:	2014–17
Wheel arrangement:	Bo-Bo
Weight:	85 tons
Height:	12ft 7in (3.82m)
Length:	67ft 3in (20.5m)
Width:	8ft 10 in (2.69m)
Wheelbase:	48ft 10in (14.9m)
Bogie wheelbase:	9ft 3in (2.8m)
Bogie pivot centres:	38ft 8in (11.83m)
Wheel diameter:	43in (1.1m)
Min curve negotiable:	4 chains (80.46m)
Engine type:	Caterpillar C175-16
Engine output:	3,755hp (2,800kW)
Maximum tractive effort:	71,260lb (317kN)
Continuous tractive effort	56,200lb (250kN)
Maximum speed:	100mph (160km/h)
Brake force:	88 tons
Route availability:	7
Main alternator type:	ABB WGX560
Traction motor type:	4FRA6063
No of traction motors:	4
ETS index	96
Fuel tank capacity:	5,600 litres

Class 69

TOPS number range:	69001–016

Design Code:	69-0AA
Built by:	EMD
Years introduced:	2020-21
Wheel arrangement:	Co-Co
Weight:	126 tons
Height:	13ft (3.96m)
Length:	63ft 6in (19.39m)
Width:	9ft 2in (2.79m)
Wheelbase:	47ft 10in (14.58m)
Bogie wheelbase:	13ft 6in (4.10m)
Bogie pivot centres:	37ft 8in (11.48m)
Wheel diameter:	3ft 9in (1.14m)
Min curve negotiable:	4 chains (80.46m)
Engine type:	GM 12N-710G3B-EC
Engine output:	3,300hp (2,462kW)

Power at rail:	3,000hp (2,238kW)
Tractive effort:	tba
Maximum speed:	80mph (128km/h)
Brake force:	tba
Route availability:	7
Main alternator type:	GM-EMD AR8
Traction motor type:	Brush TMH73-62
No of traction motors:	6
Gear ratio:	tba
Fuel tank capacity:	1,150gal (5,228lit)

Note: the statistics for the Class 69 is based on a Class 56 body and bogies and a Class 66 engine, but certain aspects could be subject to change.

Class 70

TOPS number range:	70001–020/099, 70801–817

Design Code:	70-0AA
Built by:	General Electric, Erie, Pennsylvania
Years introduced:	2009–12
Wheel arrangement:	Co-Co
Weight:	129 tons
Height:	3.94m
Length:	21.71m
Width:	2.64m
Wheelbase:	17.18m
Bogie wheelbase:	4.28m
Bogie pivot centres:	14.48m
Wheel diameter:	1.07m
Min curve negotiable:	80m
Engine type:	GE Powerhaul P616LDA1
Engine output:	3,820hp (2,848kW)
Power at rail:	2,700hp (2,014kW)
Tractive effort:	122,000lb
Maximum speed:	75mph (120km/h)
Brake force:	96.7 tons
Route availability:	7
Main alternator type:	GE 5GTAZ6721A1
Traction motor type:	AC-GE 5GEB30B
No of traction motors:	6
Gear ratio:	87:16
Fuel tank capacity:	1,333gal (6,000lit)

Class 73/9

TOPS number range:	73951/952

Rebuilt by:	Loram
Years introduced:	2015
Wheel arrangement:	Bo-Bo
Weight:	76–77 tons
Height:	12ft 5in (3.79m)
Length – buffers retracted:	52ft 6in (16.00m)
Length – buffers extended:	53ft 8in (16.96m)
Width:	8ft 8in (2.64m)
Wheelbase:	40ft 9in (12.42m)
Bogie wheelbase:	8ft 9in (2.66m)
Bogie pivot centres:	32ft (11.27m)
Wheel diameter:	3ft 4in (1.01m)
Min curve negotiable:	4 chains (80.46m)
Power supply:	660–850V DC third rail
Electric output (nom):	1,600hp (1,193kW)
Electric power at rail (Cont):	1,200hp (895kW)
Electric power at rail (Max):	2,450hp (1,830kW)

Engine type (73951/952)	2 x Cummins QSK19
Engine output:	1,500hp (1,119kW)
Diesel power at rail:	1,005hp (750kW)
Electric tractive effort:	179kN (40,000lbf)
Diesel tractive effort:	179kN (40,000lbf)
Maximum speed:	90mph (144km/h)
Brake force:	31 tons
Route availability:	6
Main generator type:	EE824-3D
Auxiliary generator type:	EE908-3C
Traction motor type:	EE546-1B
No of traction motors:	4
Gear ratio:	61:19
Fuel tank capacity:	500gal (2,260lit)

Class 73/9 MTU

TOPS number range:	73961–971
Rebuilt by:	Brush Traction
Years introduced:	2012–14
Wheel arrangement:	Bo-Bo
Weight:	77 tons
Height:	12ft 5in (3.79m)
Length – buffers retracted:	52ft 6in (16.00m)
Length – buffers extended:	53ft 8in (16.96m)
Width:	8ft 8in (2.64m)
Wheelbase:	40ft 9in (12.42m)
Bogie wheelbase:	8ft 9in (2.66m)
Bogie pivot centres:	32ft (11.27m)
Wheel diameter:	3ft 4in (1.01m)
Min curve negotiable:	4 chains (80.46m)
Power supply:	660–850V DC third rail
Electric output (nom):	1,600hp (1,193kW)
Electric power at rail (Cont):	1,200hp (895kW)
Electric power at rail (Max):	2,450hp (1,830kW)
Engine type (73961–971)	MTU R4000L 8V43
Engine output:	1,600hp (1,194kW)
Diesel power at rail:	1,072hp (800kW)
Electric tractive effort:	179kN (40,000lbf)
Diesel tractive effort:	179kN (40,000lbf)
Maximum speed:	90mph (144km/h)
Brake force:	31 tons
Route availability:	6
Main generator type:	EE824-3D
Auxiliary generator type:	EE908-3C
Traction motor type:	EE546-1B
No of traction motors:	4
Gear ratio:	61:19
ETS index	38
Fuel tank capacity:	450gal (2,025lit) 73961–965, 600gal (2,700lit) 73966–971

Class 88

TOPS number range:	88001–010
Design Code:	88-0AA
Built by:	Stadler, Valencia
Years introduced:	2016–17
Wheel arrangement:	Bo-Bo
Weight:	86 tons
Height:	12ft 7in (3.82m)
Length:	67ft 3in (20.5m)

Width:	8ft 10 in (2.69m)
Wheelbase:	48ft 10in (14.9m)
Bogie wheelbase:	9ft 3in (2.8m)
Bogie pivot centres:	37ft 7in (12.10m)
Wheel diameter:	42in (1.06m)
Min curve negotiable:	4 chains (80.46m)
Engine type:	Caterpillar C27
Engine output:	940hp (708kW)
Maximum tractive effort:	71,260lb (317kN)
Continuous tractive effort:	56,200lb (250kN)
Maximum speed:	100mph (160km/h)
Brake force:	73 tons
Route availability:	7
Main alternator type:	ABB AMXL400
Traction motor type:	4FRA6063
No of traction motors:	4
ETS index	96
Fuel tank capacity:	1,800 litres

Class 93

TOPS number range:	93001–010
Design Code:	93-0AA
Built by:	Stadler, Valencia
Years introduced:	2020–21
Wheel arrangement:	Bo-Bo
Weight:	tba
Height:	12ft 7in (3.82m)
Length:	67ft 3in (20.5m)
Width:	8ft 10 in (2.69m)
Wheelbase:	48ft 10in (14.9m)
Bogie wheelbase:	9ft 3in (2.8m)
Bogie pivot centres:	37ft 7in (12.10m)
Wheel diameter:	42in (1.06m)
Min curve negotiable:	4 chains (80.46m)
Engine type:	Caterpillar C32
Engine output:	1,205hp (900kW)
Power at rail:	tba
Maximum tractive effort:	tba
Continuous tractive effort:	tba
Maximum speed:	110mph (176km/h)
Brake force:	tba
Route availability:	7
Main alternator type:	tba
Traction motor type:	tba
No of traction motors:	4
Gear ratio:	tba
ETS index	96
Fuel tank capacity:	tba

Note: The Class 93s were not ordered as this book went to print, the relevant stats based on a Class 88 are listed but could be subject to change.

Names and liveries

This lists all the liveries and names carried by all post-privatisation new build – and rebuilt – locos, correct to June 2019. Locos marked * no longer carry these names, while those marked ** have been disposed of.

MTU Class 43s liveries and names

Liveries

First Group blue with wavy lines: 43004/009

First Group all-over blue with Angel Trains branding: 43009/175 (did not run in traffic like this)

First Group all-over plain blue: 43002–005/009/010/012/015–018/020–037/040–042/053/056/063/069–071/078/079/086–088/091–094/097/098, 43122/124–156/158–165/168–172/174–177/179–183/185–198

First Group blue with Diamond Jubilee: 43186

First Group blue with Hewlett Packard advertising wrap: 43148/186

First Group blue with Singapore Airlines advertising wrap: 43163

First Group blue with Visit Plymouth advertising wrap: 43163

First Group blue with Building a Greater West advertising wrap: 43144/146

First Group blue with Bristol 2015 Advertising wrap: 43012/126/148/192

First Group blue with Queen 90th birthday decals: 43027

Great Western Railway green: 43004/005/016/040-042/092-094/097/098, 43122/153-155/170/186-189/192/194/198

Great Western Railway green with Welsh dragons: 43187/188

Great Western Railway green with Old Oak graphics: 43093

Great Western Railway First World War tribute: 43172

Retro BR blue, grey and yellow: 43002

Retro InterCity Swallow: 43185

Virgin Trains red: 43006–008/013/014/062/063/065/067–071/078–080/084/086–094/097–099, 43100–104/121–123/153–162/166/178/180/184/193–198

CrossCountry Trains brown and silver: 43207/285, 43301/303/304/321/357/366/378/384

Great North Eastern Railway with gold lettering: 43208/238/290/296, 43300/306/309/313–315/316/318/320/367

Great North Eastern Railway blue with Leeds–London advert: 43290, 43300

Great North Eastern Railway blue with National Express white stripe: 43208/238/296, 43306/309/313–315/316/318/320/367

National Express: 43206/208/238/239/251/257/277/295/290/296/299, 43300/302/305–320/367

National Express with East Coast branding: 43206/208/238/239/251/257/277/295/296/299, 43302/305–320/367

East Coast grey: 43206/238/239/251/257/272/274/277/290/295/296/299, 43300/302/305–320/367

East Coast grey with Craigentinny special branding: 43300

East Coast grey with Virgin branding: 43239/272/277, 43305/306/307/317/320

National Express with Virgin branding: 43206/208/277/305/307

Virgin Trains East Coast red: 43206/208/239/251/257/272/274/277/290/295/296/299, 43300/302/305–320/367

Virgin Trains East Coast NRM special: 43238

Virgin Trains red with Spirit of Sunderland branding: 43274

Virgin Trains East Coast with Craigentinny branding: 43300

Virgin Trains East Coast advertising livery: 43257

Virgin Trains 'Perth is the place' branding: 43295

Grand Central black with orange solebar stripe: 43423/465/467/468/480/484

Network Rail yellow: 43013/014/062

ScotRail Seven Cities: 43003/012/015/021/026/028/030-037, 43124-152/163/164/168/169/169/175-177/179/181-183

Revised East Midlands Trains blue: 43423/465/467/468/480

Names

43002	Sir Kenneth Grange
43003	ISAMBARD KINGDOM BRUNEL *
43004	First for the Future/First ar gyfer y dyfodol *
43009	First Transforming Travel *
43012	Exeter Panel Signal Box 21st Anniversary 2009 *
43013	Mark Carne CBE
43014	The Railway Observer
43017	Hannahs discoverhannahs.org *
43020	mtu Power Passion Partnership
43022	The Duke of Edinburgh's Award Diamond Anniversary 1956–2016
43023	SQN LDR HAROLD STARR ONE OF THE FEW
43024	Great Western Society 1961–2011 Didcot Railway Centre *
43025	INSTITUTION OF RAILWAY OPERATORS 2000–2010 TEN YEARS PROMOTING OPERATIONAL EXCELLENCE *
43026	Michael Eavis *
43027	Glorious Devon *
43030	Christian Lewis Trust *
43033	Driver Brian Cooper 15 June 1947–5 October 1999 *
43037	PENYDARREN *
43040	Bristol St Philip's Marsh
43041	Meningitis Trust Support for Life
43053	University of Worcester *
43056	The Royal British Legion *
43062	John Armitt
43070	The Corps of Royal Electrical & Mechanical Engineers *

43087	*11 Explosive Ordnance Disposal Regiment Royal Logistics Corps**
43093	*Old Oak Common HST Depot 1976–2018*
43097	*Environment Agency*
43132	*We Save the Children – Will You?**
43132	*Aberdeen Station 150th Anniversary*
43139	*Driver Stan Martin 25 June 1950–6 November 2004**
43140	*Landore Diesel Depot 1963 Celebrating 50 Years 2013**
	Depo Diesel Gland r 1963 Dathlu 50 Miynedd 2013
43141	*Cardiff Panel Signal Box 1966–2016**
	Blwch Signalau Panel Caerdydd 1966–2016
43143	*Stroud 700**
43147	*Royal Marines Celebrating 350 Years**
43155	*The Red Arrows 50 Seasons of Excellence**
43156	*Dartington International Summer School**
43160	*Sir Moir Lockhead OBE**
43163	*Exeter Panel Signal Box 21st Anniversary 2009**
43165	*Prince Michael of Kent**
43172	*Harry Patch The last survivor of the trenches*
43175	*GWR 175th ANNIVERSARY**
43179	*Pride of Laira**
43185	*Great Western**
43189	*RAILWAY HERITAGE TRUST**
43194	*Okehampton Castle*
43198	*Oxfordshire 2007**
43198	*Driver Brian Cooper 15 June 1947–5 October 1999/Driver Stan Martin 25 June 1950–6 November 2004*
43206	*Kingdom of Fife**

43208	*Lincolnshire Echo*
43238	*City of Dundee**
43238	*National Railway Museum 40 Years 1975–2015*
43257	*Bounds Green*
43274	*Spirit of Sunderland*
43290	*mtu Fascination of Power**
43296	*Stirling Castle**
43300	*Craigentinny 100 YEARS 1914–2014**
43306	*Fountains Abbey**
43308	*HIGHLAND CHIEFTAIN*
43309	*Leeds International Film Festival**
43313	*The Highlands**
43314	*East Riding of Yorkshire**
43316	*The Black Dyke Band**
43318	*City of Kingston upon Hull**
43320	*National Galleries of Scotland**
43367	*DELTIC 50 1955–2005*
43423	*VALENTA 1972–2010*
43467	*British Transport Police Nottingham/Nottinghamshire Fire and Rescue Service*
43480	*West Hampstead PSB*
43484	*PETER FOX 1942–2011 PLATFORM 5**

Notes: ScotRail Class 43s still in First Group blue will be repainted in to Seven Cities livery while those remaining GWR 43s still in First Group blue will be repainted into GWR Green.

As this book went to print, Great Western Railway was starting a programme of namings for its Castle HSTs. The planned list of namings is thus, but could be subjects to change. 43198 will retain its existing names. 43194 was the first to be named.

43004	*Caerphilly Castle*
43092	*Cromwell's Castle*
43005	*St. Michael's Mount*
43016	*Powderham Castle*
43040	*Berry Pomeroy Castle*
43041	*St. Catherine's Castle*
43042	*Tregenna Castle*
43093	*Castle-an-Dinas*
43094	*St. Mawes Castle*
43097	*Castle Drogo*

43098	*Walton Castle*
43122	*Dunster Castle*
43153	*Chûn Castle*
43154	*Compton Castle*
43155	*Rougemont Castle*
43158	*Kingswear Castle*
43170	*Chepstow Castle*
43186	*Taunton Castle*
43187	*Cardiff Castle*
43188	*Newport Castle*
43189	*Launceston Castle*
43192	*Trematon Castle*
43194	*Okehampton Castle*
43198	*Brian Cooper & Stan Martin*

Class 57 liveries and names

Liveries

Freightliner green and yellow: 57001–012

Porterbrook silver and purple: 57601

Virgin silver and red: 57301–316

First Great Western green: 57602–605

First Group purple: 57602–605

Great Western Railway Brunswick green: 57604

Great Western Railway green: 57602/603/605

West Coast Railways light maroon with black stripe: 57601

West Coast Railways dark maroon: 57001/006, 57313–316, 57601

Arriva Trains Wales turquoise: 57314/315

Arriva Trains Wales turquoise unbranded: 57313/316

West Coast Railways Northern Belle umber and cream: 57601

Advenza blue: 57005/006

Direct Rail Services Compass: 57002–004/007–012, 57302/304/308/309/311

Direct Rail Services Compass with Colas Rail Freight logos: 57002

Direct Rail Services Compass with cable thieves awareness branding: 57307

Direct Rail Services revised Compass: 57002/003/007/010, 57301–304/306–311

Direct Rail Services 20 years: 57307

Direct Rail Services Northern Belle umber and cream: 57305/312

Network Rail yellow: 57301/303/305/306/310/312

Names

57001	*Freightliner Pioneer**
57002	*Freightliner Phoenix**
57002	*RAIL Express*
57003	*Freightliner Evolution**
57004	*Freightliner Quality**
57005	*Freightliner Excellence**
57006	*Freightliner Reliance**
57007	*Freightliner Bond**
57007	*John Scott 12.5.45–22.5.12*
57008	*Freightliner Explorer**
57008	*Telford International Railfreight Park June – 2009**
57009	*Freightliner Venturer**
57010	*Freightliner Crusader**
57011	*Freightliner Challenger**
57012	*Freightliner Envoy**
57301	*SCOTT TRACY**
57301	*Goliath*
57302	*VIRGIL TRACY**
57302	*Chad Varah*
57303	*ALAN TRACY**
57303	*Pride of Carlisle*
57304	*GORDON TRACY**
57304	*Pride of Cheshire*
57305	*JOHN TRACY**
57305	*Northern Princess*
57306	*JEFF TRACY**
57306	*Her Majesty's Railway Inspectorate 175*
57307	*LADY PENELOPE*
57308	*TIN TIN**
57308	*County of Staffordshire**
57308	*Jamie Ferguson*
57309	*BRAINS**
57309	*Pride of Crewe*
57310	*KYRANO**
57310	*Pride of Cumbria*
57311	*PARKER**
57311	*Thunderbird*
57312	*THE HOOD**
57312	*Peter Henderson**
57312	*Solway Princess*
57313	*TRACY ISLAND**
57314	*FIREFLY**
57315	*THE MOLE**
57316	*FAB1**
57601	*Windsor Castle*
57602	*Restormel Castle*
57603	*Tintagel Castle*
57604	*PENDENNIS CASTLE*
57605	*Totnes Castle*

Class 66 liveries and names

Liveries

English Welsh, Scottish Railway red and gold: 66001–250

EWS unbranded with DB stickers: 66002/012/014/023/031/039/040/043/053/078/080/084/088/090/095/096/098/099, 66103/108/109/111/112/114/121/127/139/143/145/155/156/168/172/174/176/188/197, 66200

DB Schenker Stobart (third variant): 66048

DB Schenker: 66001/058/097, 66101/114/118/152/185, 66200

DB Schenker red without yellow ends (Poland): 66163/178/189, 66220/227/248

DB Cargo red: 66001/009/016-021/027/034/035/041/044/055/065/066/070/074/077/078/082/085/094, 66100/104/105/107/113/115/117/124/128/130/131/134/135/137/149/150/165/167/175/182/185/192, 66206/230

DB Cargo with China–London branding: 66136

DB Cargo Maritime blue: 66005/047/051, 66142

DB Cargo PD Ports blue: 66109

Freightliner green and yellow: 66501–599, 66601–625, 66951–957

Freightliner green and yellow Shanks Waste: 66522

Freightliner blue Bardon Aggregates: 66623

Freightliner blue logos: 66623

Freightliner unbranded green and yellow: 66601/612, 66738–741

Freightliner Powerhaul (UK): 66414/416/418/420, 66504/528

Freightliner Powerhaul (Poland): 66411/412/417

Genesee & Wyoming light orange and black: 66413

Genesee & Wyoming dark orange and black: 66415/419, 66623

Ocean Network Express: 66587

Direct Rail Services Compass: 66401–434

Direct Rail Services Stobart (first variant): 66411

Direct Rail Services Stobart (second variant): 66414

Direct Rail Services unbranded: 66401–404/410

Direct Rail Services base blue: 66411/414

Direct Rail Services Malcolm (first variant): 66405

Direct Rail Services Malcolm (second variant): 66412

Direct Rail Services Malcolm (third variant): 66434

Direct Rail Services plain blue with white compass logos: 66301–305, 66421–434

GB Railfreight: 66701–717

GB Railfreight Medite black and orange: 66709

GB Railfreight Medite Sorrento wrap: 66709

GB Railfreight Golden Jubilee: 66705

GB Railfreight Metronet: 66718–722

GB Railfreight First Group: 66723–732

GB Railfreight Emily livery: 66720

GB Europorte: 66702–708/710/712/713/715/719/722/728–746/747–778/781/786/788

GB Railfreight all-over grey: 66747–749

GB Railfreight unbranded blue: 66750/751

GB Railfreight LUL tube map: 66718

GB Railfreight LUL museum black: 66721

GB Railfreight Aggregates industries: 66711

GB Railfreight Brunswick green: 66779

GB Railfreight Royal Scotsman: 66743/746

GB Railfreight Maritime blue with large numbers: 66727

GB Railfreight revised, with F231 branding: 66775

GB Railfreight revised, with ZA723 branding and Chinook graphics: 66723

GB Railfreight revised: 66724–726

GB Railfreight revised, with Charity Railtours branding: 66782

GB Railfreight BR 'Large logo blue': 66789

GB Railfreight Biffa red and orange: 66783

GB Railfreight Cemex blue & white: 66780

GB Railfreight Newell and Wright turquoise and white: 66747

GB Railfreight Pride: 66773

Fastline Freight grey and black: 66301–305, 66434

Colas Rail Freight: 66742–746, 66841–850

Advenza blue: 66841–844

Advenza unbranded blue: 66843/844

Plain black: 66048 (withdrawn)

Names

66002	*Lafarge Buddon Wood* *
66002	*Lafarge Quorn* *
66005	*Maritime Intermodal One*
66022	*Lafarge Charnwood* *
66035	*Resourceful*
66042	*Lafarge Buddon Wood* *
66047	*Maritime Intermodal Two*
66048	*James the Engine* **
66050	*EWS Energy*
66051	*Maritime Intermodal Four*
66055	*Alain Thauvette*
66058	*Derek Clark* *
66066	*Geoff Spencer*
66077	*Benjamin Gimbert GC* *
66079	*James Nightall GC*
66100	*Armistice 100*
66109	*Teesport Express*
66152	*Derek Holmes Railway Operator*
66172	*PAUL MELLANY*
66185	*DP WORLD London Gateway*
66200	*RAILWAY HERITAGE COMMITTEE* *
66301	*Kingmoor TMD*
66411	*Eddie the Engine* *
66413	*Lest We Forget*
66414	*James the Engine* *
66418	PATRIOT – IN MEMORY OF FALLEN RAILWAY EMPLOYEES
66421	*Gresty Bridge TMD*

66501	*Japan 2001*
66502	*Basford Hall Centenary 2001*
66503	*The RAILWAY MAGAZINE*
66506	*Crewe Regeneration*
66526	*Driver Steve Dunn (George)*
66527	*Don Raider* *
66528	*Madge Elliot MBE Borders Railway Opening 2015*
66532	*P&O Nedlloyd Express*
66533	*Hanjin Express/Senator Express*
66534	*OOCL Express*
66540	*Ruby*
66552	*Maltby Raider*
66576	*Hamburg Sud Advantage* *
66581	*Sophie* *
66585	*The Drax Flyer* *
66587	*AS ONE, WE CAN*
66592	*Johnson Stevens Agencies*
66593	*3MG MERSEY MULTIMODAL GATEWAY*
66594	*NYK Spirit of Kyoto*
66597	*Viridor*
66601	*The Hope Valley*
66612	*Forth Raider* *
66614	*1916 POPPY 2016*
66618	*Railways Illustrated Annual Photographic Awards Ian Lothian* *
66618	*Railways Illustrated Annual Photographic Awards Derek Gorton* *
66618	*Railways Illustrated Annual Photographic Awards Alan Barnes*
66619	*Derek W Johnson MBE*
66623	*Bill Bolsover* *

66701	Railtrack National Logistics*
66701	Whitemoor*
66702	Blue Lightning
66703	Doncaster PSB 1981–2002
66704	Colchester Power Signalbox
66705	Golden Jubilee
66706	Nene Valley
66707	Sir Sam Fay
66708	Jayne
66709	Joseph Arnold Davies *
66709	Sorrento
66710	Phil Packer BRIT
66711	Sence
66712	Peterborough Power Signalbox
66713	Forest City
66714	Cromer Lifeboat
66715	VALOUR
66716	Willesden Traincare Depot *
66716	LOCOMOTIVE & CARRIAGE INSTITUTION CENTENARY 1911–2011
66717	Good Old Boy
66718	Gwyneth Dunwoody *
66718	Sir Peter Hendy CBE
66719	METRO-LAND
66720	Metronet Pathfinder *
66721	Harry Beck
66722	Sir Edward Watkin
66723	Chinook
66724	Drax Power Station
66725	SUNDERLAND
66726	SHEFFIELD WEDNESDAY
66727	Andrew Scott CBE *
66727	Maritime One
66728	Institution of Railway Operators
66729	DERBY COUNTY
66730	Whitemoor
66731	interhubGB
66732	GBRf The First Decade 1999–2009 John Smith MD
66733	Cambridge PSB
66734	The Eco Express **
66735	PETERBOROUGH UNITED
66736	WOLVERHAMPTON WANDERERS
66737	Lesia

66738	HUDDERSFIELD TOWN
66739	Bluebell Railway
66740	Sarah
66741	Swanage Railway
66742	ABP Port of Immingham Centenary 1912–2012
66744	Crossrail
66745	Modern Railways The first 50 years
66747	Made in Sheffield
66748	West Burton 50
66750	Bristol Panel Signal Box
66751	Inspiration Delivered Hitachi Rail Europe
66752	The Hoosier State
66753	EMD Roberts Road
66754	Northampton Saints
66755	Tony Berkeley OBE RFG Chairman 1997–2018
66756	Royal Corps of Signals
66757	West Somerset Railway
66758	The Pavior
66759	Chippy
66760	David Gordon Harris
66761	Wensleydale Railway Association 25 Years 1990–2015
66763	Severn Valley Railway
66771	Amanda
66772	Maria
66773	Pride in GB Railfreight
66775	HMS Argyll
66776	Joanne
66777	Annette
66778	Darius Cheskin *
66778	Cambois Depot 25 Years
66779	EVENING STAR
66780	The Cemex Express
66783	The Flying Dustman
66784	Keighley & Worth Valley Railway 50th Anniversary 1968–2018
66788	LOCOMOTION 15
66789	British Rail 1948–1997
66847	Terry Baker
66849	Wylam Dilly
66850	David Maidment
66957	Stephenson Locomotive Society 1909–2009

Notes: Freightliner Class 66s are expected to be repainted in to Genesee & Wyoming livery, EWS Class 66s are expected to be repainted into DB Cargo livery and locos from all owners may be repainted in customer/special liveries

Class 67 liveries and names

Liveries

English Welsh Scottish Railway: 67001–030

Wrexham, Shropshire and Marylebone Railway grey and silver: 67010/012–015

English Welsh Scottish Railway Royal Train dark plum: 67005/006

English Welsh Scottish Railway Managers' train silver with EWS logos: 67029

DB Cargo Managers' train silver with DB logos: 67029

DB Schenker red with maple leaf logo: 67018

DB Schenker red: 67004/010/013/015/027

DB Schenker Arriva Trains Wales unbranded: 67001–003

DB Schenker Diamond Jubilee silver: 67026

DB Schenker Caledonian sleeper blue: 67004/010

DB Cargo with Leading the next generation of rail freight branding: 67028

DB Cargo with First choice for rail freight in the UK branding: 67010

DB Cargo Royal Train dark plum with red solebar stripe: 67005/006

DB Cargo Revised Royal Train dark plum: 67005/006

Colas Rail Freight: 67023/027

Transport for Wales: 67025

Names

67001	Night Mail *
67002	Special Delivery *
67004	Post Haste *
67004	Cairn Gorm *
67005	Queen's Messenger
67006	Royal Sovereign
67010	Unicorn *
67012	A Shropshire Lad *
67013	Dyfrbont Pontcysyllte *
67014	Thomas Telford *

67015	David J Lloyd *
67017	Arrow *
67018	Rapid *
67018	Keith Heller
67023	Stella
67025	Western Star
67026	Diamond Jubilee
67027	Rising Star *
67027	Charlotte
67029	Royal Diamond

Notes: More Class 67s may be repainted in to DB Cargo livery

Class 68 liveries and names

Liveries

Direct Rail Services new style Compass: 68001–009/016–025/033/034

Chiltern Railways silver and grey: 68010–015

ScotRail blue Saltire: 68006/007

Plain Direct Rail services blue: 68026–032

TransPennine Express silver, blue and purple: 68019–032

Names

68001	Evolution
68002	Intrepid
68003	Astute
68004	Rapid
68005	Defiant
68006	Daring
68007	Valiant
68008	Avenger
68009	Titan
68010	Oxford Flyer
68016	Fearless
68017	Hornet
68018	Vigilant

68019	Brutus
68020	Reliance
68021	Tireless
68022	Resolution
68023	Achilles
68024	Centaur
68025	Superb
68026	Enterprise
68027	Splendid
68028	Lord President
68029	Courageous
68030	Black Douglas
68031	Felix
68032	Destroyer

Class 70 liveries and names

Liveries

Freightliner Powerhaul: 70001–020

All-over dark green: 70099

Colas Rail Freight: 70801–817

Names

70001	PowerHaul
70004	The Coal Industry Society

Nameplates are mounted on the solebar.

Note: Freightliner Class 70s are expected to be repainted in to Genesee & Wyoming livery.

Class 73/9 liveries and names

Liveries

GB Railfreight blue and orange: 73961–965

Network Rail yellow: 73951/952

GB Railfreight plain blue: 73962 (did not run in traffic like this)

Caledonian Sleeper blue: 73966–971

Names

73951	*Malcolm Brinded*
73952	*Janis Kong*
73961	*Alison*
73962	*Dick Mabbutt*
73963	*Lisa*
73964	*Jeanette*

Class 88 liveries and names

Liveries

Direct Rail Services new style Compass: 88001–010

Names

88001	*Revolution*
88002	*Prometheus*
88003	*Genesis*
88004	*Pandora*
88005	*Minerva*
88006	*Juno*
88007	*Electra*
88008	*Ariadne*
88009	*Diana*
88010	*Aurora*

UK Class 66s

This table lists the Class 66s that have worked in the UK regardless of whether they were new to UK operators or are still working in the country. Also listed are those locos ordered by UK-based companies/subsidiaries.

Company	Locos ordered	Locos redeployed	Locos acquired from others	Locos returned to leasing co	Locos sold	Locos scrapped	Locos in UK traffic 2018
English Welsh Scottish Railway (now DB Cargo)	250 66001–250 (1998–2000)	80 (notes 1 and 2)			10 (note 3)	1 (66048)	159
Direct Rail Services	34 66401–434 (2003–08)		5 66301–305	20 66401–420			19
GB Railfreight	60 66701–732, 66772–779 2001–16)		29 (notes 3 and 7) 66733–751, 66780–792			1 (66734)	91
Freightliner	131 (note 5) 66501–599 66601–625 66951–957 1999–2008)	17 (note 4)	10 (note 9) 66411–420	9 66573–581		1 (66521)	115
Fastline Freight	5 66301–305 (2008)			5 66301–305			0
Colas Rail Freight			10 66841–850	5 66841–845			5
Advenza Freight			5 (note 6) 66841–845	5 66841–845			0
Locos from UK affiliated companies in use abroad							
ECR	60 (8)		64 (1)				124
FL Poland	7 (8)		17 (4)				24
DB Polska			16 (2)				16

1. 66010/022/026/028/029/032/033/036/038/042/045/049/052/062/064/071–073, 66123/179/190/191/193/195, 66201–205/208–219/222–226/228/229/231–236/239–247/249 to Euro Cargo Rail in France

2. 66146/153/157/159/163/166/173/178/180/189/196, 66220/227/237/248 to DB Polska

3. ex-DB Cargo locos 66008/016/046/058/081, 66132/141/184, 66238/250

4. 66411/412/417, 66527/530/535/582–584/586, 66608/609/611/612/624/625, 66954 to Freightliner Poland

5. 66554 was a direct replacement for 66521

6. 66845 (ex-66410) was earmarked for Advenza but did not join the company before it went bust

7. 66733–737/742–746 are ex-DRS 66401–410, 66738–741 are ex-Freightliner 66578–581, 66747–751/790–792 were acquired from mainland Europe, 66780–789 ex-DB Cargo (see note 3)

8. These locos never operated in the UK

9. ex-DRS locos, 66411/412/417 are now in Poland

Pool codes used

Code	Operator	Class	Depot	Owner	Notes
AWCA	WCR	57	CS	West Coast Railways	Operational Diesel Locomotives
AWCX	WCR	57	CS	West Coast Railways	Stored Diesel Locomotives
COLO	Colas Rail	66/70	RU	Colas Rail	Hire Locomotives
COTS	Colas Rail	67	ZE	Colas Rail	Locomotives for Refurbishing
DDHH	Freightliner	70	FD	Macquarie	Heavy Haul
DDHJ	Freightliner	66	FD	Porterbrook/Beacon Rail	Restricted Use
DDHM	Freightliner	66	FD	Porterbrook/Eversholt	Heavy Haul
DDHN	Freightliner	66	FD	Eversholt/Beacon Rail	Heavy Haul Modified
DDHS	Freightliner	66	FD	Porterbrook/Eversholt	Heavy Haul
DDII	Freightliner	70	FD	Macquarie	Intermodal
DDIM	Freightliner	66	FD	Porterbrook/Eversholt	Intermodal
DFEP	Freightliner	66	PN	Porterbrook/Halifax Assets	Locomotives in Poland/Being Prepared
DFGH	Freightliner	70	LD	Macquarie	Heavy Haul
DFGI	Freightliner	70	LD	Macquarie	Intermodal
DFGM	Freightliner	66	FD	Eversholt/Porterbrook	Intermodal
DFGP	Freightliner	66	FD	Eversholt/Porterbrook	Heavy Haul
DFHG	Freightliner	66	FD	Beacon Rail	Heavy Haul
DFHH	Freightliner	66	FD	Eversholt	Heavy Haul
DFHJ	Freightliner	66	FD	Eversholt	Fitted with Tripcocks
DFIM	Freightliner	66	LD	Porterbrook	Intermodal Modified
DFIN	Freightliner	66	FD	Macquarie/Beacon Rail/Lloyds	Intermodal Low Emission
DFRT	Freightliner	66	FD	Eversholt/Porterbrook	Network Rail Infrastructure Contracts
DHLT	Freightliner	66/70	FD	Freightliner/Porterbrook	Locomotives Stored/Surplus/Not in Main Line Use
EFOO	FGW	57	OO	Porterbrook	
EFPC	FGW	43	LA/LE/OO	Angel/Porterbrook/FGW	
EHPC	XCT	43	EC	Angel/Porterbrook	
EMPC	EMT	43	NL	Porterbrook	
FGXP	First Group	43		First Group	Stored HST Power Cars
GBBR	GBRf	73/9	SE	GBRf	CLASS 73/9 – Brush Repowered
GBBT	GBRf	66	RR	GBRf/Porterbrook	UK Cab – Long-Range Fuel Tanks
GBCM	GBRf	66	RR	Eversholt	Commercial Contracts
GBCS	GBRf	73/9	EC	GBRf	Caledonian Sleeper locomotives
GBDR	GBRf	66	RR	Beacon Rail	Locomotives from Germany
GBEB	GBRf	66	RR	GBRf/Beacon Rail	Euro Cab – Long-Range Fuel Tanks
GBEL	GBRf	66	RR	GBRf	Euro Cab – Standard Fuel Tanks
GBFM	GBRf	66	RR	GBRf	RETB Fitted Locomotives
GBHL	GBRf	66	RR	Eversholt/Porterbrook	Hire Locomotives
GBLT	GBRf	66	RR	Belmond/Porterbrook	UK Cab – Standard Fuel Tanks
GBNB	GBRf	66	RR	Beacon Rail	New-Build Locomotives
GBNL	GBRf	66	RR	GBRf	New Locomotives – ex-Netherlands
GBNR	GBRf	73/9	SE	GBRf	For Network Rail Use
GBOB	GBRf	66	RR	GBRf	Ex-DB Cargo Large Fuel Tanks, Buckeye Couplers
GBRT	GBRf	66/7	RR	GBRf	Restricted Locomotives
GBSD	GBRf	66/7	RR	Eversholt	Scottish Operation (RETB Fitted)
GCHP	GCR	43	HT	Grand Central Railway	
GROG	ROG	57	LR	Rail Operations Group Operational Locomotives	
HAPC	ScotRail	43	HA	Eversholt/Porterbrook	Power Cars

Code	Operator	Class	Depot	Owner	Notes
IECP	LNER	43	EC	Angel Trains	HST power cars
IWCA	VWC	57	LO	Porterbrook Operational Locomotives	
IWLA	FGW	57	LE	Porterbrook	
IWRP	FGW	43	LA/LE/PM	Angel Trains	
MBDL	non-TOC	various	various	non-TOC Private Owner – Diesel Locomotives	
MBED	non-TOC	73	PR	non-TOC Private Owner – Electro-Diesel Locomotives	
MBEL	non-TOC	various	various	non-TOC Private Owner – Electric Locomotives	
QADD	Network Rail	57	DF	Network Rail	Diesel Locomotives
QAED	Network Rail	73	DF	Network Rail	Operational Locomotives
QCAR	Network Rail	43	EC	Network Rail	HST Power Cars
RCJB	Fastline	66	RR	Fastline	Operational Fleet
SAXL	Eversholt	various	HQ	Eversholt	Off-lease
SBXL	Porterbrook	various	HQ	Porterbrook	Off-lease
SCEL	Angel Trains	various	HQ	Angel Trains	Off-lease
WAAK	DBC	67	TO	DB Cargo	Construction
WAAN	DBC	67	TO	DB Cargo	Network
WABC	DBC	67	CE	DB Cargo	RETB Fitted
WABN	DBC	67	TO	DB Cargo	Network – RETB Fitted
WACC	DBC	67	CE	DB Cargo	Chiltern Hire Contract
WAFN	DBC	67	TO	DB Cargo	Locomotives on Hire to FGW
WATN	DBC	67	TO	DB Cargo	Locomotives on Hire to Arriva Trains Wales
WAWC	DBC	67	CE	DB Cargo	Locomotives on Hire to Arriva Trains Wales
WAWN	DBC	67	TO	DB Cargo	Locomotives for Marylebone Services
WBAE	DBC	66	TO	DB Cargo	Fitted with Stop/Start Technology
WBAI	DBC	66	TO	DB Cargo	Awaiting Stop/Start Fitting
WBAK	DBC	66	TO	DB Cargo	Stop/Start Fitted
WBAL	DBC	66	TO	DB Cargo	Logistics
WBAM	DBC	66	TO	DB Cargo	Energy
WBAN	DBC	66	TO	DB Cargo	Network
WBAR	DBC	66	TO	DB Cargo	Remote Condition Monitoring Equipment
WBAT	DBC	66	TO	DB Cargo	General
WBBE	DBC	66	TO	DB Cargo	RETB & Stop/Start Technology Fitted
WBBI	DBC	66	TO	DB Cargo	Industrial – RETB Fitted
WBBK	DBC	66	TO	DB Cargo	Construction – RETB Fitted
WBBL	DBC	66	TO	DB Cargo	Logistics – RETB Fitted
WBBM	DBC	66	TO	DB Cargo	Energy – RETB Fitted
WBBN	DBC	66	TO	DB Cargo	Network – RETB Fitted
WBBT	DBC	66	TO	DB Cargo	RETB Fitted
WBEI	DBC	66	TO	DB Cargo	Euro Cargo Rail UK – Euro Mods Fitted
WBEL	DBC	66	TO	DB Cargo	Industrial – ECR UK Locomotives
WBEN	DBC	66	FN	DB Cargo	Euro Cargo Rail France – Euro Mods Fitted
WBEP	DBC	66	RK	DB Cargo	Euro Cargo Rail Poland – Euro Mods Fitted
WBFA	DBC	66	AZ	DB Cargo	Euro Cargo Rail – UK
WBES	DBC	66	TO	DB Cargo	Sandite Pool – ex-ECR France
WBLI	DBC	66	TO	DB Cargo	Industrial – Auto Couplers Fitted
WBLE	DBC	66	TO	DB Cargo	Lickey Bankers with Stop/Start Technology
WBLT	DBC	66	TO		
WBRT	DBC	66	TO	DB Cargo	RHTT Duties
WBSN	DBC	66 67	TO	DB Cargo	RHTT Duties
WBST	DBC	66	TO	DB Cargo	RHTT Duties – Tripcock Fitted
WBTT	DBC	66	TO	DB Cargo	RHTT – Tripcock Fitted

Code	Operator	Class	Depot	Owner	Notes
WFMS	DBC	various	TO	DBC	Fleet Management Unit – Holding Pool
WFMU	DBC	various	TO	DBC	Fleet Management Unit – Operational
WGEA	DBC	66	AZ	DBC	Euro Cargo Rail
WGEP	DBC	66	PN	DBC	Poland
WHPT	DBC	various	various	DBC	New Locomotives – Pre-acceptance
WNQX	DBC	various	various	DBC	Quarantined Main-Line Locomotives
WNSO	DBC	various	various	DBC	Sold Awaiting Movement
WNTR	DBC	various	HQ	DBC	Stored – Locomotives on Maintenance
WNTS	DBC	various	TO	DBC	Stored – Tactical – Unserviceable
WNWX	DBC	67	CE TO	DBC	Stored – Requiring Heavy Repairs
WNXX	DBC	various	HQ	DBC	Stored – Unserviceable/For Sale
WNZX	DBC	various	HQ	DBC	Locomotives Withdrawn/Disposed/For Sale
WQAA	DBC	various	HQ	DBC	Locomotives Stopped Serviceable – Group 1A
WQAB	DBC	various	HQ	DBC	Stored Locomotives Group 1B
WQBA	DBC	various	HQ	DBC	Stored Locomotives Stored Serviceable – Group 2
WQCA	DBC	various	HQ	DBC	Stored Locomotives for Component Recovery – Group 3
WQDA	DBC	various	HQ	DBC	Stored Locomotives Surplus – Group 4
XHAC	DRS	various	KM	DRS	Operational Locomotives – ETS equipped
XHCE	DRS	68	KM	DRS	Hire to Chiltern Railways
XHCK	DRS	57	KM	DRS	Operational Locos
XHHP	DRS	various	KM	DRS	Holding Pool Locos
XHIM	DRS	66	KM	DRS	Intermodal Locos
XHNC	DRS	57	KM	DRS	Nuclear Traffic
XHSS	DRS	various	KM	DRS	Stored Locos
XHTP	DRS	68	KM	DRS	For hire to Transpennine Express
XHVE	DRS	68 88	KM	DRS	Vossloh Locos
XHVT	DRS	57	KM	DRS	West Coast Thunderbird Locos

Bibliography

Modern Locomotives Illustrated issues 182, 188, 198, 204, 205, 209, 234, 236 (Colin Marsden)

The Allocation History of BR Diesel and Electrics, Parts 1–5, 6a, 6b and Third and Final Edition (Roger Harris)

Traction Transition – The Story of GM Power in the UK and Ireland (Colin Marsden)

The Class 66 Story (Ken Carr)

EWS – From Privatisation to DB (Paul Shannon)

Freightliner (Paul Shannon)

Platform 5 Combined Volumes 1985–2019 (Fox, Hall & Pritchard)

Various issues of *Railways Illustrated*, *RAIL* and *Modern Railways*

Websites used

AB Rail database

Mainlinediesels.net

Six Bells Junction

Wikipedia

WNXX.com

Index

255